HANDBOOK OF ALASKA

KENNIKAT PRESS SCHOLARLY REPRINTS
Dr. Ralph Adams Brown, Senior Editor

Series on
MAN AND HIS ENVIRONMENT
Under the General Editorial Supervision of
Dr. Roger C. Heppell
Professor of Geography, State University of New York

The Giant Moose.

(The largest mammal in North America.)

From painting in possession of Biological Survey, U. S. Department of Agriculture.

HANDBOOK OF ALASKA

ITS RESOURCES
PRODUCTS, AND ATTRACTIONS
IN 1924

BY

MAJOR-GENERAL A. W. GREELY, U. S. A.

Third Edition

WITH NEW CHAPTERS ON FISHERIES, FUR-FARMING, FUR SEALS
GAME, GOLD-MINING, PETROLEUM AND
COAL, RAILROADS, REINDEER, AND VOLCANOES

Illustrated

KENNIKAT PRESS
Port Washington, N. Y./London

HANDBOOK OF ALASKA

First published in 1909, 1925
Reissued in 1970 by Kennikat Press
Library of Congress Catalog Card No: 70-118420
ISBN 0-8046-1372-9

Manufactured by Taylor Publishing Company   Dallas, Texas

KENNIKAT SERIES ON MAN AND HIS ENVIRONMENT

PREFACE TO THIRD EDITION

NEARLY a score of years have passed since the first edition of this Handbook was written. Then a country in the course of exploitation by adventurous prospectors, with few permanent settlements, without outside communication for most sections during eight months annually, Alaska was currently viewed as a mining territory, lacking in elements essential to future Statehood.

The doubts of the armchair prophets were not without good grounds. The fur seal and other fur-bearing animals were near extermination through reckless exploitations. Most of its few railroads were aided into bankruptcy by an annual federal tax of one hundred dollars per mile. Every business, however simple and unremunerative, paid a federal license. Gold was the only productive mineral. Federal restrictions were such that ownership was practically impossible for a homestead, business site, an oil well, a coal mine, a timber lot, or a fox farm. Agriculture was deemed impracticable, and industries were non-existent, save mining and fishing.

The white settlers were ruled by federal proclamations and bureaucratic decrees. The Territory had neither any local government nor any court of final Territorial resort. The natives were perishing yearly in large numbers through famine or imported epidemics. Congress was granting them three cents daily for each native for education and relief when destitute.

Fortunately, when disappointed placer prospectors left, the remaining whites were largely men of American stock, who held fast; their courage and energy have brought Alaska to such material conditions as to insure a prosperous future.

This Handbook has been practically rewritten, and presents Alaska as it is in 1924.

New chapters treat such subjects as Fur Farming, Fur Seals, Reindeer, Forests, Volcanoes, and Reorganized Transportation. The new trend of affairs relative to coal and oil lands is set forth with reference to recent leasing laws. The rapidly changing conditions of gold mining—placer and quartz—are treated fully for thirty-four separate districts, with tabular statements of product up to 1924, the tabular statements being drawn from official reports. These indicate the growth as well as the prospective decadence or continued prosperity.

Local legislation and laws are briefly treated. It is believed that no subject of importance in Alaska has been neglected.

A. W. GREELY,
Major-General.

CONTENTS

CONTENTS

ILLUSTRATIONS

REPRODUCTION OF PHOTOGRAPHS THROUGH THE COURTESY
OF THE COAST AND GEODETIC SURVEY, THE BIOLOGICAL SURVEY,
THE BUREAU OF EDUCATION, THE BUREAU OF FISHERIES, THE
COPPER RIVER RAILWAY CORPORATION, THE GEOLOGICAL SUR-
VEY, THE NATIONAL GEOGRAPHIC SOCIETY, AND THE SIGNAL
CORPS OF THE ARMY.

ix

MAPS

HANDBOOK OF ALASKA

CHAPTER I

GENERAL DESCRIPTION

It is unnecessary to narrate here the history of Alaska, especially as existent conditions in the Territory are entirely disassociated with the past as to material interests and as to its administrative, judicial, or religious methods. However, Table No. 1* gives such matters of historical interest and dates of occurrence as are of special importance.

It is difficult to give an idea of the geography of Alaska that shall be brief and adequate, or satisfactory, owing to its vast area and its divergent conditions.

All are familiar with the accurate but misleading statement that Attu Island, Alaska, is farther west of San Francisco than that city is west of Eastport, Maine. The Alaska known to the tourist is a strip of coast and fringe of islands of about 425 miles by 100 miles, extending from Ketchikan north to Mount St. Elias—in fact, about one-twelfth of Alaska. The main Territory just begins at St. Elias, stretching northward about 700 miles to the Arctic Ocean and the same distance to the westward to Bering Sea, its total area being given by Gannett as 590,884 square miles. Perhaps some idea of its great extent may be had from the statement that its area is one-third

* See end of volume.

greater than that of the Atlantic States from Maine to Florida. While the northernmost land, Point Barrow, is more than 300 miles within the Arctic Circle, with the sun absent forty days, its extreme southern point, at the entrance to Portland Canal, is in practically the same latitude as Hamburg, Germany.

Generally speaking, the southern two-fifths of Alaska consist of rugged, precipitous mountains, somewhere glacier-covered but more often densely wooded. The northern fifth is the largely treeless and barren shores of the Arctic coast. Intervening between these regions the remaining two-fifths are the watersheds of the great Yukon and the lesser Kuskokwim rivers. Other distinctively separate areas are the Seward (Nome) Peninsula and the chain of Aleutian Islands. The general features of Alaska are evident from the map at the end of the volume.

For the purpose of description the following are adopted as districts, in view of their distinct and separate entity from the standpoints of resources, business, and transportation:

1. Sitkan Alaska, covering the mainland and outlying islands from Ketchikan northward to Skagway. This is Alaska as known to the tourists, though only about one-twelfth of the Territory.

2. Southwestern Alaska—the watersheds draining into the Pacific, from St. Elias westward to the Alaska Peninsula and the outlying islands.

3. The Aleutian and Pribilof Islands.

4. The Yukon and Kuskokwim watersheds.

5. The Seward Peninsula (Nome region).
6. The Arctic watersheds.

Sitkan Alaska includes the mainland and outlying islands from Ketchikan northward to Skagway. The mainland is a narrow strip, scarcely averaging twenty miles in width of available ground, overshadowed by the high, snow-capped mountains that separate Alaska from British Columbia. The whole of the Sitkan region is of the fiord type, the shores rising abruptly hundreds, often thousands, of feet above the sea or straits, with bordering or entering fiords of such great and sudden depths as permit large-draft ships safely to skirt the very shore. The land surfaces are most irregular, and it is with difficulty that a square mile of fairly level land can be found. The whole country is more or less densely wooded to the height of several hundred feet above the sea.

Southwestern Alaska is also a fiord region, marked by three great inlets, Yakutat Bay, Prince William Sound, and Cook Inlet. While Yakutat Bay lies under the very shadow of the St. Elias Alps and its enormously debouching glaciers, it is favored with heavy forest growth wherever there is ice-free land. The continuity of the fiord coast is broken at the Copper River delta, where there is a great projecting shelf, with moderate depth seaward and shallows at the river mouth. To the west Prince William Sound and Cook Inlet, with the Kenai Peninsula between the two sounds, are magnificent in their fiord aspects and glacier formations, which excel in beauty the more extensive glacial fields of St. Elias. In the inlet country, along and adjoining the glaciers, woodland regions are also extensive. The extreme west of the mainland, Alaska Peninsula, between Cook Inlet to the east and Bristol Bay, Bering Sea, to the north, is a mountain ridge of several hundred miles with sharply descending spurs and sides to the very sea. Its northeastern borders are divided between coast forests and lake districts, but seven-eighths are up-turned stratified beds, with many volcanic peaks whose destructive activities are not wholly of the past, as instanced by Iliamna and Katmai, by adjacent Bogoslof and Grewingk. To the south of the peninsula are the forest-covered isle of Afognak, and beautiful Kodiak, 3,642 square miles—largest of Alaskan islands, though some claim that it is second in size to Prince of Wales Island—the forests of their northern coasts thin rapidly to the southward.

The Aleutians stretch as a long, bow-shaped chain of seventy treeless islands, excluding islets, for a thousand miles from Alaska Peninsula to the coast of Kamchatka; they extend so far that two groups —Nearer and Rat—are in the Eastern Hemisphere. From west to east the groups are Nearer Islands, W. of 175° E., of which probably Attu is best known owing to its basketry and from its extreme western position, which in June holds the setting sun until it rises in Maine. Between 175° E. and 180° E. are Rat Islands, of which Semisopochnoi, or Seven Peaks, is one. The Andreanofski, of which Atka is well known, with its beautifully woven baskets and mats, lies between 180° W. and 172° W. The most important and best known, however, are the Fox Islands, which lie to the westward of Alaska Peninsula. Of these is Unimak, washed by the pass of that name, which is the route to and from Nome; and Unalaska, on which Dutch Harbor is located, formerly the base of operations for trade and travel in the Bering Sea region. Scarcely more than a score of the Aleutian Islands are inhabited. In general the islands are desolate and scraggy, with many hot springs and other evidences of their volcanic origin, while several craters show minor activity.

While the Pribilof group, better known as the Seal Islands, are some 200 miles north of Unalaska, they appear to pertain rather to the Aleutian than to any other system; they are considered elsewhere (Chapter XIV).

Seward Peninsula. As one proceeds northward into Bering Sea the shore conditions materially change beyond Bristol Bay. The coast forests disappear and the low shores continue treeless to the Arctic Ocean, excepting a woodland fringe on the east shore of Norton Sound and in the eastern portions of Seward Peninsula.

The great sounds of Norton to the south and Kotzebue to the north bound Seward Peninsula, a region of about 20,000 square miles. Its flat-topped uplands, from 800 to 2,500 feet elevation, drain most largely to the south through broad valleys of the tundra type. The coasts are low and sandy, unsuited even in the few bays for shipping except very light draft boats. Kotzebue Sound receives two quite large streams, the Noatak to the north, with scant timber, and the more important Kobuk (Kowak) to the south, where considerable bits of forest and abundant game are found. For further references see Chapter X.

The most northerly and important cape of the Arctic coast is Point Barrow, 71° 25′ N. From Kotzebue Sound to Barrow the shore is low and sandy; thence eastward along the Arctic Ocean to the Canadian boundary the coast is low, without harbors, and fringed with outlying shoals. To the east of Barrow the country is practically uninhabited, although the interior forests, which begin about one hundred miles inward, and the watercourses are visited by Esquimaux hunters. As is elsewhere shown (Chapter XVI), Point Barrow obtains its importance as a base of operations for whaling and, possibly, oil industry.

The Yukon watershed comprises nearly one-half of Alaska, the river running in a bow-shaped, generally western course for 1,500 miles from the Canadian boundary to Norton Sound. It is separated from the Arctic coast by low ranges of mountains, in which find their sources, far to the northeast in Canada, the Porcupine, and in the north the Koyukuk, a parallel stream to the Yukon for several hundred miles. To the southeastward the watershed is limited by the lofty Alaska range, from whose glacial coverings flows the Tanana northward, joining the Yukon at Fort Gibbon. The Yukon watershed is practically covered with small timber, except in the lower reaches

Juneau, the Capital of Alaska.

of a hundred miles or so in the delta country. In general the country is rough, and apart from the mountain masses consists largely of low hills. Where it is not mountainous, as in the extensive flats near Fort Yukon, the plateaus are almost wholly tundra. The Kuskokwim watershed, while much smaller than the Yukon, is of the same general character; in its more elevated parts near the McKinley range forest-covered and rough; but in the coastal region a tundra country interspersed with lakes, with many belts of timber, although its immediate delta is treeless.

Among the many interesting features of Alaskan geography there are four which are notable, owing to their practical absence from the physical features of the United States. These unique characteristics are the fiords, the glacial fields, the volcanic ranges, and the tundra regions.

The sharply indented fiords have great depth of water, are confined by lofty, precipitous cliffs, and many are from twenty to one hundred miles in length. With many ramifications they intersect the mountainous coasts of the Alaskan mainland from Portland Canal northward to Prince William Sound. Their beauty and picturesqueness are set forth elsewhere (Chapter XXXI).

The Alaskan mainland as far north as the Alaska Peninsula presents ideal conditions for extensive glaciation. The shores rise precipitously from the open sea, while the atmospheric pressures are so distributed that the vapor-laden winds are normally drawn upward over the mountain ranges. Largely through the cold of elevation, the prevailing fogs and clouds in their passage deposit their moisture as snow. So frequent are such cloud-bearing currents that enormous snowfalls occur, exceeding in many places a hundred feet or more annually (see Chapter III); hence the great glacial fields, or névés, of Alaska, which are nowhere else equalled on the North American continent. While such conditions obtain to a greater or less extent over an area of more than 40,000 square miles—of which one-fourth is ice-clad —the deepest snowfalls and the maximum resulting névés are between Icy Strait, south of the Fairweather range, and the Kenai Peninsula to the west of Prince William Sound.

Apart from the larger glaciers, numbering 200 and more, Muir writes:

In the iciest region the smaller glaciers, a mile or two to ten or fifteen miles in length, once tributary to large ones, now fill in countless thousands all the subordinate cañons and upper hollows of the mountains.

The grandeur and splendor of these wonderful remnants of the great Ice Age are set forth in Chapter XVIII.

In striking contrast to the great glaciers of the central névé region are the adjacent peaks of fire and lava. From smoking Wrangell of to-day there stretch westward for a thousand miles a series of volcanic-formed peaks, mute witnesses of the terrific internal forces which rent the earth, displaced the sea, and re-formed lands of considerable extent. Dead craters they are mostly termed, but ever-changing Grewingk Island and Mt. Katmai afford living evidence that the days of lava torrents, flame columns, uprising ridges, and tidal waves have not passed for aye. The awe-inspiring exhibitions of volcanic forces are considered in Chapter XXVI, in connection with the subject of Alaskan mountain masses.

Wonderfully dissimilar to peaks of fire and rivers of ice, as well as to striking conformations of cañon and fiord, are the immense coastal plains scarcely rising above the level of Bering Sea, and the gently undulating plateaus bordering many reaches of the Yukon and Kuskokwim. As English speech found no name for our Western prairies, so Americans have adopted the Siberian tundra to describe the Alaskan lowland. The tundra is a marshy, practically unbroken plain, overgrown with vegetation, which, though level to the eye, presents surfaces most irregular in form and hence most difficult to traverse. Collier thus describes it:

On the lowland plains and portions of the upland where drainage is imperfect a thick mat of vegetation, composed of mosses, lichens, sedges, dwarf shrubs, and some grass, overlying peat beds, covers the surface and forms the tundra. The underlying soil is perpetually frozen, as the mat of vegetation and peat protects it from changes of temperature, but during the open season the tundra is difficult to traverse on account of its soft, swampy surface.

In many places the tundra is covered with great, detached bunches of rough grass, known as niggerheads, and travel is possible only by stepping from one bunch to another—a most exhausting method, owing to irregular distances between the niggerheads and the uncertain footing afforded by them.

While glaciers and volcanoes, fiords and tundra are impressive features, there are others of equal or superior importance. Alaska contains extraordinary material related to the past history of the earth, evidences equal in variety and extent to those of any other limited area. Among subjects affording unlimited fields for scientific research, and of material value, are mineral deposits, forestal products, prehistoric fossils, and the biological problems of its land and sea life.

BIBLIOGRAPHY.—Baker: Geographic Dictionary of Alaska; Bulletin No. 299, United States Geological Survey, 1906. Brooks: Geography of Alaska; Professional Paper 45, United States Geological Survey, 1906. Gannett: Geography of Alaska; Harriman Alaska Expedition, 1901. Dall: Alaska and Its Resources. Elliott: Our Arctic Province; Alaska and the Seal Islands.

CHAPTER II

GOVERNMENT AND LAWS

In the early years of Alaska's history as a part of the United States, it suffered from the utter neglect of Congress as regards law and government, so that there were grounds for the application to the Territory of Kipling's aphorism that

Never a law of God or man
Runs north of Fifty-three.

Article III of the treaty of cession, ratified by the United States May 28, 1867, contains the provision that—

The inhabitants of the ceded territory . . . if they should prefer to remain in the ceded territory, they, with the exception of the uncivilized tribes, shall be admitted to the enjoyment of all the rights and immunities of citizens of the United States, and shall be maintained and protected in the free enjoyment of their liberty, property, and religion. The uncivilized tribes will be subject to such laws and regulations as the United States may from time to time adopt in regard to aboriginal tribes of that country.

For seventeen years Congress took no action regarding Alaska save to protect financial interests, which it did July 27, 1868, by extending to it laws relative to customs, revenue, and navigation, and their enforcement by the courts of California, Oregon, and Washington. In 1869 it established the

13

Seal Islands as a reservation and authorized their lease the year following. Then for fourteen consecutive years Alaskan legislation was totally neglected.

The President took action by sending the army in 1867 to protect Alaska (see Chapter IV), but after ten years of stormy experiences it was entirely withdrawn and Alaska was left to its fate.

Murder, rapine, and lawlessness followed, and the citizens of Sitka in one extremity appealed for aid to British Columbia, and for a time were protected by the British navy. Later the Revenue Marine Service and the United States navy alternately assumed control of local affairs.

Of conditions in Alaska from 1867 to 1897 a most competent authority, W. H. Dall, writes:

A country where no man could make a legal will, own a homestead or transfer it, or so much as cut wood for his fire without defying a Congressional prohibition; where polygamy and slavery and the lynching of witches prevailed, with no legal authority to stay or punish criminals; such in great part has Alaska been for thirty years.

He properly adds:

It will be a perpetual testimony to the character of the early American settlers in Alaska, that under the circumstances they bore themselves so well.

This tribute to Alaskans confirms statements often made by the writer, based on his frequent visits to and long experiences with Alaska, that as a whole its inhabitants are the most law-abiding body of men that he has ever known.

Congress on May 17, 1884, extended the laws of Oregon to Alaska, and provided an inadequate Territorial government, as to governor, courts, schools, etc. Where moral obligations were ignored, the discovery of gold prevailed. March 5, 1899, Congress enacted criminal and penal codes, drawn from Oregon statutes. The Act of June 6, 1900, enlarged the powers of the local officials and courts as to education, insane, lands, mines, missions, licenses and taxes. March 3, 1903, homestead entries were granted, and May 7, 1906, Alaska was recognized as a Territory and a delegate to Congress authorized.

A measure of local government was granted by the Act of August 24, 1912. It authorized a legislative assembly of eight senators, with terms of four years, and sixteen representatives with terms of two years. Elected in equal numbers from the four judicial districts, their eligibility required local residence and two years' record as electors. The governor, appointed by the President, has veto power. The legislature, meeting biennially, in the odd years, has restricted powers, and the duration of its sessions is limited. All laws enacted are submitted to the Congress of the United States, and if disapproved become void.

The main features of the Act of Congress are as follows:

The legislative power of the Territory shall extend to all rightful subjects of legislation not inconsistent with the Constitution and laws of the United States, but no law shall be passed interfering with the primary disposal of

the soil; no tax shall be imposed upon the property of the
United States; nor shall the lands or other property of
nonresidents be taxed higher than the lands or other property of residents. . . . The legislature shall pass no law
depriving the judges and officers of the district court of
Alaska of any authority, jurisdiction, or function exer
cised by like judges or officers of district courts of the
United States.

Legislation is restricted on private charters, di-
vorces, lotteries, gambling, sectarian or private
schools, credit, indebtedness, county form of government; and Territorial taxes are limited in amount.

The district court of Alaska is divided into four
divisions, each presided over by a judge appointed
by the President for four years. Probate and jus-
tices' courts, presided over by commissioners, are located in convenient precincts. They have limited
original jurisdiction in probate, insanity, minor civil
and criminal matters. A novel institution is the so-
called "floating court." The entire Territorial court,
with jurymen and lawyers, embark on a revenue cutter, and travel from place to place along the Alaska
Peninsula, Bristol Bay, and other remote settlements.
Court sessions are held on the cutter or in local buildings. Convicted prisoners are carried to the nearest
jails.

BIBLIOGRAPHY.—Department of the Interior: General Information regarding
the Territory of Alaska, 1923.

CHAPTER III

CLIMATE

THE impression is general that the climate of Alaska is arctic in its character and its severity. Several years since life insurance was refused a resident of Ketchikan on the ground that undue risks were entailed by his harsh surroundings and especially severe climate. It is difficult to convince people that there is no typical Alaskan climate, any more than there is an European or American climate. The extremes of latitude and longitude in Alaska find their parallel in Europe between Norway and Sicily—equal to the difference between Point Barrow and Ketchikan—and from western France to central Russia, about the distance from the Alaska Peninsula to Skagway.

Attempts to convey an idea of climate by the annual means of temperature, rainfall, etc., are fallacious and unsatisfactory. The temperature equability is best shown by the mean temperatures of the warmest and of the coldest month. As an illustration, it is known that San Francisco and St. Louis, which are in substantially the same latitude, have the same mean annual temperature, about 55.7°. The variations of the former place are small and inconsiderable, from 50.2° in January, the coldest month, to 59.7° in September, the warmest month—a range of less than 10° in the monthly means. In St. Louis, however, the range is from 31.6° in January to 78.4°

17

in July—a range of 46.8°, or nearly five times as great as at San Francisco. It is pertinent to note that the coldest month of Sitka, 32°, closely agrees with the coldest month of St. Louis.

As a matter of fact, the mean monthly temperatures of Alaskan stations are very high when one takes into consideration the northern latitudes of the territory. Naturally, the Aleutian Islands are favored by most equable temperatures through the influences of the Pacific Ocean. This is shown by the mean temperatures of Unalaska of 51° for August and 32° for February. Unalaska, it may be noted, is in 54° N., the latitude of southern Labrador.

While the modifying oceanic influences affect the southern Alaskan coast to the very Peninsula, it is most noticeable in Sitkan Alaska, which presents a northerly extension of the temperature conditions of the California and Washington coast region, especially during the summer. The mean temperature of San Francisco, Calif., and Port Angeles, Wash., for August is 58°, while that of Sitka is 56°, and of Juneau for July 57°.

In general, the Sitkan archipelago presents a humid, equable climate, with cool summers, warm winters, and very frequent rain or snow. Of the coast stations Sitka is typical, with its annual rainfall of 85 inches, its mean of 32° for the coldest month, January (practically identical with the January mean of St. Louis), and of 56.2° for the warmest month, August. Along the coast extremes are rarely large, the highest in forty-five years at Sitka being 87° in

August, while the lowest ever recorded is −4° in February. Compare these figures with St. Louis, 106° in August and −21.5° in January, and the equability of temperature in southeastern Alaska is obvious. Similar temperature conditions obtain in summer from the St. Elias region westward to the Alaska Peninsula, though the winters are considerably colder. Along this coast the precipitation—rain in the south and snow in the north—is frequent and heavy, being sometimes excessive. For instance, at Valdez the snowfall in the winter of 1902–1903 was 60 feet 11 inches, the maximum snowfall here observed; the average annual precipitation is 72.8 inches of rain and melted snow. At Nuchek Harbor, near by, there was a rainfall in one year of 190 inches. These large amounts of rain and melted snow indicate that over the adjacent regions there fall in some years from 60 to 150 feet of snow, which explains clearly the presence of the proportionately large number of living glaciers in Prince William Sound and Yakutat Bay.

In this connection Professor George Davidson points out the great desirability of regular climatological observations, especially with reference to sea-currents, winds, humidity, and rainfall.

Farther to the northward the coasts are washed by the Bering Sea, a cold body of water with an average temperature of about 39°. In consequence of the cold sea, its adverse winds, and the increasing northing it is natural to find a harsher climate from Bristol Bay northward. The conditions of the southern half of Seward Peninsula, of which Nome is the

business centre, are best indicated by the records of
St. Michael, one hundred miles south of Nome, where
the equable and high summer temperatures (53.6° in
July) are offset by low winter means reaching 0.0° in
February. Its rain and melted snow during the year
averages 13.2 inches.

The Arctic coasts, from their high latitude and
consequent loss of the midwinter sun, forty days at
Point Barrow, experience prolonged winter cold and
brief summers. The scanty precipitation is almost
entirely in the form of light winter snowfalls. Point
Barrow is a typical winter station, with a yearly rainfall of 5.34 inches and average temperatures of 41°
in July, the warmest month, and of −20° in January,
the coldest month. The severity and length of the
winter are shown by the fact that the average temperature is below zero from November to April, the
mean for the six months being 13° below zero.

As one enters the interior of Alaska, whether by
the Copper River, the Kuskokwim, or the Yukon,
the climate becomes continental, with great ranges
of temperature between the short, comparatively hot
summers and long, cold winters. Within a hundred
miles of the coast the oceanic influence largely dis-
appears, its gloomy humid aspects giving way to
brighter skies and decreasing rain or snow. The cul-
mination of the summer heat and of the winter cold
is found at almost the greatest distance from the
surrounding seas—in the valley of the upper Yukon.
The typical station for this region is Fort Yukon,
with its July mean of 61° and a January mean of

−31°, which, compared with Point Barrow, 300 miles to the north, shows a lower temperature of 5° in winter and a higher temperature of 25° in summer.

The rigors of the past climate are strikingly illustrated by the great depths to which the ground is frozen. In the Nome region a shaft has been sunk 120 feet without reaching ground free from frost, and near Dawson the earth was found frozen to the depth of 200 feet.

Table No. 2 gives the mean temperatures and rainfall for ten typical and well-distributed stations.

BIBLIOGRAPHY.—Dall and Baker: Pacific Coasts Pilot; Appendix 1; Meteorology, 1879. Abbe: Climate, in Brooks's Geography of Alaska; Professional Paper 45, United States Geological Survey, 1904. Annual Reports of Chief Signal Officer of the Army, 1878 to 1885. Reports of Weather Bureau, Department of Agriculture, to 1924 inclusive.

CHAPTER IV

THE ARMY IN ALASKA

A BRIEF statement as to the work of the army appears desirable, owing to its extended period of occupation and the important part played by it in the government, exploration, and development of the Territory. The general character of its services is set forth by Mr. O. P. Austin in his valuable "Commercial Alaska," where he says:

Since the foundation of our government the lines of the army have advanced simultaneously with the advance of the settler along our vast frontier. It has been the uniform policy of the government to foster the development of the country by exploring and opening up trails for emigrants and prospectors, convoying their supplies, aiding in the transmission of their mail—in all things extending a helping hand to them and in keeping step with the advance of American civilization. The army of the United States has always been the advance guard of civilization. Wherever it has gone its protection has been freely given to every American citizen.

It was General L. H. Rousseau, United States army, who formally accepted Alaska from Russia, and occupied Sitka with a military force on October 18, 1867. Military posts were established at Kenai, Kodiak, Sitka, Tongass, and Wrangell, with detachments on the islands of St. Paul and St. George; all except Sitka were abandoned in 1870.

The duties of the army were neither formulated in regulations nor authorized by law. Their scope as viewed by officers was to prevent difficulties between incoming Americans and the Indians, and properly to enforce the provisions of the Indian trade and intercourse laws regarding arms and liquor. General Howard stated that it would be easy for the army, if duly authorized, to preserve peace and establish police regulations, but authority so to do was questioned by the United States District Court, while the repeated efforts of the commanding general to secure the establishment of a civil government were steadily ignored.

The activity of the army in carrying out its orders elicited bitter criticism. Reporting on affairs at the Seal Islands, prior to the lease of the Alaska Commercial Company, it incurred enmity by officially stating that the Pribilof natives were suffering "enslavement and robbery by an unscrupulous ring of speculators." As Indian wars give local traders patronage and contracts, the tendencies to adjust troubles peacefully with the natives were viewed askant as unmilitary and unbusinesslike. To stimulate industry among the natives, it was recommended that Indians be hired to cut wood, which resulted in attacks from interested contractors. The army's insistence that Alaska was an Indian country, where neither firearms nor liquor could be imported, was bitterly fought by traders and politicians before the department, and it was years before the army's point of view was sustained by Congress and the courts.

Meantime civil regulations authorized the importation by officials of liquor in "limited quantities." Sales of "surplus" liquor, with smuggling of arms and spirits, steadily proceeded, with unfortunate results. Treasury officials sold in Sitka at public auction liquor seized by the army, and then blandly complained that the military was not suppressing the liquor traffic. Repeated requests for a steam vessel to permit raids on smugglers and liquor dealers were without avail.

Disturbed conditions due to the Stikine gold discoveries led to the reoccupation of Fort Wrangell in 1875, the impossibility of otherwise maintaining order and peace being generally recognized. Finally— happy day for the service, though not for the Territory—the army sailed away from Alaska, after, as we are told by a well-known writer, a service not highly creditable. This local judgment was natural, since the business methods of many of the early Alaskan captains of industry did not accord with army ideals as to probity and propriety.

The army's sins of omission and commission were not specified, but what it did may be stated. It had brought the Indians into a state of submission and peace—its military duty. Moreover, it had fed the starving, cared for the suffering, and nursed the sick; it had largely suppressed smuggling and illegal trade in arms and liquor; it had discouraged corrupt business methods and protested against the enslavement and robbery of natives; it had vainly besought civil government and opened day schools; finally it had fostered morality by religious teaching of children, established the first native Protestant church in Alaska, and by its initiative and petition led the Christian people of the United States to extend a helping hand to the natives of Alaska. (See Chapter XXIX.) These deeds are not strictly military duties, and while they are extra-legal acts without warrant of law, they were justified by the law of emergency and impelled by the obligations of our higher moral nature.

As General Howard wrote: "The officers of the army were denied the jurisdiction for an ordinary police, on the one hand, and held responsible for order and enforcement of the law on the other." Whether they did well or ill, at least they tried to do their duty in those early days.

Civil conditions after the departure of the army cannot be recounted without a sense of shame. A pandemonium of drunkenness, disorder, property destruction, and personal violence obtained at Sitka, which eventuated in murder, followed by a threatened Indian uprising and frantic appeals for protection, that was temporarily accorded by a British man-of-war.

The Signal Corps of the army re-entered Alaska for scientific work and occupied twenty-nine different and well-distributed climatic stations, until their discontinuance was practically directed by Congress in 1884 as useless. The contributions to Alaskan knowledge by Ray, Murdock, Turner, Nelson, and Fish were the forerunners of extensive and valuable work by the various executive departments of the United States.

The second advent of the army in Alaska arose from disturbed conditions connected with the so-called stampede to the gold placers of the Klondike. In the summer of 1897 some 20,000 men came together on the shores of Lynn Canal, a country without law, without courts, without habitations, and almost without food resources. Mostly men of character, though with many reckless adventurers, all were animated by a single aim, to reach with speed the gold fields of the Canadian Klondike, which could only be done by private transportation over almost unknown routes.

Conditions of hardship and lawlessness, of suffering and contention speedily arose, and the army was turned to as the only power that could control and ameliorate the situation. Unwilling, as always, to obtrude its activities into the domain of civil government, the Secretary of War acted promptly through a preliminary reconnoissance, which was sent to the upper Yukon via St. Michael. Two officers—Captain (later General) P. H. Ray and Lieutenant (later General) W. P. Richardson—were directed to investigate conditions and report promptly the lines and places of military operation best calculated to remedy matters.

In southeastern Alaska affairs steadily grew from bad to worse. Reports as to the number, character, and condition of the gold seekers near Skagway became so alarming, and complications regarding Cana-

dian customs so involved, that the military district of
Lynn Canal was established under Colonel (later
General) T. H. Anderson with the 14th Infantry. As
a matter of precaution Colonel (later General) G. M.
Randall occupied the military district at St. Michael
with the 8th Infantry. The presence of troops re-
stored confidence, and affairs were discreetly and
peacefully managed by the army until temporary and
stable local government was organized by the miners.

In addition, reports of starvation conditions in the
Klondike were circulated with such detailed assidu-
ity by interested parties that Congress appropriated
large sums for the relief of the Klondike miners, but
after considerable amounts had been spent for supplies and for reindeer transportation (an ill-advised
scheme that did not originate with the army), the
expedition was abandoned, as no necessity therefor
ever existed.

Meanwhile Ray and Richardson were obliged to
winter at Fort Yukon; their steamers, being unable
to proceed farther owing to low water, landed there
all their Dawson supplies. Soon a situation of great
gravity arose in connection with some five hundred
disappointed gold-seekers, fleeing from Dawson, who
arrived at Fort Yukon in straggling bands and found
further travel impracticable.

All in destitute condition, and nearly all of them
without money, they included in their number some
of the most desperate men of the North ready for
any enterprise. Unscrupulous leaders obtained possession of many of the guns, and conspired to seize and

divide the stores, with the view of providing amply for themselves without regard to the common weal.

Ray and Richardson were alone, without a single soldier, but they acted with daring promptness. Ray hoisted the American flag over the two depots of provisions, announced that he took possession of them in the name of the United States, and stated that they would be held for the benefit of all destitute persons. An organization for the resolute defense of the stores was formed, and the battle was won. Awed by the firm attitude of the officers and by this display of Federal authority, the lawless element abandoned their plans, and the winter passed quietly.

This adjustment of a serious trouble without bloodshed was the forerunner of the army's policy during the occupancy of the Yukon Valley by troops under Richardson at Gibbon, Rampart, and Circle in 1898. Assuming control in all emergencies, the army extended assistance, afforded relief, discouraged violence, and when absolutely necessary made arrests and administered condign justice.

The opening of the Nome placers and the assembling there of some 18,000 adventurous and determined men, naturally led to difficult situations. In the absence of courts, of law, and of authorized civil government, the settlement of disputed points of current and financial importance devolved on the troops, who proved equal to the occasion. Disputes involving thousands of dollars were promptly decided by officers and the decisions peacefully accepted.

The most striking instance of army methods in the

interests of order was that displayed by a young lieutenant. Several hundred disappointed and idle gold-
seekers called a mass meeting, naturally not attended
by the busy miners, for the understood purpose of
vacating all miners' locations and throwing them
open to the first—or in this case to the last—comers;
a procedure that was certain to result in a miners'
war. When the discussion ended and the resolution
·was to be put, the resolute and clear-headed lieutenant, Oliver L. Spaulding, Jr., declared the meeting
adjourned and dispersed the assembly with his squad
of only seven soldiers. This ended claim-jumping by
mass meeting.

Under such emergencies the army continued its
alert and supervisory control over affairs until Congress passed the Alaskan Civil Code and established
courts at Nome and on the Yukon in 1900. This
unauthorized exercise of general police authority over
interior and western Alaska was not only accepted as
indispensable for the security of person and property,
but was also viewed as fully justified by the law of
the frontier. Moreover, it was so impartially and
judiciously administered as to give almost universal
satisfaction, and, indeed, a desire for a return of military sway was not infrequently heard during the first
unfortunate and stormy year of scandalous actions
by the Federal court at Nome.

Commercially the greatest service rendered Alaska
by the army was the construction and operation of a
military telegraphic service, open to private telegrams, which brings every important business inter-

est of the Territory in connection with the world. The system aggregates about 4,500 miles at present, and extends from Seattle via Sitka, Skagway, and Valdez to Nome, in the west, and to Eagle, on the Canadian frontier in the east. (See Chapter XXX.) These lines are due to the acumen of Secretary of War Root in approving the plans and securing the money, especially for the Seattle-Skagway cable; to General G. M. Randall for urging the system and very greatly facilitating construction work by the line of the army, and to the activities and energy of the men and officers of the Signal Corps, of which the writer was the chief, during the four critical years of construction and installation. This system has made modern Alaska possible, as without it not one-quarter of the present business could be satisfactorily and economically done. The extent and importance of the service may be judged from the fact that the tariffs on private telegrams amount to about $250,000 annually, while government telegrams amount to at least $100,000 additional in tariff value. (See Chapter XXX.)

So efficient and economical has been this service that the civil departments have failed to relieve the army of a duty that years since ceased to be military. Of its value Governor Bone in 1924 reported that the "system in the progress and development of Alaska cannot be overestimated." Yet this task rests on an overburdened army.

The invaluable services rendered by the army road commission are considered in Chapter VI.

In exploration the army began early and did much. Raymond fixed the boundary line of the upper Yukon in 1868, which checked aggression and caused the Canadian abandonment of Fort Yukon. He also made a valuable map of the Yukon Valley, having determined astronomically several points therein. Ray, during his notable service at Point Barrow, discovered the Endicott Mountains in 1882, and the next year Schwatka traced and mapped the Yukon from its source to the sea. Later Abercrombie and Glenn did work of importance, with Prince William Sound and Cook Inlet as their bases. Of geographic work done by the army, Brooks states that the expedition of Lieutenant H. T. Allen, from March to September, 1885, "was one of the most remarkable in the annals of Alaskan explorations," being provided with few men, an inadequate equipment, and at times in a half-starved condition, as they were dependent on the country for food. Brooks adds:

No man through his own explorations has added more to a geographic knowledge of interior Alaska than Lieutenant Allen. Throughout his journey he made careful surveys and noted all facts which came within his observation; and within one season he made maps of three of the larger rivers (Copper, Tanana, and Koyukuk) of the Territory, which, until accurate surveys were made twelve years later, were the basis of all maps. His reports are the work of a careful, painstaking observer.

Duty in Alaska is confining and restricted to the post, except that done along the military telegraph system. While it is monotonous and irksome, it has been performed in such a manner as to elicit general commendation from the inhabitants. Under the law the army has unique and embarrassing duties devolved on it, as in Alaska (and nowhere else) it is subject to the call of the governor (or courts) as a *posse comitatus*; again, officers of the army are liable to jury duty, and have even been summoned to either pay or work out a road tax.

In season and out of season, the officers of the army have proclaimed the obligations of the United States toward the natives of Alaska: and, in default of an authorized system and in the absence of civil officials, have assumed the difficult task of conserving, as far as possible, the interests and rights of the natives.

BIBLIOGRAPHY.—Annual Reports Commanding General, Department of Columbia, 1869–1878, 1889–1908. Compilation of Narratives of Explorations in Alaska. Fifty-eighth Congress, 1st Session, Senate Report No. 1,023, 1900.

CHAPTER V

WATERWAYS

THE entire absence of roads in Alaska, until the past few years, has made river transportation practically the only method of extended travel in the Territory. Fortunately, the river systems of Alaska are such as to facilitate very greatly personal travel and the movement of freight during the four or five months of open season. Waterways in Alaska navigable by steamers approximate 4,000 miles, of which nearly 2,700 are in the Yukon watershed.

Navigable Rivers

The great artery of summer travel and freight is through that magnificent stream, the Yukon, which divides Alaska into two nearly equal parts in its course of about 1,200 miles, flowing in a bow-shaped course, in its general direction of east to west. Formed by the junction of the Pelley and Lewes, its length from the source of the Lewes to the Yukon delta, Norton Sound, is 1,865 miles, its length in Alaska being about 1,200 miles. Flowing in its upper reaches through cañon-like valleys, it debouches shortly after entering Alaska into a plateau tundra region, where its wide and winding channels divide and flow sluggishly—especially in the great flats near Fort Yukon; there the islands and cut-offs make the river from ten to thirty miles wide—again to find precipitous, confining mountains in the so-called rampart region, near Fort Hamlin. From Fort Gibbon to Norton Sound the river valley grows steadily wider, until the vast, treeless delta region is reached, about one hundred miles inward from Norton Sound. The delta has an area of about 9,000 square miles, greater in extent than any one of the States of New Jersey, Massachusetts, Maryland, Vermont, and New Hampshire.

Although one of the largest rivers of North America, exceeded in length or volume by only the Mississippi, Mackenzie, St. Lawrence, and Winnipeg, yet the usefulness of the Yukon, though navigable throughout its entire extent, is largely restricted by its very shallow mouths, which admit boats drawing not over three or four feet of water. In consequence all freight shipments for the Yukon watershed are transferred from the ocean steamships to river steamboats which run to St. Michael, ninety miles seaward from the Apoon mouth of the delta.

The Yukon navigation is divided into two sharply separated systems—the Canadian and the American —with Dawson, Yukon Territory, as the line of demarcation. This is caused by the customs and navigation laws, which practically necessitate the transshipment of everything in and out of Alaska via the upper Yukon, at Dawson; and again every boat coming into the Alaskan Yukon is obliged to stop and submit to customs examination at Eagle, about one hundred miles below Dawson.

The Canadian system is also affected by the spring
and summer conditions of the chain of lakes which
forms the extreme upper Yukon (or Lewes), through
early autumn freezing and late break-ups in the
spring. The more rapid, as well as the more northerly, river keeping open longer than the lake section,
part of the steamers are wintered north of Lake Le-
barge, near the mouth of the Hootalinqua, ninety
miles north of White Horse—which is the terminus
of the White Pass and Yukon Railway. In six years'
consecutive record, the average period between the
dates of the first [boat and the last boat from White
Horse to Dawson was four months and nineteen days
—from June 4 to October 23. The average date of
the first boat from Hootalinqua to Dawson was
May 13—thus lengthening the navigation period by
twenty days. The earliest date that the first boat
has reached Dawson was May 16 from Hootalinqua,
but in two years it was delayed until May 26. The
average date of the last boat arriving at White Horse
from Dawson is October 28, although in 1902 a boat
arrived as late as November 4.

At Fort Gibbon (Tanana P. O.), junction of the
Yukon and Tanana, the two rivers are open on the
average by May 13 and closed by November 1, an
interval of five months and nineteen days. In eight
years the opening of navigation ranged from May 7
to 24, and its closing from October 21 to November 9.

The period of navigation from Fort Gibbon up the
Yukon River to Dawson is materially longer than
it is down river toward Norton Sound; its mean

duration in three consecutive years being four months
and fourteen days to Dawson, from May 21 to October 5.   Toward St. Michael the time of navigation
averages three months and fifteen days, from June 15
to September 30.   The arrival of the first boat from
Dawson has ranged from May 19 to 23, and from
St. Michael from June 2 to 24.

Between Fort Gibbon and Fort Egbert (Eagle
City), 575 miles up the Yukon, the boats usually run
up river from June 1 to October 6, and down from
May 16 to September 17.   In general it takes twice
as long to go up the Yukon by steamboat as it does
to come down the same distance.

The most northerly important affluent of the Yukon, within Alaska, is the Porcupine, which joins it
at Fort Yukon, just north of the Arctic Circle; it is
navigable for light-draft steamboats for about one
hundred miles.   On this, as on other rivers, small
poling boats are available for navigation to much
greater distances, dependent largely on freshet-water
conditions.

From its volume of water, length of course, and its
commercial relations, the Tanana is far the most
important tributary of the Yukon.   First navigated
in its lower reaches in 1893, it was opened to Chena
in 1898, and regular summer navigation has been
had since 1901 with Fairbanks, about 300 miles up
the river.   Occasional steamboats have carried supplies up the Tanana to Delta River, and one reached
the junction of the Nabesna, about 700 miles from
the mouth of the Tanana.   If mineral developments

should ever justify, the Tanana and its main upper fork, the Chisana, could be navigated by very light draft boats for a distance of about 750 miles. Among the Tanana's affluents, the Kantishna has been navigated about 200 miles, while the Chena, Tolovana, and lower Volkmar are likewise practicable for light steamers, and most other tributaries for small boats.

The period of navigation on the Yukon is exceeded in duration by that on the Tanana. For three years between Fort Gibbon (Tanana post-office) and Chena or Fairbanks, its usual duration was five months. The average date of opening was May 14 and of closing October 14. A boat has reached Fort Gibbon from Chena as early as May 8, and as late as October 17.

Of the Yukon watershed, as is shown in Chapter VI, it is to be noted that the completion of the Alaska Railroad practically eliminated its river transportation, both of the Canadian boats from Dawson in the upper Yukon, and of the American lines of the lower river from St. Michael. The United States is undertaking the replacement of the former efficient systems by governmental lines of steamers. Several years must pass before such lines can become entirely satisfactory.

In Cook Inlet region the Susitna, with a basin of 8,000 square miles, has been navigated by steamers to the mouth of the Chulitna, and its main tributary, the Yentna, to the mouth of the Kichatna. In Lynn Canal the Chilkat is practicable for very small steamers to Klutwan, twenty-five miles from the mouth.

The Copper River has been navigated during the months of July and August, in conjunction with the Copper River Railway, from the head of Abercrombie Rapids to Copper Centre, while the mouth of the Gulkana can be reached. It is thought that the upper Copper, now practicable for poling boats, can be utilized for very light draft steamers. The Chitina, a tributary of the Copper, is navigable to the Nizina, and possibly the mouth of the Tana may be reached.

The Alsek, Kvichak, Unalaklik, and many other small rivers are practicable for poling boats.

Portages

In no country are portages of greater importance than in Alaska. The following are the most important:

Chipp—Colville; Cook Inlet—Illiamna Lake; Copper—Tanana; Koyukuk—Kobuk; Kuskokwim—Nushagak and thence to Chulitna; Kuskokwim—Togiak Lake; Nushagak—Chulitna; Tanana—Kuskokwim; Tanana—Copper; Yukon—Lynn Canal; Yukon—Mackenzie; Yukon—Kuskokwim; Yukon—Koyukuk; Yukon—Tanana; Yukon—Norton Sound.

CHAPTER VI

ROADS AND RAILROADS

INTERIOR Alaska necessarily remained an unknown country as long as its roving inhabitants saw, from their boats, only the bordering regions of its great rivers. It was the adventurous gold-prospectors who, pack on back or rifle in hand, blazed under extraordinary hardships the devious paths which led to the interior valleys and streams of this vast country. Then in time came mining trails over which travel with pack animals was possible.

It was only when the United States, urged by material interests, took action that roads were constructed over which eventually passage was practicable by wagon or auto in summer and by sled or sleigh in winter.

Roads and Trails

The necessity of supplementing river transportation by roads was always recognized theoretically, but nothing was done in this direction until the gold discoveries made Alaska a new El Dorado. Then it was the army of the United States which initiated the work and, with wise, remarkable foresight, selected a route that has proved to be of the greatest benefit to the Territory, from the Gulf of Alaska to the Yukon Valley.

In 1898 a military detachment began the exploration and construction of a trail from Valdez, Prince William Sound, to Eagle, on the Canadian border in the upper Yukon.

A committee of the United States Senate, after two months' examination of Alaska, reported in 1904 that: "Outside the few scattered towns there is not to be found a single public wagon road over which vehicles can be drawn, winter or summer. The only approach to one is the military trail extending from Valdez, on the Pacific, to Eagle, on the Yukon, constructed by the War Department in 1899–1900." It may be added that the greatest value of the trail was the fact that it passed entirely through American territory, all land travel previously having been over the Canadian Klondike route.

As an outcome Congress in 1904 enacted a law providing for the construction of military post-roads and trails in Alaska, constituting the Alaska Road Commission under the War Department. The expense of the work was to be divided between Federal appropriations and allotments from the Alaska Fund— which fund was formed from Federal licenses granted for business in the Territory.

Fortunately the presidency of the commission was filled by Major (later General) Wilds P. Richardson, a man of wide Alaskan experience. His executive acumen, business ability, skilful supervision, and discriminating judgment made the work of the commission of great and permanent value to Alaska during his service from 1904 until 1917, when he was called to field duty in the World War. No single man has

contributed so largely as he to the development of
the Territory as a whole. His problems were difficult and conflicting, involving the relative importance
of mail service, transportation routes, mining trails,
and local needs.

Up to June 30, 1924, there had been spent in road
work $8,363,500, of which amount Alaska contrib-
uted $3,162,674. A ten-year programme, looking to
a future annual fund of $1,000,000, will care for the
most important needs, if Congress authorizes.

There have been constructed 9,625 miles of roads
and trails, with necessary bridges, ferries, and tramways. There are 1,498 miles of wagon roads, 1,088
sled roads, 6,326 permanent and 712 flagged trails.
Of these, 800 miles have a gravel surface and are
practicable for light automobile traffic. The main
branch is the Valdez-Fairbanks military road, appro-
priately known as the Richardson Highway, connecting the interior during the entire year with Prince
William Sound, which is always open to navigation.
This roadway, of 410 miles, connects by a branch at
Chitina with the Copper River and Northwestern
Railway. With its branches and trails this main road
connects with practically all settlements west of the
141st meridian, including the important mining districts of Circle, Iditarod, Innoko, Kuskokwim, Nome,
and Susitna.

Unfortunately, under the unco-ordinated Alaskan
activities, there are four other bodies engaged in road
building, a manifest waste of administrative energy.

Over the Richardson Highway, from Valdez to

Fairbanks, practically the whole route is settled, though sparsely, and roadhouses are situated at intervals of ten to twenty miles, where most comfortable accommodations are found. Many of these enterprising proprietors have made homestead entries, are keeping stock, growing grain fodder, and raising vegetables which are often abundant and excellent. Their presence and facilities tend to the thorough exploration of the adjacent mineral fields by the ever present and persistent prospectors.

The main mail artery, passing through Hot Springs and Fort Gibbon, continues down the Yukon via Nulato, and over the Kaltag portage to Unalaklik, whence, St. Michael being reached by a side route, the shores of Norton Sound are practically followed to the settlements of Seward Peninsula and Nome.

In the vicinity of Fairbanks there are eight local roads, aggregating 64 miles in length. Longer separate routes are the sled roads from Cleary to Birch Creek, 54 miles; from the mouth of the Salcha to Caribou, 45 miles; and the road from Hot Springs to Gulch Creek region, 22 miles. The Fairbanks-Fort Gibbon road of 160 miles passes through Circle. It is passable its entire length in winter for double bobsleds, and for 100 miles for wagons in summer.

Fairbanks is really the centre of the road system of Alaska, as from that point roads and trails lead not only to the adjacent mining districts but also eastward to the Salcha Valley; northeastward to Circle, Eagle, and Dawson; and northwestward to Hot Springs. This last road is the most important, the

Seward.

(Southern terminus of the Alaska Railroad.)

great winter mail route to Fort Gibbon (Tanana); to the entire Yukon Valley except Eagle and Fortymile, which are reached via Dawson; to the Koyukuk region; to Seward Peninsula and Arctic Alaska—Point Barrow, etc.

In addition to its connection with Fairbanks, before mentioned, Eagle can now reach Fortymile over an American road, though previously nearly all travel and all supplies passed through Canadian territory.

On Seward Peninsula, Nome is connected with all important mining camps not reached by railway. There arc on the peninsula sixteen roads, aggregating 50 miles in length. Freighting is now practicable over the greater portion of the peninsula, where packing was formerly the only method of transportation. In 1924 the Nome-Sheldon tramway became Territorial property and was opened to public traffic. The Tolovana tram road was purchased the same year, and was being rehabilitated for public use.

The flagging of winter trails in this bleak and treeless tundra country has rendered travel in the winter darkness, during periods of storm, much less hazardous. The difficulties of safe travel on Seward Peninsula are very great during the period of winter and almost sunless days over a gently rolling, unbroken tundra, where there is no tree, bush, or even stone to mark the trail or relieve the unvarying monotony. In earlier years scores of bewildered travellers have wandered from the dim, snow-covered trail and miserably perished in the winter blizzards.

The extent of such travel and the length of routes are conveyed by the statement that nearly 500 miles of such trails are annually flagged—slight sticks provided with red flannel flags being planted in the snow from 50 to 100 yards apart, according to the character of the country.

The Road Commission looked in its construction to doing standard work that would be of lasting and permanent benefit. So it has built good country roads 16 feet wide, winter sled roads 12 feet wide, trails 8 feet, and bridges 14 feet wide.

In southeastern Alaska conditions have so improved that the Governor in 1924 reported that "Juneau, with thirty-odd miles of road, has nearly 300 licensed automobiles, and all coast towns maintain a taxi service."

Railroads

There can be no stronger evidence of the permanency of the population and industries of Alaska than the construction of railroads in this far-distant Territory. The law of May 14, 1898, granted to duly incorporated railways, wagon roads, and tramways a right of way of 100 feet on each side of the road. Ten corporations have built railways aggregating 446 miles of completed road.

The Federal tax of $100 per mile, costly fuel, and reduced mining output caused the abandonment of the following roads: Council City and Solomon River, 33 miles; Golovin Bay, 7 miles; Seward Peninsula, 97 miles; and Cook Inlet and Coal-Fields, 10 miles.

Cordova, Prince William Sound, and the Copper River Railroad, October, 1908.

(Chugach Mountains in the background.)

The following systems were absorbed and form part of the U. S. Alaska Railroad: Tanana Railroad, 45 miles, and the Alaska Northern, 72 miles.

Private lines in operation in 1924 were: Yakatut Southern, standard gauge, 12 miles, from Minto Bay to Situk Bay—a freight road running part of the year only; the Copper River and Northwestern (with which has been consolidated the branch of 7 miles from Katalla), the most important private line in the Territory, 195 miles. It connects the open navigation at Cordova with the rich copper district at and near Kennicott, Nizina valley. White Pass and Yukon Railroad, Skagway, to boundary, 20.5 miles, and thence 90.5 miles to White Horse, head of navigation on Yukon River. Dawson is reached from White Horse by steamboats in summer and by stage in winter.

The United States Alaska Railroad

The only very large expenditure made by the United States in Alaska has been in the construction and operation of the governmental Alaska Railroad. Criticized as to the wisdom of the project, as to the selected route, and the enormous cost over the original estimates, it has been an undertaking of tremendous difficulty, and its success has been creditable to American engineers. Years must elapse before its receipts will meet the cost of maintenance and operation.

Congress authorized in 1913 an investigation by the Alaskan Railroad Commission of the various routes suggested. In 1914 there was enacted a law to construct a railroad to connect an open port on the Pacific with a navigable river in the interior. Although the commission estimated that a suitable road could be built for $26,800,000, Congress appropriated $35,000,000 and left the selection of the route to the President. In 1915 the route from Seward to Fairbanks was designated, and the construction was placed under the Alaskan Engineering Commission.

Progress was facilitated by the purchase at a cost of $1,154,188 of the Alaska Northern road, extending from Seward to near Anchorage, and for $300,000 of the Tanana Valley road, from Chena to Chatinika; both roads were necessarily rebuilt. Largely owing to war prices, Congress increased the appropriation by $17,000,000, and, through supplementary funds and material transferred from Panama and elsewhere, the total amount was raised to $52,460,159.

The construction of the great steel bridge across the Tanana River at Nenana opened, in February, 1923, the main trunk line from Seward to Fairbanks, 467 miles in length. The length of the entire system is 537 miles, including the Matanuska-Chickaloon branch, 38 miles; Happy-Chatinika, 32 miles; and the Eska branch, 3 miles. Other short branches are planned to reach rich deposits of coal.

To develop coal mines, as fuel could not be bought, in the Matanuska district $1,130,242 was spent. Later, coal was obtained irregularly as private mining was prosecuted.

Repair shops were built at Anchorage, the headquarters of the system. The completion of the rail-

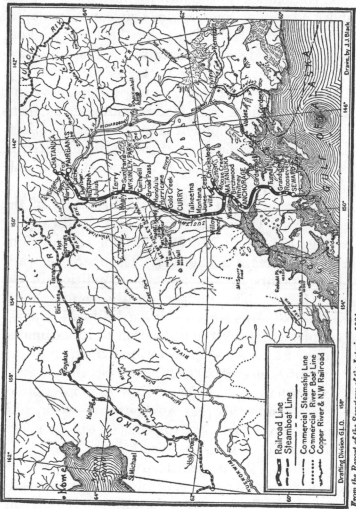

Map 1.   The Alaska Railroad.

way made river transportation unprofitable for commercial companies, so the railway authorities had to establish a summer river service between Nenana, on the Tanana, and Holy Cross, on the lower Yukon, where commercial service continued. The total revenue of the railway during 1921 was $480,000, and in 1922, $715,000. Floods, bank-erosion, cave-ins, rock and snow slides have made maintenance expensive. Travelling equipment is modern and comfortable. Trains between Seward and Fairbanks are run twice a week in each direction, on a two-day schedule with a stop-over at Curry.

In his annual report for 1924 the Secretary of the Interior says: "Operating revenues for the fiscal year were $907,174, as against $758,031 for the previous year, or an increase of $149,142. This increase, while not large, points to a more stable condition in the railroad belt." The budget for the coming fiscal year, 1925–26, asks for the Alaska Railroad $2,000,-000 supplemented by the utilization of its estimated receipts of $1,200,000. The estimated expenditures are: Maintenance $2,200,000; river steamers, $95,-000; construction, $500,000. Recent inspection of the railroad indicates that several years' work, with an expenditure of nearly $10,000,000, will be necessary to place it in first-class condition.

Fortunately, the appointment of an expert engineer and executive as general manager tends to increase its efficient administration. The road, however, cannot be expected to meet its costs of maintenance for several years, at least.

CHAPTER VII

MINING IN GENERAL—GOLD, COPPER, AND COAL

In connection with the mining industries of Alaska, very brief though inadequate allusion is made to the United States Geological Survey, both on account of its intimate relations with mineral products and also for its invaluable labors in the interests of the Territory. Its able officials have mapped the topography and geology of over one-third of Alaska's total area of 585,400 square miles. They have investigated every producing mining district in the Territory and mapped many in detail. The results of such surveys have been incorporated in 380 or more separate publications, which cover the subjects and areas under consideration with such fulness, practicality, and accuracy as to elicit the highest commendation. These volumes have been most beneficial to the mining public, and are invaluable to all Alaskan interests. It may be added that practically all the data now discussed have been drawn from the official publications of the Geological Survey.

Alaska surpasses any other equal area of the United States in the variety, extent, and value of its mineral resources. Among the mines now operated are those of gold placers, gold lodes, copper, silver, lead, nickel, tin, palladium, platinum, bismuth, quicksilver, marble, gypsum, coal, and petroleum. Other mines temporarily closed are those of antimony, barites, chromite, graphite, molybdenite, and tungsten, which await higher prices of minerals and lower cost of production.

There have been two periods of unreasonable views on Alaskan mining. The early period of bonanza discoveries and great fortunes therefrom led the general public to expect a continuance of such rich deposits of gold, which were very largely exploited in a few years. The succeeding era of depression was accentuated by the disaster to the great Treadwell mines, and the failure of some of the large auriferous quartz mines near Juneau. The failure to develop rapidly the coal and oil resources of the Territory has also had a misleading effect on those unfamiliar with existing conditions.

The aggregate mineral output of Alaska, to include the year 1924, is valued at $535,600,000. To include the year 1922 the Geological Survey distributes it as follows: gold, $335,526,000; copper, $145,479,000; silver, $8,834,000; coal, $2,273,000; tin, $938,000; lead, $772,000; antimony, $237,000; marble, gypsum, petroleum, etc., $3,476,000. Attaining a value of $1,000,000 in 1892, the maximum mineral output of $48,632,212 was in 1916. The annual values fell irregularly to $17,000,000 in 1921, recovered to $19,500,000 in 1922, and to $20,330,643 in 1923.

Gold was the most productive metal until 1916, when the imperative war demands caused the copper output to rise to $29,484,000 as against $17,242,000 gold product. The third metal in value, silver, has generally been a side product from the gold and copper ores. The recent discovery of high-grade silver deposits in various regions, promises soon to develop another special and profitable mining industry. Silver and copper are treated fully in connection with mining districts.

Enormous as are the coal fields, and promising as are the prospects for petroleum, they are as yet unimportant mineral factors. They are elsewhere treated in Chapter XIII.

Interior mining is done under great disadvantages of severe climate, short season (about four months each year), costly transportation, insufficient water, expensive fuel, frozen ground, and uncertain labor. These adverse conditions particularly affect placer mining, which produces about 85 per cent of the gold output. Along the southeastern coast, however, where transportation is rapid, freights low, and fuel comparatively cheap, mining operations are conducted at a minimum cost, as is illustrated later in the account of the Treadwell mines (Chapter VIII).

The costly, elaborate plants which are found in all rich placer districts make Alaska a rich man's country. Bonanzas are exceedingly rare, and to an increasing extent the product comes from mines operated by men of considerable capital. In general the cost of production is double what it is in the United States proper. During nearly eight months of the long winter the demand for labor is very greatly reduced in the Yukon Basin and on Seward Peninsula, which causes thousands of men to leave each autumn for the "outside," with a consequent uncertainty of their return the following season. With constantly changing force and the necessity of using much new and untrained labor, the situation has been aggravated in some years by labor strikes. As the extended journey out and back from Fairbanks costs about $200, and entails a loss of time exceeding a month, the enhanced cost of production is obvious. Mining industries in southeastern and southwestern Alaska are free from these disadvantages.

The completion of the Alaska Railroad reduces the cost of transportation to such an extent that the mineral output of interior Alaska must largely increase in the near future. Up to 1924 the cost of gold production has been so great that only the richest ground could be profitably mined.

The enormous area of Alaska and the distinctive and varying features of widely separated regions make it advisable to consider gold and copper mining by districts.

BIBLIOGRAPHY.—Brooks: Annual reports of Alaskan Mining Industry, U. S. Geological Survey.

CHAPTER VIII

SOUTHEASTERN ALASKA

HERE began in 1880 the mining industry of the Territory, and the sectional prosperity of the region has depended on the discovery and successful exploitation of the gold and copper bearing lodes. As elsewhere, the industry has been subject to vicissitudes, but it has very largely increased and holds its own as one of the great mineral producers of North America.

In the public mind Alaska is the country of placer bonanzas, but its original ventures and future success are inseparably associated with quartz mining. Already the lodes practically equal the placers from an industrial standpoint, values produced and men employed being considered. In 1922 the lodes produced gold and silver to the value of $3,087,557, against $4,421,369 from placers. It is to be noted that there were employed throughout the year an average of 1,200 men in connection with the lodes, while the force of 2,600 employed on placers for one hundred days during summer was reduced to 402 employed the entire year.

Of quartz mining Brooks says:

Though the developed gold-ore reserves are small, the discovery of promising auriferous lodes in so many widely separated localities is auspicious for a large lode gold-mining development. Silver-bearing galena ores are also widespread.

The mineral output of southeastern Alaska to date considerably exceeds $100,000,000. In 1922, a year of mining depression, the mineral product was $3,084,369. There were operated seven gold-quartz mines, one copper mine, one gypsum mine, a few placers, and a group of extensive marble quarries.

The Juneau District

The oldest American settlement in Alaska is Juneau, and it has the most evident signs of that permanency which casual visitors are fond of denying to Alaskan towns. As the capital of the Territory, the metropolis of southeastern Alaska, and the centre of mining operations, Juneau was properly named for Joseph Juneau, whose discriminating eye and mining skill discovered the quartz and placer riches that have made this region famous.

Dominated by Mount Juneau, against whose background of sheer 3,000 feet the town is outlined as seen from the sea, the capital city is picturesque and interesting. The adjacent coasts of the Alaskan mainland are so steep that the average rise from the sea is about one foot in ten, while mountains a mile high are not unusual within five miles of the ocean, and even nearer in extreme cases. Juneau is built on the slope of a steep mountain, and within its limits there cannot be found a naturally level spot one hundred feet square. Its prominent courthouse is perched on the top of a high hill. The streets are necessarily winding in some places and in others rise sharply and in terraces, one above another. The roadways are plank-covered, and many vine-clad or flower-embowered cottages are reached by gray-mossed stairways. Altogether sightseeing is a vigorous and necessary exercise, for horses are few in Juneau.

With good hotels, indifferent variety shows, excellent restaurants, well-stocked curio shops, Indian basket pedlers, and a hospitable community, the town affords all comforts and many luxuries to visitors. For its residents there are schools, several churches, good markets and shops, a fine water supply, electric lights, an efficient telephone service, and cable connection with Seattle.

Moreover, Juneau is the commercial and supply centre for adjacent mining camps; has banks, assay offices, transportation facilities, hospitals, and other institutions. Here live the governor and other Federal officials for the transaction of judicial, administrative, and mining business. Two daily papers keep march with the world's progress, the chamber of commerce discusses trade and other public matters, the women assemble in their clubs, the few sick (for all Alaska is phenomenally healthy) are well cared for in hospitals, the children are in well-taught schools, the library is fair, and the community is hospitable, orderly, and enterprising. In ten visits there have been experienced no importunity by beggars, no affront from the mythical border ruffian, and no offensive drunken scenes or street disorders. In short, Juneau is a well-governed, intelligent, thriving, self-respecting town, with a population varying between two and three thousand—from summer to winter.

In addition to being on the through line of travel from Seattle to Skagway and to the upper Yukon, Juneau is the point of departure for the westward— to Yakutat, Cordova, Valdez, Cook Inlet, Kodiak, Unalaska, and in summer to Bristol Bay. Adjacent mining camps, canneries, etc., are reached by local steamers—all travel in these regions being by water.

The Juneau gold-bearing areas extend along the mainland from Port Houghton to the head of Lynn Canal, and include the outlying islands, such as Douglass and Admiralty.

The Juneau mining industries owe their birth to placer and quartz discoveries made by Joe Juneau and by Richard Harris in 1880, the first ledge located being now worked by the Alaska-Juneau Company in the Silver Bow region.

Lode Mining

The centre of quartz mining was long on Douglass Island, across a narrow inlet to the west of Juneau. Here is located the famous Treadwell mine, which in the height of its operations was one of the most productive gold mines in the world. At one time it had 880 stamps in operation, and its efficiency was such that for years its average cost of mining and milling was about $1.30 per ton of ore. Among its annual outputs of interest since 1891 are the minimum of $738,049 in 1898, and its maximum of $2,007,482 in 1905, which it is said was very largely exceeded in later years. An excellent account of the methods of mining and of reduction in the Treadwell group was written by A. H. Kinzie (see *Transactions American Institute of Mining Engineering*, Vol. 34).

At the height of its production the Treadwell system was disrupted by the great disaster of 1917, when two of its largest mines were ruined by caving and sea-flooding. Despite this great disaster Juneau continued to be the centre of quartz mining, and in 1923 it produced about two-thirds of all the lode output of Alaska.

While the low value of gold and the enhanced cost of mining have affected the Juneau district, yet it continues to develop new mines, of which in late years the Perseverance and the Alaska-Juneau are most widely known. The Perseverance closed its operations in 1921.

The Alaska-Juneau has continued its operation and has seemingly solved the problem of making ore with low gold content profitable by improved machinery and efficient administration. The mine is developed by a 7,000-foot adit, and is equipped with a concentrating mill giving a daily capacity of 8,000 tons. Its production lately is as follows: 1921, 904,323 tons of ore milled, producing gold, silver, and lead to the value of $1,035,251; 1922, 1,108,559 tons, producing $1,388,679. In these two years 1,211,000 tons of coarse tailings were rejected.

A few placer mines are regularly worked in the Juneau District, but their output has not been important.

The Ketchikan District

Apart from its mining interests, which naturally centre there as the official headquarters, Ketchikan is an incorporated town of about 1,300 inhabitants, with quite extensive business interests. It is by law the first port of call for all steamers doing business with southeastern Alaska, which are required here to make entry of cargo and passengers. It has two good hotels, several large outfitting stores, canneries, a fish-plant, sawmills, and is the commercial distributing point for adjacent regions. It is well provided with educational and religious institutions; has waterworks, electric-light plants, telephonic service, and other modern equipment. Picturesquely located, with its famous salmon stream and forested hills, Ketchikan is an attractive place. Built with some difficulty, owing to the broken, hilly ground, it has an excellent system of boardwalks and roads, most creditable to the town. By almost daily steamers in summer and semi-weekly in winter, Seattle is reached 660 miles to the south and Juneau 240 miles to the north. Local lines of steamers run with some regularity to Port Simpson, up the Skeena River, and to Prince of Wales Island.

The centre of copper-mining in this district is on Prince of Wales Island, where very extensive plants were built, including smelters, tramways, repair shops, sawmills, etc. At one time there were ten copper-producing mines, and developments were made in other deposits. Many of these mines are

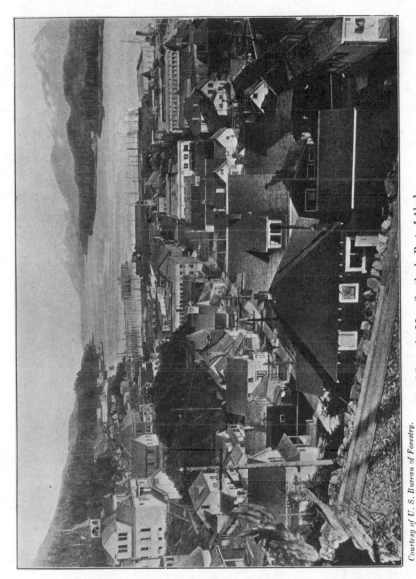

Ketchikan, the Most Southerly Port of Alaska.

permanently closed, and others await increased prices
before active operation. Of all these mines only the
Rust and Brown Company has been able to continue
these many years a regular and profitable output. It
holds its position as the fifth mine in its production
of copper.

Of the silver-lead deposits, those of the Moonshine
Mine, on Prince of Wales Island, are the only ores
which have reached a stage of production, and that
on a small scale. The Palladium Mine, in the hands
of a receiver, has made no output for several years.
The gold ores have not yet been developed to a paying basis.

The most promising improvement of recent years
in the Ketchikan District has been the development
near Hyder, in the Portland Canal region, of quite a
number of properties, carrying chiefly gold, silver,
and lead ores, with some other valuable minerals.
The prospects of profitable development are reported
as most favorable. On the Canadian side of the
canal, close to the international boundary, the Pre-
mier Mine produced in 1921, 4,356 tons of ore, which
is officially reported to have "yielded 35,000 ounces
of gold and 1,200,000 ounces of silver, valued at
$1,400,000."

The molybdenite deposits near Shakan, Prince of
Wales Island, are yet in the developing stage.

A new industry of southeastern Alaska pertains to
building materials, the non-metallic minerals of ce-
ment, gypsum, clay, and granite being widely distributed. Marble quarries have been located and

opened at various points on Prince of Wales Island, though very promising deposits are elsewhere in process of exploitation. The most extensive operations have been made by the Alaska Marble Company, whose quarries near Shakan have been worked since 1905. They have ample installation and plant in the shape of a gravity railroad, dressing and cutting machinery, with suitable shipping facilities. The importance of the industry is shown by the increase of shipments of marble and gypsum.

Wrangell District

The Ketchikan District originally included this district, which is now separate and has as its northern limits Frederick Sound and Chatham Strait. The two districts were separated in 1901 by order of the United States Supreme Court, such action being calculated to facilitate the business of each district.

The most valuable mineral of the Wrangell District are the copper deposits on Kupreanof Island. Although well developed, their regular operation awaits improved prices. There are also rich and extensive silver-lead ores, which promise to be economically valuable in the near future. On Castle Island, Duncan Canal, barite deposits have been fully developed, but await the perfecting of title by patent, lately asked for, before active operation.

The town of Wrangell, near the mouth of the Stikine River, is the centre of a region rich in fisheries, furs, and timber. It has considerable trade with the Stikine valley of British Columbia.

The Sitka District

Sitka itself is most interesting, but its situation on the outer edge of the islands, which made it convenient to Russia, puts it at a disadvantage with other Alaskan towns. In 1867 it was the capital of Alaska, the headquarters of the military district and of the Treasury agents, and the recognized centre of Alaskan interests. The establishment of a mission with school and hospital, the location of an agricultural experiment station, its selection as the diocesan residence of Bishop Rowe, and the establishment of cable communication, all added to its importance, while its designation as a naval station, with marine garrison and coal depot, was thought to have insured its prosperity. Suffering from the diversion of trade, it is, however, gradually losing its commercial importance.

Neglected though it be by trade, Sitka is the most interesting Alaskan town for tourists from the southland. It is reached by the inland passage through winding channels, hedged in by emerald shores and fascinating islets that charm every lover of the beautiful and unusual.

The town itself has a striking background of mountains, which is greatly enhanced in attractiveness under the rays of the not too frequent summer sun. Westward one looks on a landscape made beautiful by the graceful blue slopes of volcanic Mount Edgecumbe, especially when from its extinct snow-filled crater there drift down alabaster streaks of newly fallen snow, or when a vanishing storm leaves its summit adorned by drifting bannerets of fleecy clouds.

The Bay of Sitka can scarce be equalled for scenery: in fine weather for its mingled softness of beauty and rugged picturesqueness, or on dark, stormy days for its stern and sombre grandeur.

On shore first of all are the Indian curio women, with varied wealth of articles—quaint, graceful, and original, or harsh, common, and barbaric, as run the taste and judgment of the visitor.

Sitka town presents few structures of interest beyond the moss-covered log buildings of a past age and former régime and the severely simple Greek church. Externally the church is a green-roofed, bulbous-domed building, with a clock-faced tower and sharp spire, attractive as a novelty to most tourists. Its interior and the furnishings appeal to every one appreciative of unusual art forms or interested in either the method or the outcome of religious systems. To one class appeal the interior arrangements —the holy of holies, the screens, the silver-cased icons, the ancient vestments wrought of cloth of gold, and the artistic silver censers—all enhanced æsthetically by the external and surrounding simplicity of the building itself. In contemplative and susceptible minds, however, rise up holy memories of the Russian priest who furnished the church, Veniaminof, the combined St. Paul and St. John the Baptist of Alaskan natives. The consideration of such a life of consecration, devotion, and self-sacrifice is a benison to any soul.

Turning from Russian to American efforts, the road to other churches and to the Industrial Training School (see Chap. XXIX) winds partly by the shore of the bay and partly by shady paths along Indian River through a park of charm and beauty. Indian River Park is so thoroughly sylvan and so unexpected in its aspects as to be strikingly impressive. One looks skyward through tangled vistas of tall, dark spruces, fragrant yellow cedars, or sombre, graceful pines, and turns his eyes earthward to enjoy the dense flower-covered sward and extended patches of edible berries, in great variety. Meanwhile the ear is filled with the murmur of babbling brook or by sound of gentle waterfall, and gladdened by such melodious and full bird song as is rarely heard elsewhere in Alaska. Unfortunate the Sitkan tourist who has not been there favored by bright sun and these other delightful experiences, for he fell on evil days.

Sitkan Mines

In this district the large Chichagoff gold mine continued in 1924 its productivity, under new ownership. Productive work was continued the same year on the Hirst-Chichagoff, with a five-stamp mill, and the installation of a ten-stamp mill at the Apex El-Nido Mine, near Lisianski Strait. While the prospecting of nickel-bearing copper has not reached a commercial value stage, further exploration is justified. The nickel occurs with pyrrhotite and chalcopyrite. Widely separated nickel deposits are found in Bohemia basin, Yakobi Island, and at Surge, Tanakis, and Snipe Bays. The gypsum mine on Chichagoff Island has been profitably operated for several successive years. Altogether the mining future of the Sitkan District seems most encouraging.

Skagway District

The construction of the Alaska Railroad decreased the commercial importance of the town of Skagway, at the head of Lynn Canal, the American ocean terminus of the White Pass and Yukon Railway.

Placer mining continues on an individual and small scale in the drainage basin of the Chilkat at Lituya Bay and a few isolated camps.

It is to be noted that the gold production of southeastern Alaska is almost entirely from lode. In this connection the Geological Report of 1924 states: "In 1924, 29 quartz mines in Alaska produced $2,750,000 in gold, an increase of more than $400,-000 over the output for 1923. This increase is largely credited to the Alaska-Juneau mine."

CHAPTER IX

THE BERING SEA REGION

UNDER this heading are included the bays, sounds, and sea north of the Aleutian chain, the Seward Peninsula, the Kuskokwim watershed, and the Alaskan coast, except the lower Yukon Valley. It has been a matter of surprise that this remote and desolate region—arctic and subarctic—shut out from the rest of the world for the greater part of the year, should be the most productive of the Alaskan districts. Yet such is the economic story of this vast area.

From its shores and waters have come the fur seals (see Chapter XIV) and other sea animals, the salmon (see Chapter XV) and whale fisheries, the furs of land animals, the reindeer herds, the placers and silver-bearing ores of the Kuskokwim, and the wonderful bonanzas of Seward Peninsula, which in the aggregate exceed in value the products of any other Alaskan region.

Placer Mining in Alaska

Since 1880 the placer mines of Alaska have yielded $234,000,000, and as the first great stimulus to this enormous industry was made on the shores of Bering Sea, it is well to summarize the various phases as seen by the Alaskan expert, Brooks.

He says:

Other bonanzas than those of Nome were soon discovered, and by 1906 the value of the annual output of placer gold had reached $18,600,000, and the industry employed about 8,000 men. Declining, by 1913 its value was reduced to $10,680,000 and the miners to 4,700. From 1914 to 1917 the average annual output was about $10,000,000. The war affected Alaskan industries seriously, and placer mining reached its minimum, only $3,873,000. It increased to $4,395,000 in 1922.

With the rapid exhaustion of the bonanzas, successful alluvial mining necessitated a greater use of power-driven machinery to harvest Alaska's large reserves of low-grade auriferous gravels, but this work is possible only in easily accessible districts.

A large number of the placer deposits occur in semi-arid regions, where the annual precipitation is only from ten to twenty inches. An extra-dry season always curtails gold production.

The cost of operation was constantly lowered by improved methods of mining, especially in gold-dredging, the output of which increased from $20,000, in 1903, to $2,200,000, in 1913.

In 1922 Alaska gold dredges produced $1,767,753 gold; in 1923 a gold output of $1,848,596 was made by twenty-five dredges. The new dredges include two, installed at Nome, of the largest ever built in Alaska. In spite of adverse conditions, gold-dredging is on the increase in Alaska.

The outlook for large-scale placer mining is very encouraging, yet in many districts the day of profitable small operations is passing.

As to future placers, he says:

A rough estimate, which includes only the auriferous gravel whose gold content is large enough to be profitably exploited by methods now used, shows that there is still about $350,000,000 worth of placer gold in the ground of Alaska.

Placer Mining on Ester Creek, near Fairbanks.
(Washing up the cump, or frozen gravel, mined in winter.)

The percentage of placer gold produced by dredges has risen from 12 in 1911 to 40 in 1922.

Mines of Seward Peninsula

Seward Peninsula is especially a region of placer

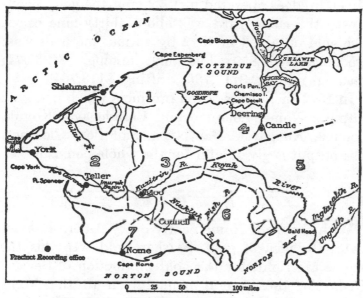

Map No. 2.   Mining Precints of Seward Peninsula.

mining, though with the decadence of the placers more or less successful efforts have been made at lode mining. In 1922 there was a producing galena mine in the Fairhaven precinct.

Methods and conditions of mining have radically changed since pioneer days. Under sluice-box and shovel methods ground producing less than one dol-

lar per cubic foot could not be profitably mined.
Mining has largely passed to corporations, who have
introduced dredges, scrapers, steam shovels, steam
thawers, pumping plants, and hydraulic elevators.
Ground can be worked, if in quantities, when producing twenty-five cents per cubic foot. There were
fifteen dredges operated in 1922, and the gold recov-
ery to the cubic yard was about thirty-nine cents.
The gold obtained in 1922 by various methods was:
dredging, $609,859; hydraulic mining, $426,671;
open-cut mining, $117,736; drifting, $110,734.

In 1922 there were seven precincts which had gold
outputs: Nome, Solomon and Casadepaga, Koyuk,
Council, Kougarok, Fairhaven, and Port Clarence.
The output is given later for the whole peninsula.

Nome Precinct

With the word Nome nearly every American associates the idea of gold, Alaskan gold. In this the
people are right, for the gold production of Seward
Peninsula, the general name given to the Nome
region, aggregated to 1921 the enormous sum of
$82,000,000, a materially larger output than any
other Alaskan district has yielded. Moreover, it is
of interest that the earliest discoveries in Council
District, on Ophir Creek, and in Nome, on Anvil
Creek, long held their own as the largest producers.
Indeed, they have yielded three-fourths of the gold
values of Seward Peninsula—as shown by the outputs of three years, 1902–1904, $13,425,000, of which

nearly 60 per cent came from the Nome District and 19 per cent from Council.

The details connected with the increase of the gold output from $75,000 in 1898 to $2,800,000 the following year, and the growth in a single season of a mining camp of a few score men into a, mushroom town of 18,000 or more, are not parts of this book, though the author was a Nome visitor in the fateful year of 1900.

Indeed, it would take volumes to tell the story, with its countless incidents, whose true and graphic portrayal would exceed in thrilling interest the wildest romance of the age. Among these were the scheme of late comers to overthrow by vote in mass meeting all claims located by their fortunate predecessors; the active jumping of claims; the disputing of locations; the despair of thousands of hungry, disappointed men; the epidemic of typhoid; the home shipment of indigents; the impracticable mining machinery; the speculative schemes; the gold-brick mining companies; the camp dissipations; the displacement of the natives; the astounding discovery of the golden sands of the beach; the judicial system of receiverships with consequent ejectment of original owners and of their machinery from fabulously rich claims. These and more are parts of a history alternately comic and tragic, corrupt and straightforward, generous and hateful, disorderly and law-abiding. The sterling qualities of the American miner were never displayed to greater advantage than in the development and transition of Nome into a successful and permanent mining district, with so little of cruelty, dishonesty, and crime, at a minimum cost of human life and suffering.

The population fell from 2,600, in 1910, to 852, in 1920, but is said to be increasing.

Nome city is the commercial centre of Nome District, which includes the southwestern part of the peninsula. The most astonishing yield of this region was from the ruby beach sands, which in two years produced gold to the value of $2,000,000. The richest placers have been those of Anvil Creek, which, yet productive, had an output of more than $6,000,-000 up to 1905. Of this more than $1,000,000 came from an area one-tenth of a mile square. Very rich placers were found on the three beach lines, two ancient beaches being far from the sea, each producing several millions of dollars.

The Nome Precinct maintains its standing as the most productive of the precincts. The gold product fell from $585,000 in 1921 to $485,000 in 1922, the number of summer mines being reduced from 42, with 230 miners, to 26, with 164 miners. Two very large dredges were installed in 1922, making six in all.

This was followed by an increase in 1923, when the output was $1,275,000 from 60 summer-placers, worked by 606 miners. It is estimated that the gold values of 1924 are slightly higher.

Council Precinct

This precinct includes the southeastern part of the peninsula. Its output decreased from $420,000 in

1921 to $375,000 in 1922. While Nome is an untim-
bered country, Council is favored by a considerable
area of spruce forests. Five dredges are now regularly used in the precinct.

Fairhaven Precinct

This precinct, with an area of 7,500 square miles,
lies to the south of Kotzebue Sound, along which it
extends about 150 miles east, from Goodhope Bay.
Reached via Bering Strait and the Arctic Ocean during a short summer season, it is a most promising region. It increased its product of $120,000 from 20
mines in 1921 to $150,000 from 26 mines in 1922. In
this precinct was the only gold-lode producing mine
of the peninsula in 1922. Some lignitic coal was
also mined for local use.

Koyuk Precinct

This precinct lies to the north of Norton Bay, in
the southeast of the peninsula. In 1921, 17 mines
produced $152,000, which was reduced to $109,000
in 1922, due to the closing of 6 mines. The greater
part of the deep mining of the region is here done,
and therefrom was obtained the only platinum of
1922.

Solomon and Casadepaga Precinct

This new precinct, to the east of Council Precinct,
produced in 1921 $120,000 from 12 mines, which was
reduced to $111,000 from 14 mines in 1922. Three
dredges are now installed in this precinct.

Kougarok Precinct

The production of $45,000 from 20 mines in 1921 fell to $32,000 from the 11 mines worked during 1922. One dredge only was used. The precinct is an interior one, lying to the east of Port Clarence. It has summer travel by boat up Mary River, from Port Clarence as far as Davidson.

Port Clarence Precinct

This precinct is the largest, and includes the northwestern peninsula. Teller, where the first reindeer station (see Chapter XIX) was established, is the only deep harbor of the peninsula. Its placer output is insignificant, falling from $8,000 from 7 mines in 1921 to $3,000 from the 5 mines worked during the summer of 1922. Here are located the only producing tin mines, and from this precinct has been obtained nearly the entire tin, valued at $936,664, of Alaska. The low price of tin temporarily closed these mines, but in 1924 a few tons of stream tin were mined.

Arctic Ocean Districts

These mineral deposits lie to the north of Seward Peninsula, but are intimately associated therewith, as the peninsula is the travel route to them. The coal deposits of Cape Lisburne and the petroleum properties near Cape Barrow are elsewhere recorded (see Chapter XIII). The placer mines of the Kobuk River basin are being developed in a small way, the total output being annually about $8,000 in gold. Hydraulic plants, it is said, are to be installed for full exploitation.

Gold Output

The gold and silver productivity of Seward Peninsula from 1897 to 1922, inclusive, amounts to $83,380-185 gold and $279,608 silver. As shown below by

DETAILED PRODUCTS, GOLD AND SILVER, 1897–1923

	Gold	Silver
1897	$15,000	$52
1898	75,000	56
1899	2,800,000	9,752
1900	4,750,000	17,097
1901	4,130,700	14,747
1902	4,561,800	14,035
1903	4,465,000	13,052
1904	4,164,600	14,021
1905	4,800,000	16,997
1906	7,500,000	29,005
1907	7,000,000	16,828
1908	5,120,000	10,905
1909	4,260,000	10,853
1910	3,500,000	10,971
1911	3,100,000	9,718
1912	3,000,000	10,710
1913	2,500,000	7,305
1914	2,700,000	8,667
1915	2,900,000	8,878
1916	2,950,000	9,391
1917	2,000,000	11,340
1918	1,108,000	6,022
1919	1,360,000	7,773
1920	1,300,000	7,426
1921	1,455,085	6,411
1922	1,265,000	6,790
1923	1,270,000	*6,000

* Estimated.

the table of annual outputs, the maximum gold output, $7,500,000, was attained in 1906, since which year there had been an almost uninterrupted decrease to $1,108,000 in 1918, due to the war.

Fuel Conditions

The extensive deposits of coal and petroleum are treated in Chapter XIII.

In the eastern part of Seward Peninsula there is a scattering growth of spruce, the largest trees not exceeding 16 inches in diameter and 50 feet in height. However, the steam sawmill at Council has been able to meet local demands and compete with imported lumber.

Among the unexploited fuel resources of Seward Peninsula, as indeed of Alaska in general, may be mentioned peat, which is available in the tundra regions in enormous quantities. As yet either wood or coal is the more economical fuel, but, with increasing demands for fuel and a steady decrease in the supply of wood, the development of a peat industry is not improbable in northern Alaska.

Nome City

There is not much to be said of Nome City beyond the statement that it has all the modern comforts and most of the luxuries for physical well-being, with amusements and social pleasures pertaining to a wealthy, intelligent community. Springing into existence as a city of 18,000, it now numbers about 1,000 in winter and double that number of inhabitants when the arctic sun of June gives it the glory of continuous daylight. It is the commercial, judicial, and educational centre of Seward Peninsula.

How Nome is Reached

There is frequent steamer service between Seattle and Nome, the first boat reaching Nome, in a voyage from eight to ten days, about June 15, and the last boat leaving there about October 15. The distance is about 2,741 miles. The approximate fares are $75 to $100 for first-class and $35 for steerage. Travel in and out by land is via St. Michaels, Holy Cross, and Fairbanks, whence by Alaska Railway and Seward. In summer the journey to Fairbanks is by river, and in winter by dog-sledge. Summer communication from Nome with the Yukon and Tanana Valley is via St. Michael, 115 miles distant, from which point boats run very irregularly up the Yukon, leaving from June 20 to September 20, and arriving from June 10 to September 30.

Kuskokwim District

The mining is done in the upper tributaries of the Kuskokwim River. This water-shed is divided into two regions. The lower, below Bethel, is low-lying tundra plain. Above this the river, one of the largest in Alaska, is a rapid stream fed by many tributaries. The rolling country, with many areas of birch, spruce, and willow, rises to a mountainous region. The lower region is given to fishing, the upper to mining.

Bethel, 80 miles from the sea, is the centre of activity—judicial, school, trading, and missionary work (see Chapter XXIX). Akiak, 40 miles above, is a native village, with hospital and school. In 1920 Bethel had a population of 221, and Akiak 150.

In 1922 there were about 30 placer mines operated by 137 men. Dredge work is possible for five months. Lode mining is steadily developing, and the mine at Nixon Fork is operating an amalgamating and concentrating mill. The quicksilver deposits of the lower Kuskokwim are being developed.

The placer gold produced in the Kuskokwim District from 1908 to 1923 aggregates $2,262,000. The number of mines operated, men employed, and output in recent years are as follows: 1918, 19 mines, 87 men, $100,000; 1919, 22, 104 and $350,000; 1920, 32, 126 and $305,000; 1921, 31, 106 and $520,000; 1922, 30, 137 and $542,000; 1923, 30, 110 and $292,000. The decrease of 1923 is attributed to the very dry season, and consequent failure of water for hydraulic power. The Whalen mine, formerly operated as the Nixon mines, produced considerable gold in 1924.

CHAPTER X

THE YUKON BASIN

THE Yukon River has rendered possible the exploitation of the mineral resources of the interior of Alaska through its wondrous facilities for cheap and reliable transportation. The river and its tributaries are navigable by steamboats nearly 3,000 miles, with as much more additional water channels that are traversed by poling boats. There is not a mining camp in all the great watershed of the tributaries of the Yukon that is 100 miles distant from navigable water. The length of the navigable season of the Yukon is surprising, considering its high latitude. At Circle, near the Arctic Circle, in nine years the Yukon opened between May 11 and 22, while it does not close until early November.

The borders of the great river furnish scanty results to the gold seeker, while the few placer-paying tributaries flow from the south, the ice-clad flanks of the high Alaskan range being more prolific of gold than the lower mountains to the north.

The principal settlements in the Yukon Valley merit brief allusions. Eagle, a town of about 100, near the Canadian boundary, is the customs office for the region, and a trade centre for Fortymile and other camps. Tanana, at the junction of the Yukon and Tanana rivers, is the site of St. James Episcopal mission, adjoining old Fort Gibbon, now abandoned. Other towns are mentioned in their respective mining districts.

Gold Mines

The watershed of the great Yukon River is a region of vast extent, and deposits of gold are widely distributed in paying quantities. In 1922 there were no less than 18 separate mining districts in active and profitable operation. While the most widely known districts are Fairbanks, Iditarod, Innoko, and Tolovana, half a dozen others are of growing economic importance.

Gold constitutes practically the mineral putput of the entire Basin. The mineral product of the Yukon Basin from 1886 to 1922 inclusive amounts to $137,-580,598. It is thus distributed: Gold from placers, $134,331,000; from lodes, $1,357,090. Silver from placers, $682,093; from lodes, $248,787. Coal, $416,845. Antimony, copper, lead, platinum, tin, and tungsten, $544,783.

In the summer of 1922 there were operated 321 gold-placers and 8 gold-lode mines, as well as 2 coal-mines. Districts producing more than $100,000 were: Fairbanks, $693,000; Iditarod, $280,000; Innoko and Tolstoi, $224,000; Tolovana, $221,000; Koyukuk, $132,000; Ruby, $123,000; and Circle, $121,000.

There was a notable increase in 1922, the values being $2,303,755 in 1922, as against $2,093,088 in 1921, the principal gain being $278,275 in gold. The increase of 20 per cent in Fairbanks in 1922, as compared with 1921, shows what may be expected in the immediate future from the reduction of mining costs brought about by the completion of the Alaska Railroad. It is not unreasonable to forecast the Yukon Basin as the greatest mineral producer, in the future, of the Alaskan districts.

Fairbanks District

Owing to its special importance, this district is described separately in Chapter XI, under "*The Tanana Basin.*"

Chandalar District

This camp is within the arctic circle, being about 100 miles up the Chandalar River, which enters the Yukon near Fort Yukon. Although within the reach of light-draft steamers, it is difficult of access. Its output, 1906 to 1922, was $254,519, with its maximum of $83,574 in 1922. This seems small, but it has steadily improved the past four years, and its prospects are excellent for future development. For years promising gold-quartz lodes have been held, but the remoteness of the region and the excessive cost of bringing mining machinery into the camp have retarded lode-mining development. Brooks says: "There are indications that eventually the Chandalar region will be included in the list of gold-lode camps."

In 1920 Chandalar village had a population of 20, while the district had 257.

Chisina District. See "*The Tanana Basin,*" Chapter XI.

Circle District

The settlement of Circle, on the southwest side of the Yukon and near the arctic circle, is the centre of the Birch Creek mines, which are among the oldest placers worked in Alaska. Its production has been large, aggregating from 1894 to 1922, $6,814,170, $49,505 being silver. It reached its maximum in 1896, $706,780. The annual output never fell below $136,000 until its minimum of $55,506 in 1920. With the introduction of dredges its 15 summer and 8 winter mines produced in 1922, $122,007. Recent discoveries give promise of future increases.

In 1920 the population of the district was 594, including Fort Yukon, Circle, and Black River villages.

Eagle District

The town of Eagle, near the Canadian boundary, is the customs centre for the eastern territory. It is the trade centre for Fortymile and other mining camps in extreme northeastern Alaska. The post of Fort Egbert is no longer occupied by the army.

Mining has been carried on for fifteen years, with no very large results. It now depends largely on the Seventy-Mile valley, which is sometimes called a separate district. The output from 1908 to 1922 was $348,808, of which $1,808 was silver. From fourteen summer mines in 1922 there was produced, largely by hydraulic methods, $24,159, a material increase from $16,093 in 1921. Much is expected from the upper basin of Seventy-Mile River.

In 1920 the population was 185, including both white and native villages.

Fortymile District

This district is directly south of Eagle, and its exploitation was long conducted under special difficulties, as Fortymile Creek enters the Yukon in Canadian territory. Conditions were remedied by the Richardson Commission, which finally succeeded in making a practicable all-American trail between Fortymile and Eagle.

The Fortymile is one of the oldest mining fields in Alaska, and its continued profitable output is remarkable, considering its remoteness and the long period of placer working. From 1885 to 1922 it produced $6,506,133, $35,133 being silver. Its maximum was $308,360 in 1904, and the annual output fell below $100,000 in 1914. The average 1914 to 1922 was $54,000. In 1922, 24 summer and 18 winter mines produced $50,423. Scarcity of water has somewhat affected hydraulic operations, which are expected to replace scrapers.

The population of the district in 1920 was 317, including Tanana Crossing village.

Hot Springs District. See "*The Tanana Basin,*" Chapter XI.

Iditarod District

This district is in the watershed of Iditarod River, located south of the Yukon and to the east of the Innoko. It is one of the richest placer regions of the

Yukon, and is surpassed in its production by Fairbanks only. The Iditarod aggregates values of $19,-
107,946—silver $87,946—from 1910 to 1922. Its
maximum of $3,518,313 was in 1911. In 1922 the
output from 13 mines, $282,041; the second year to
fall below half a million dollars. The greater part of
the 1922 output was mined by two dredges on Otter
Creek, working 163 days. Five steam scrapers and
six hydraulic plants are used. Lode ores are present,
but high freight charges into this remote region make
their working unprofitable at present. In the upper
Iditarod is one of the two quicksilver mines in Alaska,
the other being in an adjacent region on the Kuskokwim River.

The annual outputs of gold, including small values
of silver, have been as follows in Iditarod: 1910,
$502,297; 1911, $2,511,273; 1912, $3,518,313; 1913,
$1,865,769; 1914, $2,065,849; 1915, $2,055,337; 1916,
$1,956,589; 1917, $1,509,105; 1918, $1,249,000; 1919,
$730,937; 1920, $508,954; 1921, $352,482; 1922,
$282,041.

In 1920 the Otter District, including the incorporated town of Iditarod, 50, and Flat Village, had a
population of 346.

Innoko and Tolstoi Districts

These rich placers are in the upper valley of the
Innoko, the largest southeasterly tributary of the
lower Yukon. This stream enters the main river
near the Holy Cross (see Chapter XXIX), the most
successful of the missions in contributing to the

agricultural development of the natives of the lower Yukon.

The Innoko camps are from 50 to 300 miles beyond the head of navigation by steamboats—the Indian village of Deekakat, 200 miles from the Yukon. Freight from this village is poled up the river in summer, a portion of the way to the productive creeks— Anvil, Gaines, Little, Ophir, and Yankee. Under these disadvantages it appears surprising that from 1907 to 1922 there should have been an output of $3,022,825, with a maximum of $340,908 in 1909. The product of the Tolstoi District is small, the four mines being a one-man property operated by the owner. The minimum output of $110,560 in 1920 has been followed by improvement as shown by the following annual values: The product of the 18 summer and 4 winter mines, $225,264 in 1922, was the result of a dredge in Yankee Creek. Another dredge, to be operated by hydro-electric plant, is expected to increase materially the output. The difficulty of establishing such dredges is shown by the experiences in 1922, when steam-dredge material, which had to be sledded hundreds of miles to Gaines Creek, was landed in the autumn at Tacotna. Placer values of the Innoko and Tolstoi Districts: 1907, $13,044; 1908, $72,196; 1909, $340,908; 1910, $325,901; 1911, $250,681; 1912, $250,681; 1913, $280,869; 1914, $200,658; 1915, $190,495; 1916, $220,744; 1917, $175,917; 1918, $120,608; 1919, $140,803; 1920, $103,577; 1921, $110,569; 1922, $225,264.

In 1920, Ophir District had a population of 145.

Koyukuk District

Among the instances of energy of the American miner are to be especially recorded mining work in the watershed of the Koyukuk, the most important northern tributary of the lower Yukon River. This district is probably the most northerly gold camp of the world. The principal activities are on the creeks of the headwaters of the Koyukuk, on the southern flank of the Endicott Mountains. The richest placers are more than 600 miles from the mouth of the river, which is navigable for a few months of the summer as far as Battles, which is the commercial centre of mining activities. The chief operations lie around Coldfoot, which is 100 miles further north and is reached as to its freight by poling boat in summer and by dog-sled in winter. The placer regions are entirely within the arctic circle, yet they have been systematically exploited for a quarter of a century, without exhausting the placer resources of this remarkable region.

In 1920 the Koyukuk District had a population of 349, including Alatna, 32; Allakaket, 85; and South Fork, 29.

The output from 1900 to 1922 amounts to $4,904,147, of which $20,147 was in silver. The maximum was $433,806 in 1913, and in these years has fallen below $100,000 but twice. The following data show how well the Koyukuk mines have held up: 1900 to 1909, $2,208,993; 1910, $160,598; 1911, $150,551; 1912, $225,457; 1913, $433,806; 1914,

$286,091; 1915, $291,017; 1916, $321,458; 1917, $255,421; 1918, $153,880; 1919, $114,881; 1920, $91,161; 1921, $78,119; 1922, $132,214.

In 1922 there were operated 36 summer and 10 winter mines, and their material increase over 1921 was due to the discovery of new rich bench ground on the famous Nolan Creek. Hammond and Sixty-Mile Rivers afford prospects favorable to the continued success in this arctic region. Galena ore deposits exist in the valley of Wild River, 20 miles west of Coldfoot. Three hydraulic plants have been established in the placers.

The establishment of the Episcopalian mission at Allakakct, on the arctic circle, is mentioned in Chapter XXIX.

Marshall District

This district is on the lower Yukon, and with it is included the Stuyahok camp, about 40 miles to the northeast, 10 miles from Tuckers Landing on the Yukon. The production from 1914 to 1922 was $1,133,526, with a maximum of $427,719 in 1917. The minimum output in 1922 from 12 summer mines was but $22,134. A hydraulic plant and scraper have been introduced, and increased production is expected.

Rampart District

The town of Rampart, on the Yukon, just south of the arctic circle, has long been the commercial centre of the adjacent mining industries, and the site of the federal crop activities. By its labors the officials of the experimental station of the Department of Agriculture have successfully proved the practicability of raising good crops of grain and of vegetables.

Mining has been carried on in this district for many years, and the output since 1896 has been $1,610,202; silver values, $7,202. In 1922 the production was only $18,062 from 14 mines. The installation of dredge machinery is expected to increase the output.

The population of the district in 1920 was 274, including the villages of Rampart, 121, and Stevens, 103.

Richardson District. See *"The Tanana Basin,"* Chapter XI.

Ruby District

This camp lies south of the lower Yukon River, about thirty miles from Louden, the nearest settlement. The placers produced, 1907 to 1922, $5,452,-189, of which silver was $26,189. In 1922 there were operated 24 summer and 13 winter mines. The original richness of the placers appears from the annual production since 1912, when it was fully operated: 1912, $175,712; 1913, $788,134; 1914, $1,003,655; 1915, $702,345; 1916, $853,697; 1917, $880,046; 1918, $403,000; 1919, $166,406; 1920, $171,213; 1921, $171,158; 1922, $123,819.

Very promising galena veins have been prospected, and the Perseverance mine produced in 1922 very high-grade lead-silver ore, to the amount of 50 tons, which was sledded to the Yukon.

The population of the Nulato District in 1920 was 994, including the villages of Kaltag, 89; Koyukuk, 124; Louden, 64; Nulato, 258; and Ruby, 128.

Tolovana District. See "*The Tanana Basin,*" Chapter XI.

Coal

From time to time there have been expectations of the utilization of the extensive coal-beds of the Yukon, of which the known area approximates 400 square miles. However, oil has tended to displace coal as supplementary fuel to the 30,000 cords of wood used annually by Yukon steamboats. (See Chapter XIII.)

CHAPTER XI

THE TANANA BASIN

THE watershed of the great Tanana River contains natural resources of specially important character in the evolution of a permanent community, and for the upbuilding of a populous State in the future. It is favored with rich gold placers, promising gold-quartz, silver-bearing galena ores, immense coal-beds, considerable timber, and extended agricultural areas under cultivation. It has a permanent population, engaged in local industries of profitable value. Its past disadvantages of limited and expensive transportation have been largely removed by the building of local roads and the completion of the Alaska Railroad. It is now better able than ever before to transact its local business, and is kept in direct and constant relations with the outside world. Its future seems assured by its attractiveness as a region where there will be a rapid development in riches and in population.

The output of precious metals mined to date in this basin exceeds $86,000,000, which is more than one-fourth of the gold and silver produced in all of Alaska. Its enormous deposits of coal are in process of rapid exploitation. (See Chapter XIII.)

Besides many scattered prospects, it has six organized mining districts—Bonnifield, Chissana, Fairbanks, Hot Springs, Kantishna, and Tolovana, which produce values exceeding $500,000 annually.

The explorations and discoveries of Allen in 1885, by Brooks and Peters in 1898, by Pedro in 1902, and Barnette's establishment of a trading post on the site of Fairbanks in 1901, are the successive factors which led up to the wonderful development of the Tanana Basin, which once had an annual yield of $10,000,000 in gold, a larger amount than has been elsewhere mined in an Alaskan district.

Bonnifield District

This district extends eastward from the Nenana River to and including the Wood River Basin, and in general is co-extensive with the Nenana coal field (see Chapter XIII). The two coal-mines put forth in 1922 about 20,000 tons of lignitic coal.

The gold and silver mines are less important economically than the coal deposits. The output of the precious metals has always been small, aggregating from 1903 to 1922 $286,422, with a maximum of $50,309 in 1909. In 1922, seven mines had an output of $29,200. There are eight open-cut mines, and the working season is about 140 days. Two hydraulic plants, established in 1922, are expected to increase the output. A gold-bismuth quartz prospect, about ten miles from the Alaska Railroad, is promising in lode development. Considerable work was done on it in 1924, but transportation costs forbid its present exploitation.

In 1920 the Nenana District had a population of 1,258.

Chisana District

This new district, situated northeast of the Wrangel Mountains, is in the watershed of the Chisana, a tributary of the upper Tanana River. It produced from 1913 to 1922, $648,511, the maximum of $251,609 being in 1914. Soon decreasing, the average output for five years, 1918 to 1922, was $23,000. The nine summer mines produced in the last-named year $29,200. Mining is principally done by automatic dams, which, washing away the overburden, leave the bedrock to be cleaned by pick-and-shovel methods. The active mining period is short, May to August. In 1920 Chisana village had a population of 148.

Hot Springs District

Among the many hot springs of Alaska, that on Baker Creek, near the mouth of the Tanana, is the most important. By these waters the immediate neighborhood is so warmed that about fifty acres are susceptible to a high degree of agricultural cultivation. Efforts have been made to make the springs a winter watering place for interior Alaska. The discovery of very rich placers turned it into a mining camp, known as Hot Springs.

The production from 1902 to 1922 was $6,298,965, $30,565 being silver. The maximum of $806,534 in 1916 was followed by steady decreases to the minimum of $35,348 in 1921. This was succeeded by an increase in 1922, when 25 mines produced $55,631. Material increases are expected in the immediate future through the replacement of drift by open cut mining, the introduction of hydraulic machinery, and the reduction of excessive overhead freight-costs, by the completion of the Alaska Railroad. Then many placers of lower grade can be profitably worked. The population of the district in 1920 was 198.

In 1924, some stream tin was recovered as a by-product of gold-mining in this district.

Kantishna District

This is a remote interior camp, situated to the north of Mt. McKinley, west of the Chulitna, a tributary of the Susitna River. Consequently, its output from 1903 to 1922 aggregates only $512,060, the silver valued at $3,060. The introduction of hydraulic machinery resulted in the maximum product, $32,403 in 1922. Overhead expenses have been excessive, as supplies are brought in over a bad trail by caterpillar traction from Diamond, the head of launch navigation on Bearpaw River. The Alaska Railroad is now within about 60 miles of the camp.

Sulphide-bearing lodes have been prospected. They lie about 14 miles from timber, but fortunately are near lignite beds. More than 1,100 tons of a galena deposit were mined a few years since, but it had to be carried by horse-sleds to the Kantishna River, and later by light-draft steamers to the Tanana. Only hand-picked ore was thus handled, which gave $3.25 gold and 140 ounces of silver to the ton. The population of the district was 120 in 1920.

Richardson District

This district is south of Fairbanks, near the junction of the Tanana and Little Delta rivers.

The aggregate production from 1906 to 1922 is $1,738,156, silver values being $10,156. It attained its maximum, $377,447, in 1907. Its output since 1917 has never exceeded $10,000, and at present its product is from prospects, no mines being regularly operated in 1922.

Tolovana District

This new district is located on the north side of the Tanana River, to the east of Hot Springs. Its production from 1915 to 1922 amounts to $4,054,469, of which silver was valued at $18,469. It attained its maximum of $1,156,946 in 1917. In 1922 its 25 mines, mostly open-cut, produced $221,913. The richest of the old placers are decreasing in output, and the future increase is dependent on late prospects.

The population of the district in 1920 was 263, including Livengood village, 131.

Fairbanks District

Far the greatest gold producer is the Fairbanks District, of which the centre is Cleary Creek, about nine miles from the city of Fairbanks. Herein is located the Pedro placer, the first paying discovery to

which the district owes its prosperity. Cleary stands
first with its production of $10,000,000 or more of
gold, from a creek seven miles long. Among other

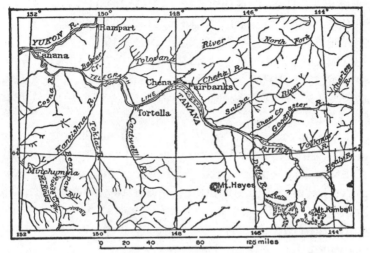

Map No. 3. Fairbanks Mining District

creeks which are very large producers are Ester,
Dome, Fairbanks, Goldstream Vault, and others.

Mineral Products of Fairbanks District

The value of the total mineral output for twenty
years, 1903 to 1922, is $74,015,674, of which $71,973,-
000 was in gold and $367,053 in silver. The maxi-
mum value was $9,695,375, and for four successive
years exceeded nine millions. The minimum product
of $573,941 was in 1921, followed by an increase of
$125,000 next year. The output of 1922, $697,783,
came from the six leading creeks, as follows: Cleary,
$23,198,000; Goldstream, $15,085,000; Ester, $11,-

443,000; Dome and Fairbanks, $16,486,000; Vault, $2,701,000; Little Eldorado, $2,360,000.

The annual products follow: 1903, $40,188; 1904, $602,281; 1905, $6,028,212; 1906, $9,042,318; 1907, $8,037,616; 1908, $9,243,151; 1909, $9,695,375; 1910, $6,128,683; 1911, $4,527,690; 1912, $4,179,632; 1913, $3,312,245; 1914, $2,516,050; 1915, $2,464,241; 1916, $1,807,276; 1917, $1,311,904; 1918, $805,708; 1919, $735,820; 1920, $584,218; 1921, $573,941; 1922, $697,783.

The placer output of 1922 came from 62 mines; the gravel sluiced had an average gold content of about $1.34 to the cubic yard. Modern methods are employed, the 45 drift mines operating 2 dredges; 10 open-cut mines using steam scrapers; 5 mines were worked hydraulically, and 11 only had no mechanical equipment.

Lode Mines

From lode mines there have been produced from 1910 to 1922, $1,337,059 gold, and $9,864 silver. The maximum output, in 1912, was $395,628, followed for three years by an average annually of $266,000. The war and high costs closed many mines, but the output increased from $20,000 in 1920 to $54,000 in 1922.

No tungsten was mined in 1922, though it has been earlier produced, as well as antimony and lead.

Of the future of quartz mining, Brooks says:

In the Fairbanks District the completion of the Alaska Railroad, and the assurance of comparatively cheap fuel from the Nenana coal field have stimulated lode development; there are in the district at least a score of lode properties which are worthy of further exploration.

Mining Institutions at Fairbanks

The primary importance of the Tanana Basin has been officially recognized both by the federal and the territorial authorities. When Congress, under the act approved March 3, 1916, authorized ten new mining experiment stations under the Bureau of Mines, one was established at Fairbanks. This mining station serves to solve mineral problems, prevent wasteful methods in mining processes, and aids in the efficient application of hydro-electric power.

In 1922 the territorial legislature established its first institution of higher education, the Alaska Agricultural College and School of Mines, which is located at Fairbanks. By legislation this college has for its leading objects:

Such branches of learning as are related to agriculture; the mechanic arts and household economics; to promote a practical education. . . . It shall be opened to both sexes for equal educational opportunities.

The development of the college has been rapid and inspiring. In 1924, three new faculty positions were created, additional buildings for instruction and experiments constructed, a library of over 5,000 volumes installed, while the enrollment increased to 84 students.

The supervising engineer of the U. S. Bureau of

Mines inspected the college, and pronounced its fitness for scientific investigations. On July 1, 1924, the college began the work of assaying, ore-testing and mineral determination.

The Town of Fairbanks

Fairbanks is a well-built town, especially within its fire limits. An electric plant furnishes light and power; the telephone service includes nearly 300 stations in the city and extends by long-distance lines to seven adjacent towns; a central steam plant heats the business quarters and many private residences; the fire system has a capacity of 15 streams at 140 pounds pressure; there is a good supply of water distributed in the business section by mains; three banks, with assay offices, and foundries cover the material side of life. Among the moral elements are five religious denominations, with pastors and churches, excellent schools for about 150 pupils, two efficient hospitals open to all, three newspapers (two dailies), and a quarterly religious magazine. The papers publish the cable news of the world, which appears in creditable form through typesetting machines and cylinder presses. There are comfortable hotels, excellent restaurants, and a variety of stores from which almost everything can be obtained. A large theatre, social clubs, baseball park in summer, curling and skating halls in winter, supplement the more quiet amusements of the many attractive homes. Adjoining Fairbanks more than 60,000 acres have been homesteaded, from which are now

Fairbanks Town, Tanana Valley, on July 4th.

annually produced large crops of potatoes and other vegetables, while hay, forage, and grain are regularly grown. Of the agricultural possibilities, Georgeson, the expert of the Department of Agriculture, said in 1923:

The Tanana Valley contains the largest area of agricultural land that can be reached at reasonable expense in the interior, and the whole stretch of the valley is available for settlement. At the town of Tanana, at the junction of the Tanana and Yukon, there is a considerable settlement [see Chapter XXIX], and some farmers are located in this region. The main settlement between Fairbanks and Tanana is Nenana (where the Alaska Railroad crosses the Tanana River), which will be a centre of a considerable farming region in years to come. The Tanana valley will produce grain crops—barley first; oats second; spring wheats third; and then winter rye and winter wheat.

Around Fairbanks there have been built eight local roads, 75 miles in length, connecting every important town or camp with Fairbanks or the railway.

Important as are the roads, they are secondary in point of transportation to the Tanana Valley Railway, a system of 45 miles, which is now a section of the Alaska Railroad. Commenced in 1905, it has since been operated continuously, winter and summer. Connecting the deep-water port of Chena and Fairbanks, the main line follows the placer mining region to Gilmore and Chatinika, thus reaching all the large producing placers. More than 54,000 passengers and about 15,000 tons of freight passed over the road in one season. When the railway was opened the local freight rate was $3 per ton mile, which has been steadily reduced by the railway from 88 cents per ton mile in 1906 to 58 cents in 1908. An idea of the enterprise of the railway builders, and of the cost involved, may be had from the statement that much of the material was moved 6,000 miles, while the freight thereon cost twice the initial value of the rails.

CHAPTER XII

SOUTHWESTERN ALASKA REGIONS

WITHIN the past few years the watersheds draining into the Gulf of Alaska have steadily advanced in economic prominence and in productive wealth. The wonderful copper deposits of the Copper River basin and of Prince William Sound, the high-grade coal-veins of Bering River and of the Matanuska Valley, the petroleum resources—active and prospective—of Katalla, Anchorage, and the Alaska Peninsula, justify the prediction made a score of years since that these regions would eventually lead in the mineral products of the Territory. First explored for gold, these lands now lead in copper, and may in time find petroleum a close rival.

The development of all this region has hitherto been slow and unsatisfactory. The gold output from 1895 to 1920 can scarcely exceed $9,000,000. In 1921 the approximate output was about $500,000, and in 1922 $700,000. What it lacks in later years in gold and silver is more than counterbalanced by copper. It is beyond reasonable doubt, however, that the mineral productivity of this part of Alaska will be largely increased, and that within a few years.

For convenience the districts will be treated under sub-headings of *Copper River Region, Prince William*

Sound, Cook Inlet Region, and *Susitna Basin.* The important minerals, coal and petroleum, are described separately in the succeeding chapter.

Copper River Region

The largest and oldest settlement of this region is Cordova, situated on the eastern shore of Prince William Sound. Being the ocean terminus of the Copper River and Northwestern Railroad, which extends 197 miles to the Kennicott copper mines in the Chitina Valley, all freight and travel to and from these mines pass through the town. It is a modern place, has two newspapers, and a population of over a thousand. It has considerable fishing interests connected with the canneries operated near here. About 135 miles southeast of Cordova is the small settlement of Katalla, the only oil-producing district in Alaska (see Chapter XIII). Chitina, about 125 miles up the Copper River Railroad, is the southeastern terminus of the Richardson Highway, over which Fairbanks, 317 miles distant, is reached by autos in summer and by sleighs in winter. The great copper industry of this region is adjoining the town of Kennicott in the upper Chitina Valley. In 1920 the population of the Copper Center District was 511, Cordova District 1,555, and of Kennecott District 904.

Copper River Gold

The earliest mining in this region was that of gold placers. Data are uncertain as to the aggregate output, but to 1922 it probably does not exceed $5,000,-000. In late years the number of summer mines and the placer product were: 1920, 9 mines, $200,000; 1921, 7, $220,000; 1922, 8, $165,000. Hydraulic min-

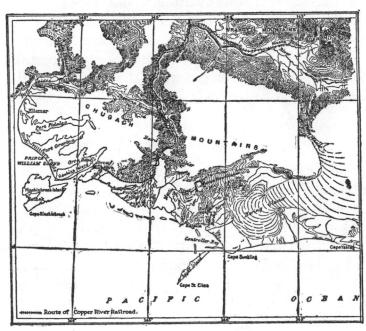

Map No. 4.   Lower Copper and Chitina Valleys.

ing continues on the Nizina placers, and also in the Chistochina District and on Chititu Creek, and is being introduced elsewhere.

Of the Chitina District Moffit reports: "In Berg Creek have been found silver-gold deposits, occurring as veins of iron and copper sulphides, in which the silver predominates largely in quantity over gold."

He adds that the Berg mill was started for copper, but gold and silver predominated in value.

The mining interests of the Controller Bay region built up Katalla as a rival to Valdez, but complications arose and disadvantages developed, which ended in the practical transfer of the railway terminus to Cordova, where a thriving, bustling town came into existence in 1908. Its future success is assured by the enormous development of the copper deposits of the Chitina watershed.

Copper Mining

The copper veins from which the greatest yield is anticipated are rich in quality and extended in distribution. Indeed, it is claimed that this district is unequalled elsewhere in its copper resources, whether viewed from the standpoints of extent of field, richness of ore, or facility of mining. The deposits are both sulphides and native copper, which are widely distributed and apparently unlimited in quantity. The copper-bearing area is included between the Nebesna watershed of the Wrangell Range and Chitina Valley to the south, and from the Kotsina eastward to the International Boundary. In both the Chitina and Kotsina basins the deposits have been systematically developed.

Owing to the decrease in the average price of the metal, the copper output fell from 86,000,000 pounds, valued at $12,630,000, in 1923, to 75,500,-000 pounds, valued at about $12,630,000, in 1924.

Chitina Copper

Scarcely second in importance to the discovery of the gold bonanzas has been the evolution of the three famous copper mines of the Kennecott Copper Corporation in the Chitina watershed. Of them Moffit says: "No other ore bodies comparable in size with those at Kennecott are known in the Chitina Valley, and none similar in size and richness have been found elsewhere." It is significant of the courage and confidence of American business men that a railroad 200 miles long should have been built by them for the exploitation of these deposits.

No complete data are available as to the production of these mines. It is reasonable to believe that of the copper valued $145,478,823, 1880 to 1922, more than $120,000,000 are to be credited to these mines.

It is impracticable to distribute the production of copper produced in the Chitina Valley, in Prince William Sound, and on Prince of Wales Island, but the following data are of interest, since the great development of this industry: In mines operated, pounds of copper produced and its value: 1911, 8 mines, 27,-267,878 pounds, $3,408,485; 1912, 7, 29,230,491, $4,823,031; 1913, 6, 21,659,958, $3,357,293; 1914, 6, 21,450,628, $2,852,934; 1915, 14, 86,509,312, $15,-139,129; 1916, 18, 119,654,839, $29,484,291; 1917, 17, 88,793,400, $24,240,598; 1918, 17, 69,224,951, $17,098,563; 1919, 8, 47,220,771, $8,783,063; 1920, 8, 70,435,363, $12,960,106; 1921, 6, 57,011,597, $7,-354,496; 1922, 5, 77,967,819, $10,525,655.

Most of the copper ore mined in 1922 was shipped to the Tacoma smelter, but a portion of the southeastern product was treated elsewhere.

Coal

The most valuable coal deposits in Alaska are those at and near Controller Bay, of which the Bering River veins are best known. The coal beds on the Matanuska River, Cook Inlet, are but slightly inferior. The Bering River fields cover an area aggregating 48.4 square miles, of which 26.6 are underlaid by anthracite and semi-anthracite. The opinion that these coals are suited for coke, steaming, etc., is fully justified by analyses. Their value and output are set forth in Chapter XIII.

Prince William Sound

The oldest town in this region is Valdez, which is the most northerly seaport of Alaska that is open the entire year. A modern town, it is the commercial centre of the important copper interests of the Sound, and of the various gold-quartz mines of the surrounding region. Here the Signal Corps cable from Seattle connects with the land lines (see Chapter XXX), which serve the greater part of the Territory. It is also the initial point of the Richardson Highway, which extends via Fairbanks to the northeastern mining fields.

In 1920 the population of the region was 1,572, including Ellamar, Fort Liscum, Latouche, Tatitlek, and Valdez.

The region of the Sound has a variety of minerals, antimony, copper, gold, and iron. The gold-lodes are widely distributed, and there are four productive mines, and many deposits are in the prospecting stage. The most valuable metal is copper. While deposits of copper are widely scattered, the most productive mines are on Latouche and Knight Islands. The only output in 1922 was from the Beatson-Bonanza, which is one of the four great copper-producing mines of Alaska. The ore mined in 1922, 274,863 tons of copper, assaying 1.88 per cent copper, yielded 23,147 tons of concentrates, assaying 18.99 per cent copper.

Prince William Sound is a most remarkable region as regards glacial phenomena and living glaciers. (See Chapter XVIII.)

Region of Cook Inlet

To the east of the inlet is Kenai Peninsula, of which the principal town is Anchorage, on Knik Arm, population 1,856 in 1920. It is a large and thriving town, built up by the construction and operation of the Alaska Railroad; here are the repair shops and headquarters of the operating force. In Anchorage also centre the trade interests of the agricultural and mineral industries of the Matanuska and Susitna valleys.

Next in importance is Seward, population 652 in 1920, located on Resurrection Bay on the south coast of the peninsula. It is the transportation centre of the Gulf of Alaska and its bordering lands. Being the southern terminus of the government railroad, all freight and passengers to and from the States pass through this deep-water harbor. From Seward are made the monthly trips to the local ports to the westward as far as Unalaska. The town also serves the mining and fishing interests of Kenai Peninsula and the canneries of adjacent waters.

Mining of coal is the principal industry of the Matanuska Valley, to the northeast of the inlet (see Chapter XIII), and of gold on the Kenai Peninsula. On Kenai in 1922 were operated a dozen placers, which yielded about $40,000 in gold. The gold-lodes are increasing in number and output. Besides the five mines now operating are many promising prospects. At Kachemak Bay the lignite veins of coal were worked for local use.

Susitna Basin

As the construction of the Alaska Railroad progressed, and overhead mining costs decreased, the productivity of the mineral wealth of this region has largely increased. In the Yentna basin the placer output of 1921 was $120,000 gold. In 1922, when hydraulic plants were used on some creeks, while elsewhere pick-and-shovel methods continued, there were mined 472,000 cubic yards of gravel, with a value of $222,000. While much gold quartz has been located in the Yentna field, no auriferous lodes of commercial value have as yet been developed.

Capps reports in 1924 as to Yentna: "This district has yielded a steady and increasing production of placer gold since its discovery in 1905, and the successful operation of a dredge there in recent years gives encouragement of the belief that it will long continue to be a productive mining-camp." Good coal there mined is available for local use only.

The most productive district of the Susitna basin is that of Willow Creek, where gold-lode mines have been profitably operated for 15 years. The total output from 1908 to 1922 was $2,184,997, of which $7,301 was silver. The maximum production was from 3 lodes, $300,160 in 1916. In 1922, 7 mines produced $239,500. The output for ten years follows: 1913, 3 mines, $101,193; 1914, 3 mines, $297,-919; 1915, 3 mines, $247,688; 1916, 3 mines, $300,160; 1917, 5 mines, $196,248; 1918, 5 mines, $270,348; 1919, 5 mines, $163,453; 1920, 3 mines, $63,558; 1921, 7 mines, $119,302; 1922, 7 mines, $239,500.

In this district in 1924 there were 15 mines and 23 prospects. Capps says:

The gold lodes of the Willow Creek district are by far the most important developed metal in the Talkeetna region. The gold is present in the veins largely as native gold, and much of it is recoverable directly by amalgamation. Associated with the gold in the veins are the metallic minerals pyrite, arsenopyrite, stibnite, chalcopyrite, bornite, chalcocite, galena, malachite, limonite, and cinnabar.

Describing the many lode prospects being developed, Brooks says: "The success of several mines in the district, and the projects of systematic work under way, give great hopes for the future."

Of the abundant lignite coal in the Susitna Basin, several veins are mined for local use.

Miscellaneous Mining

To the north of Cook Inlet, in the region tributary to the Alaska Railroad, there is much prospecting of gold and copper lodes, more particularly in the Talkeetna, Chulitna, Broad Pass, and Nelchina districts. A few coal banks were worked for local use in the Broad Pass region. Placers were worked for gold on Valdez Creek, and on a tributary of Knik River.

On the west side of the inlet, in the Lake Iliamna district, lode prospecting continues on a small scale. Placer mining is carried on on the beaches of Kodiak and Trinity Islands, and quartz prospecting on Kodiak. On Unga Island small amounts of copper ore are produced. The sulphur deposits of Akun Island are not worked at present. The exploitation of the petroleum deposits of the Alaska Peninsula are described in Chapter XIII.

In 1924 there were reported further quartz discoveries at Nuka Bay, Kenai Peninsula, which promises to become the centre of a large area of mineralization.

Bibliography.—Capps: Mineral Resources of the Region Traversed by the Alaska Railroad. Bulletin 755C. U. S. Geological Survey.

CHAPTER XIII

COAL AND PETROLEUM

COAL is the fourth mineral of Alaska in productive value, and the petroleum output has been practically nil, yet these essential products for Alaskan prosperity must in the near future be important factors in the development of the Territory. The coal deposits of Alaska are extensive, widely distributed, and of enormous amounts. It is probable that the coalfields already known cover an area of more than 25,000 square miles.

On recommendations from subordinate officials, President Roosevelt, to prevent predicted monopoly, withdrew all coal lands from location, and by regulations of April 12, 1907, authorized entries in strictly limited acreage. On this subject the Commissioner of the General Land Office said:

These withdrawals were occasioned by the widespread belief that public coal lands were being improvidently disposed of, and that they were even falling into the ownership of corporations able to control the output of the mines and fix their own prices on the product.

The fallacy of this belief and the unwisdom of the withdrawal are shown by the official coal data. The amount of coal mined in Alaska from 1880 to 1922 is insignificant in value and amount. Against the production of 469,880 tons in the Territory, there were imported 2,356,194 tons. The results of official discrimination against Alaskan enterprise in its efforts for local development were speedily evident.

In 1907, before the executive order went into effect, there were mined 10,139 tons; in four following years the coal output fell to 355 tons in 1912, in which year there were imported 96,093 tons. Alaskan coal mining was substantially ruined; about 1,000 claims were cancelled on alleged grounds of fraud and the work of the claimants forfeited. The 150 billions of tons of coal remained unexploited.

In 1914 Congress enacted a coal-land lease act limiting leases to 2,500 acres as a maximum, with no right of purchase. The act has failed to encourage coal mining. In six years there have been made three leases in the Matanuska field: in 1920 one had been abandoned, the second was under development, and the third had been taken over by the Alaskan Engineering Commission, as otherwise local coal was not obtainable for the Alaska Railroad. The two leases in the Bering River field were in course of development, but no coal had been marketed. The Secretary of the Interior reported that in 1920 there were only three leases in force, covering 5,940 acres. Of the many coal-mining permits there were in that year only 14 in effect, covering 140 acres.

Even now shipments of coal into the Territory continue; 30,192 tons in 1923, and 31,663 tons in 1924.

It eventually was the fate of the United States,

through force of circumstance, to restore to partial activity, at an expense of millions of dollars, an Alaskan industry that its laws had made economically impracticable for private enterprise.

The Matanuska Coal-Field

In this field, after spending about a million of dollars, the United States navy has abandoned its development for the present of its reserve coal-fields, having taken away for test purposes 5,000 tons of washed, selected coal. The only private mine in operation in 1922 was the Jones Mine, which closed down owing to a fire, thus obliging the United States to reopen the Eska Mine to provide necessary fuel for the operation of the Alaska Railroad. A small quantity of coal was produced from other prospects in this field.

Bering River Coal-Field

From the high-grade deposits of this field there were mined in 1922–1924 only small amounts for testing and development purposes.

Alaska Railroad Coal-Fields

While Alaska produced in 1923, from 12 mines, 119,826 tons of coal, the output fell off in 1924 to about 90,000 tons from 10 mines. Most of the amount was divided between the bituminous coal of Evan Jones mine, Matanuska, and the good lignite from the Healy River Corporation, Nenana.

The fuel question has been a vexatious and expensive problem for the railroad authorities. To

insure its coal the costly and unprofitable Matanuska branch was built, and even then much of its
fuel had to be obtained by operating at public expense its own mine.

Such divergent statements have been made as to
the economical value of the high-grade coal of the
Matanuska Valley, as to give importance to the investigation of a federal geologist, set forth in 1924.
This geologist, S. R. Capps, an Alaska expert, reports:

Within the lower basin there is an extensive coal-field
that has been widely credited as constituting one of the
country's greatest coal-reserves on the Pacific coast. . . .
Up to 1922 the Matanuska field has produced over 305,-
000 tons of coal, a considerable part of it from mines
operated by the government. . . . The beds so far exploited are so much faulted and broken that the cost of
mining has remained high. . . . In the meantime, the
lower-grade, but more easily mined, coals will continue
to supply the needs of the railroad and other local demands.

With abundant cheap fuel-oil on the Pacific coast, and
plentiful, more cheaply mined coals of lower-grade available along the Alaska Railroad, the higher-grade but
more difficultly mined coals of the Matanuska Valley may
be unmarketable.

At Mile 341 on the railroad, near Yanert Station,
beds of coal about 6 feet thick have been discovered
carrying about 60 per cent of fixed carbon. The
coal is good, very accessible, easily worked, and so
is commercially valuable.

The Nenana coal-deposits are among the most

valuable mineral resources adjoining the Alaska
Railroad. The coal is a lignite of very fair grade,
and is easily mined. On Healy Creek 23 veins had
an average thickness of 10 feet. The field is estimated to have 9,000,000,000 tons. It is a most
important factor in the development of central
Alaska, and the cost of fuel in the Fairbanks and
adjacent mining-districts has already been materially reduced.

Coal-Fields in Northern Alaska

In the Yukon Valley there are many small deposits
of bituminous coal, generally of inferior quality and
at points where it is of no value except for local consumption.

On Seward Peninsula there are several small mines
worked for local use, as well as one on Kobuk River,
and also at Wainwright Inlet—mostly for use by the
natives.

There are, however, very large and valuable coal
beds in the extreme northern regions. In 1922 Foran,
of the Geological Survey, discovered extended coal-
beds, supposed to be sub-bituminous, finding 13 beds
from 4 to 10 feet thick. This new field is on the arctic littoral, between Cape Beaufort and Wainwright
Inlet—evidently a northern and inland extension of
the Corwin beds. In the future it is thought that
this excellent coal might supply Nome and northeastern Siberia.

Plans have been under consideration for the utilization of the enormous deposits in the region of Cape

Lisburne, which place is open to navigation several months each summer. These deposits include very high-grade bituminous coal, as well as enormous bodies of sub-bituminous coal.

In his last official report the Alaskan expert, Brooks, thus summarizes the situation:

The mining of the lower-grade coals for local use will increase considerably, though no large market for these coals can be expected in the immediate future. Underground exploration of the higher-grade coals of Bering River and Matanuska will be continued. The mining of these coals will depend on the discovery of beds that will be cheaper to mine because they are less disturbed than those at present known, or on an increase in the demand for coal on the Pacific. Evidently such increase is involved with the future of petroleum production. The possibility of Alaska furnishing a large petroleum supply must be considered.

Existing Mining Conditions

In 1922 coal was mined at 12 places only, and but 7 mines had an output of more than 1,000 tons. Witnesses before a Congressional Committee were fully justified in their statements that:

Presidential proclamation and bureau regulations put into effect a policy of restriction and reservation that effectively stopped all development. . . . Forty-seven years passed before the Alaskan could use the great store of coal for fuel purposes without laying himself liable to prosecution.

While cabinet officers and bureau chiefs are doing what is possible to remedy existing conditions, Congress fails to remedy conditions by legislation. In 57 years only 935 acres of coal lands have been patented, less than half that have been granted to missions; what has been denied the body for daily use, has been given to the soul.

Petroleum

Alaska is believed to be a profitable field for oil production. That it needs local oil is shown by the importations from 1905 to 1922, which were in gallons as follows: Heavy oils, 284,581,705; gasoline and lighter oils, 28,209,447; other oils, 21,402,680. In 1922 the importations for the year reached 23,564,191 gallons.

The lack of native oil is due not to individual neglect, but to executive action and Congressional inaction. Prospectors began exploration in 1902, and numerous shallow wells were sunk in the Katalla, Cold Bay, and Iliamna regions. The withdrawal of all the oil-bearing lands of Alaska was made by executive proclamation in 1910, which caused the abandonment of all development. Fortunately the prospectors who had sunk a few shallow wells, from 300 to 1,400 feet deep, were able to obtain a patent to a tract of 151 acres at Katalla, from which oil amounting to about 2,000,000 gallons has been drawn to 1923. This oil is of a paraffin base and carries a high percentage of gasoline. A small refinery was established, and its products were disposed of locally.

Although indications of oil were known in the districts of Cold Bay, Iliamna, Katalla, Point Barrow, and Yakataga, they remained unexplored for the many years until Congress, in 1920, by its oil-leasing Act, threw open Alaska to the petroleum industry.

Of the distribution of oil seepages and their quality, Brooks states:

The quality of Alaska petroleum leaves little to be desired. It is a high-grade refining oil, similar in composition to that from Pennsylvania.

Petroleum seepages are known in five widely separated districts in Alaska—at Katalla, near Controller Bay; at Yakataga, sixty miles east of Katalla; near Inisken Bay on the west shore of Cook Inlet; on the Alaska Peninsula, notably near Cold Bay; and near Douglas River, southwest shore of Cook Inlet. There are also indications of the presence of petroleum in extreme northern Alaska, near Smith Bay, about one hundred miles southeast of Point Barrow.

Under the oil-leasing Act of 1920 prospecting for oil began with the enthusiasm that marked bonanza times, and much land thus claimed will doubtless prove non-productive. From the date of the leasing Act in 1920 to June 30, 1923, there were made to the Secretary of the Interior 1,197 applications for oil and gas permits in the Territory. Of these 753 were granted, 111 rejected, and the balance awaited further proof. Of the 372 permits granted in 1922, the distribution was as follows: Cold Bay, 221; Yakataga, 44; Katalla, 41; Iliamna, 37; and Anchorage, 17. In 1923 two companies were drilling in the Cold Bay region, Alaska Peninsula, and one in Katalla.

Most important has been the action of the United

States in connection with the official report that indications of oil have been found in the arctic coastal-plain region. In February, 1923, 35,000 square miles of the western part of the supposed oil-bearing region were withdrawn from entry as Naval Petroleum Reserve, No. 4. The Executive order states: "Said lands to be reserved for six years, for classification, examination, and the preparation ,of plans for development. . . . The reservation hereby established shall be for oil and gas only." In April, 1923, the Navy Department made a grant of money to the Geological Survey for an investigation, which is being made now (1924).

It is interesting to note that in Canada the most northerly producing oil well is in the Fort Norman region, 64° N., in the valley of the Mackenzie. This well in 1921 was producing about 60 barrels a day.

Oil Prospects on Alaska Peninsula

The most promising of the oil districts, as far as is shown by surveys to 1923, is the Cold Bay-Chignik District, on the east coast of the Alaska Peninsula, southwest of Kodiak Island. This region was explored during the oil excitement of 1902–1904. Four wells were then drilled, of varying depths. Some paraffin-saturated beds were penetrated and a little oil found, but the wells were not commercially productive. Exploitation in this district was made under disadvantages of lack of fuel, bad climate, poor harbors, and irregular transportation.

Seepages exist at Oil Creek—where about half a

barrel of oil exudes daily—on Rex Creek, Bear Creek, Salmon Creek, and at Pearl Creek Dome in the drainage area of Ugashik. Many other cases are reported by prospectors. Active operations are in progress in the Pearl Dome region by two large corporations. The Associated Oil Company suspended work in 1923 after sinking two wells, about 500 and 950 feet deep, but renewed work in 1924; at last accounts a depth of 2,170 feet had been reached. The Standard Oil Company of California is said to have reached a depth of 1,400 feet in March, 1924. Although drilling has been necessary to a greater depth than was originally planned, yet such showings of oil have been discovered as encourage the two companies to test the structure thoroughly.

It is reasonably hoped from the geological surveys and investigations, in Naval Petroleum Reserve, No. 4, that petroleum beds of value will be found on the arctic littoral, in the region of Point Barrow. This important field-work was under Philip S. Smith, U. S. Geological Survey, the field-work being done by three parties. Two parties went overland during the winter of 1923—1924, via Seward, Nenana, Tanana, Allakabet, and the Alatna River. Nearly 20,000 square miles of the arctic watershed were geologically surveyed and mapped, covering generally an unknown region. The surveys of the parties confirmed the report of the expedition of 1923, which discovered oil seepages on the coastal regions then visited. Laboratory stud-

ies are being made of the material gathered, and
while the experts are unwilling to express their opinion of the regions as oil-bearing in quantities, yet
the outlook is thought to be favorable.

BIBLIOGRAPHY.—U. S. Geological Survey Publications. Brooks: Annual Re-
ports on Alaskan Minerals. Martin: Petroleum in Alaska, Bulletin 719. Capps:
Cold Bay District, Bulletin 739. Smith & Baker: Cold Bay-Chignik District,
Bulletin 755.

CHAPTER XIV

FUR–SEAL FISHERIES

ENWRAPPED in constant summer sea mists, which concealed them almost absolutely from chance observation, the breeding grounds of the Alaskan fur-seal were finally discovered by a patient and persistent fur-hunter, Gerassim Pribilof, in 1786, after whom the group of four islands is named. The principal islands, St. George and St. Paul, are 30 miles apart, and near by are the lesser islet of Otter and the waterless ledges of Walrus. St. Paul has an area of some 35 square miles, its highest elevation is 600 feet, and the population numbers about 300; St. George has an area of 27 square miles, its elevation is 930 feet, and the population about 100; uninhabited Otter Islet has an area of about 4 miles, while the flat-topped Walrus reef scarcely measures a tenth of a square mile.

The group is about equidistant, 200 miles, from Unalaska to the south, St. Matthew to the north, and the Alaskan mainland to the east. This isolation, the character of the frequented beaches, and the humidity of its almost sunless climate, are elements that have done much to conserve these immense herds of fur-seal as a limitless source of wealth, until the introduction of the exterminating pelagic

or open-sea hunting, which presents another example of reckless commercial exploitation that is utterly
regardless of the welfare of future generations.

Practically the Pribilofs have two seasons only,
cool, rainy, and foggy summers from May to October,
and dry, cold, and stormy winters, with very high
winds, from November to April.

A few creeping willows are the only trees, but here
and there shrubs furnish forth black currants and
red salmon berries in good seasons. With difficulty
lettuce, radishes, and turnips are raised, while mush-
rooms grow in abundance. In addition, rank grasses,
beautiful flowers, delicate mosses, and luxuriant ferns
make much of the landscape beautiful during the
short summer season. Of animal life there are foxes
—blue and white. The lemming is found on St.
George. Reindeer, introduced in 1911, now number
several hundred.

Aside from the fur-seal, the birds of the Pribilofs
are of the greatest interest. There are two great
bird rookeries—on the face of the bluffs of St. George
and on the table-topped Walrus ledge.

"The latter place," says Eliott, "affords within
the smallest area the greatest variety of nesting and
breeding birds, for here the 'arrie,' many gulls, cor-
morants, sea-parrots, and auks come in countless
numbers. . . . Hundreds of thousands of these birds
are thus engaged [in hatching eggs], roosting stacked
up together as tight as so many sardines in a box, as
compactly as they can be stowed, each and all utter-
ing an incessant, muffled, hoarse, grunting sound.

"Here, without exertion or risk, the naturalist can observe and walk among tens upon tens of thousands of screaming waterfowl, literally ignored and surrounded by these feathered friends."

Of the eggs, Elliott relates that in 1872 six natives, in four hours, loaded a bidarka (large boat) of four tons burden, to the water's edge with the gayly colored eggs of the arrie (*lomvia arra*).

It is the otary or eared seal, commonly known as fur-seal, that is of predominating importance in these islands, this species being the most valuable of all maritime mammals in commercial productivity. The present method of rookery sealing was introduced by Pribilof in 1786, which speedily led to fierce rivalries and the settlement of the Pribilof group by 137 natives from Unalaska and Atka. The preservation of the herds from utter destruction was due to the monopoly granted the Russian Trading Company in 1799. Then the policy was adopted, which remains unchanged to-day, of restricting the killing of seals to agents of the leasing company.

In 1868 Congress made the Pribilof group a fur-seal reservation, and in the Act of June, 1870, for the preservation of fur-bearing animals, provisions were made for the leasing of the islands for a term of years. The first lease was made in 1870 for twenty years to the Alaska Commercial Company, under well-guarded restrictions to insure the preservation of the seal and to guard the welfare of the inhabitants of the islands. The company was authorized to take annually not more than 100,000 sealskins, paying

Fur-seal Rookery on St. George Island, Pribilof.

therefor on a sliding scale, while certain food, fuel, and educational facilities were to be furnished the natives, whose liberty of action and removal were likewise insured. In 1890 the lease passed to the Northern Commercial Company, whose rights expired in 1910.

The seals resort to the Pribilof Islands for breeding purposes in the early part of June. The mother has one pup, born about the end of June, which by the early days of August has learned to swim and is ready to leave for the south. Full-grown seals of four years weigh about 200 pounds, and increase somewhat in weight after that age.

Seals Killed from 1868 to 1908

During these years there were taken 3,443,202 fur-seals, valued at $50,327,537. Of these the leasing companies took 2,533,497, value $39,946,772, while the balance were captured by open-sea, or other methods. The largest year for the company was 1879, when the 110,511 fur seals taken were valued at $2,340,713. Under the slaughter caused by the poachers, their catch fell to 7,390 in 1893, value $199,530, against 30,812 killed by pelagic fishing, with a value of $385,150.

The open-sea fishing was very profitable from 1887 to 1896, when the value of that catch ranged from $235,836 in 1887 to $938,196 in 1891. During these ten years the average annual value was $500,000. In 1904, when the value of sealing fell to $232,140 for the open-sea fisheries, against $388,800 for the companies, it was evident that the sealing industry was practically destroyed, being unprofitable.

The high value of sealskins caused Canadian fishermen to attack the seals passing to and from the Pribilofs and to shoot them outside the three-mile limit, often killing both male and female; three-fourths were females. As this industry was equally important to Great Britain, where the skins are dressed and dyed, an arbitration conference was eventually held at Paris in 1893. Under the regulations there formulated, Great Britain and the United States agreed to limit pelagic sealing by prohibiting it at any time within sixty miles of the Pribilof Islands, and permitting it to be followed in the rest of Bering Sea only between May 1 and July 31 of each year. Sealers were to be licensed, and forbidden to use firearms or explosives in fur-sealing.

As pelagic sealing was still allowed, there had, however, been no practical relief by the action of the Paris conference. The destruction by pelagic and coast hunting increased from 23 per cent of the grand total in 1889 to 58 per cent in 1890. The disastrous effects were speedily evident, as the number of skins taken on the seal islands fell from 102,617 in 1889 to 7,390 in 1893, as against 30,812 taken that year by pelagic and coast hunters. That such action was destructive to all concerned, pelagic hunters as well as the authorized agents, is shown by the values of all sealskins taken in 1893, $584,680 as against $2,298,204 in 1888, showing that more than three-fourths of the industry had been destroyed in five years. The number of fur-seals killed on the islands averaged 14,969 for the five years ending with 1908, as against 104,245 in the five years ending with 1889.

The story of the destruction of the fur-seal is shown by the rapid decrease of seals captured: 1886, 133,015; 1887, 136,388; 1888, 139,693; 1889, 132,-475; 1890, 69,673; 1891, 73,794; 1892, 54,151; 1893, 38,202; 1894, 76,871; 1895, 71,137; 1896, 74,571; 1897, 43,532; 1898, 64,599; 1899, 50,980; 1900, 57,-661; 1901, 47,116; 1902, 44,994; 1903, 46,292; 1904, 24,483; and 1905, 25,383.

It is estimated that the seal herd in 1867 numbered about 5,000,000; in 1873, about 3,200,000. Pelagic, or open-sea, hunting means annihilation, as very many so killed are nursing mothers. Only a small proportion of those shot are saved, so that the whole pelagic fishery means wanton waste. As a result the seal herd at the Pribilof group scarcely exceeded 200,000 in 1905, of whom about one-third were females.

Conditions were remedied by a convention between Great Britain, Japan, Russia, and the United States, December 14, 1911, which prohibited pelagic sealing for fifteen years in the Pacific Ocean north of the 30th parallel, including the seas of Bering, Japan, Kamchatka, and Okhotsk. Resident aborigines can seal for local use, in canoes and without firearms. The results of sealing on the various islands are equitably divided between the countries named.

To enable the seal herd to recuperate from over-exploitation, Congress on August 24, 1912, instituted a closed season for five years. The reservation of Pribilof Islands and the care and exploitation of the fur-seal herds were placed under the Bureau of Fisheries, which by its wise and skilful administration has managed this important industry to the advantage of the nation. Since 1917 the surplus seals have been killed, and the pelts have been cured and dressed in the United States. The recuperation of the herd has been steady and encouraging. When the private lease expired there were left in 1910 about 200,000 seal. The growth of the herd, as shown by the census each year, has been as follows: 1912, 215,738; 1913, 268,305; 1914, 294,687; 1915, 363,782; 1916, 417,281; 1917, 468,692; 1918, 496,332; 1919, 524,269; 1920, 552,718; 1921, 581,442; 1922, 604,692; 1923, 653,008.

The number of fur-seal taken meantime were: 1911, 12,138; 1912, 3,191; 1913, 2,406; 1914, 2,735; 1915, 3,947; 1916, 6,468; 1917, 8,170; 1918, 34,390; 1919, 27,821; 1920, 26,646; 1921, 23,661; 1922, 31,156; 1923, 15,920.

Estimating the value of the skins taken since 1911 at $35 each, it would make the total value of the fur-seal fishery to date approximately $57,000,000.

Taking into consideration the seals killed for food by natives from 1911 to 1924, the total increase in the Pribilof herds must be about 600,000. It is important to note that the devastation wrought in ten years cannot reasonably be expected to be fully repaired in less than forty years, even under skilful supervision.

Pribilof Colony

This reservation, closed to the public, can be visited only by permit. Besides the resident natives, there are the government officials and laborers admitted for work during the busy season. The resident natives numbered 320 on December 31, 1922. Under governmental control they have very much improved, physically and mentally. On St. George the village is lighted electrically, has a water system, and similar improvements are planned for St. Paul. Concrete houses are under construction, and modern sanitary methods have been introduced. Medical and hospital facilities are present. In the schools are taught reading, writing, arithmetic, spelling, history, and geography. Higher education is furnished by scholarships in a training school in Oregon.

The natives are paid for all labor performed, which consists largely in the capture of seals, the caring for the pelts, and for trapping foxes. Fox farming is efficiently carried on, and about 800 animals, almost entirely blue foxes, are taken annually. Nearly $50,000 are paid the laborers each year, and about one-sixth of the adults have savings accounts. A herd of reindeer supplies fresh meat, thus supplementing the former fish diet.

BIBLIOGRAPHY.—Department of Commerce: Annual Reports Bureau of Fisheries, Alaska Fishery, and Fur-Seal Industries.

CHAPTER XV

ALASKAN FISHERIES—THE SALMON

In general the prosperity of our Alaskan investment was long thought to be dependent on the fur-seal rookeries of the Pribilof Islands. The great falling off in marketed sealskins of one-third, from 1881 to 1882, was viewed by many as the beginning of the end of Alaskan productivity.

The maximum output in value of fur-seal skins occurred in 1880, amounting that year to $2,347,687. A few far-sighted and enterprising firms of San Francisco realized the great wealth of life in the northern seas, and were endeavoring to develop the fisheries of Alaska. Despite their utmost efforts, the fishery products in 1880 were viewed somewhat askant, as they totalled less than $500,000, about one-seventeenth that of the fur-seal values.

The extension and conservation of the valuable fisheries of Alaska have been largely due to the energetic and persistent efforts of the United States Commissioner of Fisheries and his skilled assistants. Their reports are full of valuable and interesting matter, which has been largely utilized in this volume.

Few, it is thought, realize even to-day the extraordinary growth of the Alaskan fisheries, whose values aggregated in 1907 $9,500,000 as against less than $500,000 for fur-seals, the rookeries producing only one-nineteenth as much as the fisheries. In 1918, when the number of sealskins taken was but 34,890, the value of the canned salmon alone had reached the astounding amount of $51,041,949.

The extent and importance of the fishery industries of Alaska depend not alone on their productivity, but also on their personnel, capitalization, and their influence on trade. The total investment in 1907 was less than $10,000,000, with 12,732 employees, and an output valued at $10,160,183. In 1918 the investment was $73,750,789, personnel 31,213, and the products valued at $59,154,859, the maximum year of output. As the salmon industry averages in value 90 per cent of the total fisheries, it will be here treated separately, leaving the other fisheries to the succeeding chapter.

The Salmon Fishery

The salmon of Alaska are thus described by the Commissioner of the U. S. Bureau of Fisheries:

The five species of salmon found in the waters off the North Pacific range northward from southern California to the Arctic Ocean and southward to Japan on the Asiatic coast. They are: Chinook or king; blueback, red, or sockeye; silver or coho; chum or keta; and humpback or pink. *The Chinook or king salmon* is the largest of the Pacific salmons. Its average weight is about 20 pounds, but mature individuals greatly vary in size; some weighing from 70 to perhaps 100 pounds are occasionally taken. It ranges from the Sacramento River, Calif., to the Arctic Ocean. It is the principal species taken from the Sacramento and Columbia Rivers. It is found in the Unuk, Stikine, Taku, Copper, and other coastal rivers of Alaska, also in Cook Inlet and Bristol Bay, and in the Yukon River.

The red or sockeye salmon is the species most sought after by the cannery men in Alaska. Its range extends from the Columbia River northward to Bering Sea, being confined to such streams as have lakes in their courses accessible for spawning. Its average weight is about seven pounds. The run in Alaska begins in May and extends usually to the middle of August. The height of the season, however, is in the month of July, all regions considered. True to its name, the red or sockeye salmon retains its distinctive reddish color after the process of cooking and canning, a factor which makes it highly attractive to the consumer. Mature individuals vary in age from three to seven years.

The silver or coho salmon ranges from Monterey Bay, Calif., to the Yukon River. It runs later in the season than any of the other species. Its average weight is about eight pounds, with a maximum of 30 pounds. Its flesh is of excellent flavor, but paler in color than the red salmon, hence less desirable for canning purposes. It is known to the trade as medium red. Like the king salmon, the coho is frequently used for mild curing or for freezing. It is a voracious feeder, of very rapid growth, the largest individuals not exceeding three years of age.

The humpback or pink salmon is the smallest and most numerous of the five species of salmon on the Pacific coast of North America. Its weight is from 3 to 11 pounds, the average being about 4 pounds. The flesh is pale, hence its trade name of pink salmon. The range of this species is from the coast of Oregon northward to Bering Sea. It is found in greatest abundance in the waters of southeastern Alaska. Many of the canneries in that region, and some of those in central Alaska, depend chiefly upon

By courtesy of U. S. Bureau of Fisheries.

Salmon Cannery of Alaska Packing Association at Loring.

the humpback for their packs. In southeast Alaska the run begins in June and continues until September. All individuals of this species mature, spawn, and die in their second year.

The chum or dog salmon reaches a maximum weight of about 16 pounds, the average being about 9 pounds. It has a wide range, extending from the coast of Oregon to the Arctic Ocean. It is the least sought for commercial use, as the flesh turns practically white in the process of canning, and is usually very poor in oil. It is rich, however, in food values, and deserves a wider market than it obtains. It is especially good for freezing, salting, and smoking, and is much used by the natives of the Yukon and other far northern rivers.

Canned Salmon

More than 90 per cent of the salmon reach the public in cans. This industry is under governmental supervision, as its inspectors visit the canneries to prevent waste, ensure cleanliness and proper methods of preservation. A case of salmon is always understood to mean 48 one-pound cans.

The total value of the canned salmon to include the year 1923 amounts to the enormous sum of $477,-128,390. The value to include 1908 was $92,836,983. Since that year the number of cases and their values were as follows: 1909, 2,395,477 cases, $9,438,152; 1910, 2,413,055, $11,086,322; 1911, 2,823,817, $14,-593,237; 1912, 4,054,641, $16,291,927; 1913, 3,739,-185, $13,531,604; 1914, 4,056,653, $18,920,589; 1915, 4,500,293, $18,653,015; 1916, 4,900,627, $23,269,429; 1917, 5,947,286, $46,304,090; 1918, 6,605,835, $51,-041, 949; 1919, 4,583,688, $43,265,349; 1920, 4,429,-

463, $35,602,800; 1921, 2,596,826, $19,632,744; 1922, 4,501,652, $29,787,193; 1923, 5,035,697, $32,873,007.

The maximum year in product and in value was 1918. The following figures show the marked variations from year to year, giving number of canneries operated, persons employed, and salmon caught: 1920, 146 canneries, 24,423 employees, 65,080,539 salmon; 1921, 83, 12,986, 37,905,591; 1922, 123, 21,974, 72,370,400. In 1922 there was an investment of $45,207,557 in the salmon industry.

The average price per case of salmon rose from the minimum in 1913 to the maximum in 1918: Coho, from $3.45 to $11.27; chum, $2.21 to $6.82; humpback, $2.58 to $5.47; king, $4.04 to $13.13; red, $4.54 to $12.98.

Besides the fisherman the salmon has the following natural enemies: bears, gulls, predatory trout seals, and belugas.

In the past the salmon have been taken by traps, seines, gill-nets, lines, etc. In 1922 the percentages thus taken were: Traps, 41; gill-nets, 35; seines, 23; lines, etc., 1. Under the recent law and regulations (see Table 3), catches by traps and by seines are practically forbidden. Efforts are made to maintain the supply by hatcheries, which in 1922 resulted in the release of about 110,000,000 fry. In that year there were taken 72,370,400 fish in the three districts: Southeastern Alaska, 31,055,302; central Alaska, 15,-612,843; western Alaska, 25,702,255. As to kinds, they were: Red, 33,898,772; humpback, 30,589,342; chum, 5,273,883; coho, 1,838,094; king, 770,309.

Uncanned Salmon

It must not be inferred that the industries of the various forms of uncanned salmon are unimportant. In 1921 there were employed 1,600 persons in the special industries of mild-cured, pickled, frozen, fresh, smoked, and by-products of the salmon. There was an investment of $2,301,581, and the products had a value of $1,179,064. The aggregate value of these special products from 1868 to 1923 is $19,465,960. This brings up the value of the salmon, exclusive of the very large amounts consumed by the people of Alaska, to $480,154,404. With the catch of 1924 the value will far exceed half a billion of dollars.

Conservation of the Alaska Salmon

The proper conservation of such a productive source of income for the future of the American people, both fishermen and consumers, is a problem of importance and difficulty. The opinions of prominent Alaskans, of the leading officials of the great fishing industries of the Pacific, and of the experts of the Bureau of Fisheries, were set forth at length before a committee of the House of Representatives, which reported the bill "For the Protection of the Fisheries of Alaska," which became a law June 6, 1924. The official regulations now in force have been formulated under the Secretary of Commerce in accordance with that Act.

BIBLIOGRAPHY.—Department of Commerce, Annual Reports of the Commissioner, Bureau of Fisheries.

CHAPTER XVI

MINOR FISHERIES

The Cod, Etc.

THE cession of Alaska to the United States immediately stimulated and rendered permanent the hitherto desultory and experimental fishery efforts, and the fleet engaged in catching cod immediately increased from three sail in 1867 to fourteen in 1868, all from the port of San Francisco.

The great distance from the home port at which the fishery was conducted proved so expensive in time and money that the policy was adopted of establishing in Alaska shore stations, from which fishermen could operate in small boats. The first shore station was located in 1876 at Pirate Cove, in the Shumagin group. In 1907 there were no fewer than 19 such stations, situated on the following islands: 6 on Unga, 4 on Sanak, 3 each on Guinak and Sagai, 2 on Little Koniuji, and 1 on Popof. These stations are operative the entire year. The fishermen usually go out singly, in a dory, from one to five miles, where in good weather they haul trawl lines several times each day. The men thus employed furnish only the fishing-gear.

In fleet operations the fishing is usually by hand lines from dories, while each vessel carries a dressing-gang, with splitter and salter. The usual bait, both shore and ship, is halibut, sculpin, and cuttle-fish.

As better grounds—the outer banks—have been discovered, the fish prove larger, and the average weight of a codfish has risen from 2.8 pounds in 1868 to 4 pounds in 1905.

Systematic work was commenced by the Bureau of Fisheries in 1888 to locate and survey the best fishing-grounds, and the *Albatross* in the next four seasons examined and plotted many codfish banks, of which the following are the principal: Slime, Baird or Moller, and Gravel, all in Bering Sea; Davidson, Albatross, Portlock, Sannak, and Shumagin, on the southern side of the Alaska Peninsula.

Special care is necessary properly to cure the Alaskan cod to a condition equal to that of the Atlantic cod, and neglect in the past has militated against the regular marketing of the Alaskan cod in the great fish-consuming countries. Fixed standards, rigidly maintained, are essential to secure profitable markets.

The value of the product of the Alaskan cod fishery from 1868 to 1923 somewhat exceeds $13,000,000. There are, however, great fluctuations in the business from year to year, owing to foreign competition, state of market, etc.

The year of maximum activity was 1920, when there was invested in the industry $2,057,728, with 803 employees. There were caught that season 12,763,399 pounds of fish, valued at $1,117,464. This enormous production was followed by a great falling off; the catch in 1922 was only 6,134,649 pounds, and in 1923, 1,070,802 fish, valued at $99,105.

According to condition, the cod are salted, frozen, pickled, or sold fresh, as the market demands. While some tongues are preserved, there is considerable waste, as the livers, sounds, etc., are cast into the sea.

Herring

In late years there has been a marked development of the herring industry, which is carried on extensively in the waters of southeastern Alaska. In output it now stands second, being surpassed only by the salmon. The values of herring caught in late years were: 1919, $1,676,170; 1920, $1,303,604; 1921, $934,044.

The year 1922 showed a very large increase, the value rising to $2,329,116. There were 22 plants in operation, employing 1,280 persons, and the catch amounted to 43,273,915 pounds. No less than 36,-000,000 pounds were pickled by the Scotch curing-method. Of the cured herring the official report says: "The pack was of better quality, and sales were better and more promptly made than in past seasons."

Herring fertilizers were produced to the value of $98,528, and there were obtained 425,241 gallons of oil, value $144,418.

The total value of the 1923 catch of herring was $1,602,571.

Halibut

Halibut fishing is conducted both from shore stations and by fleets, power and sail. Steam trawlers have proved uneconomical, although trawls are largely and successfully used by fishermen in dories.

Eighty per cent of the catch is from shore stations, which are established on the shores of, or adjacent to, the Inside Passage between Ketchikan and Juneau, in Frederick Sound, Icy, Chatham, Peril, and Sumner Straits, with headquarters at Wrangell Narrows. Large quantities of the catch go into either the Canadian or the Puget Sound ports, and so are not of record in Alaska.

The halibut fishery was a small industry in 1907, when the value of its products was $140,751. In time it has become a most important business. Data as to the value of the fishery from 1890 to 1923 are wanting, but the amount doubtless exceeds $15,000,-000. Affected by the war, the maximum value was that of 1918, but of fish caught 1921 leads. The catch and values of recent years are: 1918, 13,869,706 pounds, $1,667,686; 1919, 14,278,791, $1,150,605; 1920, 15,295,500, $1,726,798; 1921, 17,176,274, $1,476,450; 1922, 11,075,237, $1,034,967. It is estimated that about one-third of the catch of American fishermen enters the Canadian ports, and so is not included in the above data. The Alaskan catch of 1922 was divided in sale between 3,188,473 pounds frozen, and 7,886,764 marketed fresh. The value of the catch of 1923 was $1,253,951.

Experts had for years pointed out that the continuance of the halibut industry depended on the adoption of conservation methods. It became evident that the banks were being overfished, a practice equally injurious to the best interests of both Canada and the United States.

After prolonged negotiations a treaty was concluded between the United States and Great Britain, on March 24, 1924, for the conservation of the halibut fisheries of the North Pacific Ocean. The treaty imposes a closed season from November 16 of each year to February 15 of the succeeding year. During such period of closure the taking or landing of halibut in the United States or Canada is prohibited. The agreement also provides for the maintenance of a patrol during the closed season, and imposes penalties for violations. The treaty continues in force for several years. The North Pacific halibut treaty was ratified by the U. S. Senate on May 31, 1924, and the enabling Act to put the treaty in force was approved by the President June 7, 1924.

Whales

Formerly the whale fishery was the most important of any in Alaskan waters. The fleet of 250 whalers which fished in the Arctic Ocean in 1851 had dwindled to 5 vessels in 1913, whose product amounted only to $26,250.

Shore whaling, which began in 1907, was represented in 1922 by two stations—Port Armstrong and Akutan. The products are whale oil, sperm oil, ivory, whalebone, meat (frozen), hides, and fertilizers. At the stations every portion of the animal is converted into a finished product. During the war whale meat became a staple, and 148,000 pounds were marketed in Seattle.

In 1922 there were 220 employees, and the value of all whale products was $409,618. There were 445 whales caught, of which 204 were finbacks, 95 humpbacks, 77 sulphur bottoms, and 69 sperm. The total value to 1923 since 1880 approximates $7,000,000.

Walrus

In 1877 there were killed enough walruses to furnish 74,000 pounds of ivory and 221,000 gallons of oil. Soon the killing for oil not proving very profitable, the walrus were slaughtered for their tusks and their hides. It was evident that this animal was doomed to early extermination unless protected by legislation.

Their protection is now ensured by the Acts of Congress of May 11, 1908, and May 31, 1920. It is permitted only that natives may kill the walrus for food and clothing, and miners or explorers when in urgent need of food.

Miscellaneous

The relatively unimportant minor fisheries are gradually increasing in value and importance. The Alaskan clams, crabs, shrimps, trout, etc., put on the market in 1922 exceeded $400,000—a record. The output in 1923 was nearly double in value—$788,527.

BIBLIOGRAPHY.—Annual Reports of the U. S. Commissioner of Fisheries.

CHAPTER XVII

AGRICULTURE, FORESTRY, AND HOMESTEADS

As on other points, there have been advanced optimistic and pessimistic views on the possibilities of successful agriculture in Alaska. On this subject various official reports and many verbal statements have been considered, which are supplemented by personal observations over a great variety and extent of country.

Agriculture as a whole is valuable in Alaska solely for the purpose of supplying the local market, and that in part only. There are a few successful farmers, all in well-chosen localities in the vicinity of towns of considerable size. At Kenai the cattle live exclusively on the native grasses, which are sweet and nutritious. Butter and cheese are there made, but the demand is not equal to the supply.

Parts of the Yukon are suitable for gardening to a degree astonishing to the uninformed. The best-known instance of successful farming is that at the Holy Cross Mission, on the Yukon, in 62° N. Here cattle have been raised for ten years or more, and the products of the forty acres of land under cultivation excite surprise in every visitor. All through the valley of the Yukon potatoes and other vegetables mature, when proper ground is chosen and skilled attention given.

At Fort Gibbon, at the junction of the Yukon and the Tanana, and at Fort Egbert, on the International Boundary near the arctic circle, the military garrisons have raised large quantities of vegetables, potatoes being especially successful. Even in the Koyukuk Valley similar conditions obtain, and at Coldfoot, within the arctic circle at 68° N., potatoes, cabbages, turnips, rhubarb, etc., are grown of large size and good flavor.

That the productivity of Alaskan agriculture is important both in quantity and in value is clearly indicated by the diminution in the shipment of potatoes from the United States to Alaska, which dropped from 211,215 bushels in 1906 to 167,033 bushels in 1908. Meanwhile the values of all vegetable shipments fell from $696,928 to $483,855, a decrease of more than 30 per cent. During the same period the quantity of imported hay fell from 10,405 tons to 9,165 tons, though the number of stock increased. In 1924 only 5,834 tons were imported.

Agriculture

In considering the agricultural possibilities, it has been wisely said that those considering this industry should have in mind the fact that Alaska is remote from the great markets, that its sparse population is scattered, its transportation limited, the local markets few, and the installation of an agricultural plant is as a rule excessively costly.

Naturally Alaska is not a country of grains or of tender vegetables, but it has hardy small fruits and berries in many localities. Dall, an authority on the Territory in general, reported many years since on this point. He said:

Small fruits are in the Yukon watershed in the greatest profusion. Among them may be noted red and black currants, gooseberries, cranberries, raspberries, thimbleberries. Among other berries are blueberry, salmon, twin, heath, moss and rose.

Agricultural Experiments

The agricultural possibilities of the Territory have been quite fully determined by the experimental researches of the U. S. Department of Agriculture for many years, under Georgeson. It appears that the largest and most promising areas of agricultural land are in the valleys of the Copper, Kuskokwim, Matanuska, Susitna, Tanana, Yukon, and especially on the south fork of Forty-Mile River. In 1923 in the Fairbanks district there were 48 farms, of 12,570 acres, of which 924 were under cultivation with 157 head of stock. In the Anchorage and Matanuska district 42 farms, 9,557 acres, 497 cultivated, with 262 head of stock. It is estimated that there are in the Territory 100,000 square miles of agricultural land, half farming and half grazing. In general the soil is rather poor, from the crop-producing standpoint.

Grain

Corn cannot be grown. In the interior valleys above named oats can be grown nearly everywhere,

Home Gardening at Fairbanks, Tanana Valley.

but in localities are subject to injury by early frosts. Winter rye survives when covered by 20 or more inches of snow. Hardy winter wheat requires 30 inches; when there is less not more than 50 per cent survives. Spring wheat is possible for certain early varieties which can ripen in the 100 days of growing weather. Early varieties of barley mature everywhere in normal seasons. A hybrid barley has been developed which ripens more quickly than in the States. The only failure of the grain crop in 25 years occurred in 1922. While frost and excessive rain may injure Alaskan crops, they are free from hailstorms, fungus diseases, and destructive insect pests. In 1921, 3,500 bushels of spring wheat were grown in the Fairbanks District, and local farmers erected a mill where flour was produced for interior markets.

Vegetables

Hardy vegetables of nearly every kind are grown in all valleys south of the Yukon. While they thrive well in the interior they are most successful in the coast region.

Live Stock

Cattle, hogs, and goats do well on Kodiak Island and in the Matanuska and Tanana valleys. They live on native forage, the winter food of the cattle being hay and silage made from grass. All tame grasses grow well, but smooth broom grass is best. White clover survives the winter cold, but the red does not.

Homesteads

The settler may locate 160 acres; when on unsurveyed lands he must bear the cost of surveys. For agricultural purposes he cannot encroach on reservations, missions, hot springs, or mineral lands. Residence must be established within six months. Cultivation must be started on one-sixteenth in the second year, and on one-eighth the third year. At the end of the third year proofs must be made, and governmental costs paid, ranging from $25 to $50, according to situation.

The National Forests of Alaska

As happens with all measures for the conservation of national resources, the establishment of these forestal reservations met with bitter criticism. Under wise concessions and modification of regulations, most of the misunderstandings between citizen and official have disappeared.

The extent to which the advantages of these forests have been granted to the community at large has not been generally realized. Homesteaders and residents are accorded free such timber as is needed for their personal use. Under regulation permits— revocable only for cause—there are established within the limits of the two forests in 1924, 202 residences, 173 fox farms, 76 fish canneries, and 15 farms. The following general conditions are drawn from official sources.

National Forests of Alaska

The first withdrawals from the public domain in Alaska for the purpose of establishing what are now known as national forests were made by President Harrison in 1892, when the Afognak Forest and Fish Culture Reserve was created. In 1902 President Roosevelt created the Alexander Archipelago Forest Reserve, and in 1907 the Chugach and Tongass National Forests. In 1908 Mr. Roosevelt, by executive order, consolidated the Afognak and Chugach, under the name of the latter, and the Alexander Archipelago and the Tongass under the name of the Tongass National Forest. Later Presidents have by proclamation added to or eliminated from the areas of these two forests. On June 30, 1923, the area of the Chugach National Forest was 5,129,120 acres, and the Tongass National Forest contained 15,442,429 acres.

These two national forests are under the general administration of a district forester, who, with his staff, maintains his headquarters at Juneau. Each forest is under the immediate direction of a forest supervisor, who administers the forest with the aid of a staff of rangers and guards. The headquarters of the Chugach is at Cordova, and that of the Tongass at Ketchikan.

The Chugach National Forest is the more northern of the two and is located in the Prince William Sound region. According to the latest estimate of the Forest Service, it contains the following stand of merchantable timber:

Western hemlock	4,275,000,000 feet B. M.
Sitka spruce	1,435,000,000 " "
White spruce	750,000,000 " "
Cottonwood	60,000,000 " "
White birch	50,000,000 " "
Total	6,570,000,000 feet B. M.

Notwithstanding the very small population in and adjacent to this forest and the comparative inaccessibility of its resources, nearly 900 different sales have been made of standing timber, involving a total of 54,000,000 feet. Its timber was an important factor in the construction of the United States Alaska Railroad. One hundred and thirty-six special use permits were in force in the forest during the calendar year 1923, of which 33 were for fox farms, involving 77,000 acres of land; 58 were for residences or cabins; 31 for fish canneries; 6 for agriculture; and 5 for sawmills.

The Tongass National Forest, the larger of the two, is located in the Panhandle of Alaska, in southeastern Alaska. It includes the mainland south of the Unak River, as well as the islands to the westward. According to the latest estimate of the Forest Service, the timber stand of the Forest is as follows:

Western hemlock	54,400,000,000 feet B. M.
Sitka spruce	14,700,000,000 " "
Western red cedar	2,200,000,000 " "
Alaska cedar	2,200,000,000 " "
Total	73,500,000,000 feet B. M.

Timber in the Chugach National Forest, near Cordova.

(Along Copper River Railroad.)

The Forest Service has made over 4,000 sales of timber in the Tongass Forest, involving nearly 700,-000,000 feet B. M. During the calendar year 1923, 512 special use permits of various kinds were in force. Chief among these were 140 permits for fox farms, involving 78,000 acres and 144 residence permits for houses and cabins. Other large users were fish canneries, 43 permits; tramways, 26 permits; farms, 19 permits.

Water-Power and Pulp Timber

The water-power resources of southeastern Alaska, that is, in the Tongass National Forest, were the subject of a reconnaissance survey in 1921 and 1922 by the Forest Service and the Federal Power Commission. Over 450,000 horse-power has been found and recorded to date, and a thorough power exploration of the entire forest would likely disclose the presence of many important units not now known to exist. The power sites so far investigated occur in units suitable for a wide range of pulp-mill capacity, the largest site being able to furnish 32,000 horse-power throughout the year. In a number of cases near-by sites afford opportunity to concentrate power at one manufacturing point. The power resources of the Chugach Forest and vicinity have received little study, but it is known that they are not nearly so extensive as those of southeastern Alaska. The most important known power site of this region is Eklutna Lake, near the city of Anchorage, where an estimated capacity of 20,000 horse-power is found.

The local demand for timber requires but a very small percentage of the possible timber output of the national forests of Alaska, and while this demand will always be met, the region must look forward to exporting timber products and to an extensive permanent development of industries shipping to the general markets of the United States and foreign countries. The manufacture of paper, and more particularly newsprint paper, is the wood-using industry for which this region apparently holds the best prospects. Forest Service studies indicate that the timber resources of southeastern Alaska, under proper management, protection, and utilization, can produce 2,000,000 cords of pulpwood annually in perpetuity. If converted into newsprint, it represents an annual production of 1,500,000 tons, or well over one-half of the present yearly requirements of the United States. The region has many favorable features for the development and operation of paper plants, the most outstanding of which are cheaply developed, year-round water-power, low cost of wood delivered at the plant, a sustained source of timber supply, a climate that permits of year-long operation and shipping, and the possibility of ocean transportation directly from the mill warehouses.

The management of the timber resources of the national forests of Alaska has as its prime objective (1) the development and maintenance of a permanent pulp and paper manufacturing industry commensurate with the available water-power and timber resources; (2) the furnishing of a permanent and convenient supply of timber for local consumption, with such an additional supply for the local saw-mills for the general lumber market as may be needed to justify efficient mill facilities and provide year-long operations.

Distribution of Forest Trees

The treeless wastes are the Aleutian Islands, the south half of the Alaska Peninsula, the Yukon Delta, and the mouth of the Kuskokwim, the west half of Seward Peninsula, and the coasts for a hundred miles inland from Bering Strait and the Arctic Ocean. Excepting the glaciers and high mountain summits the rest of Alaska may be called wooded.

The true forest with valuable timber is confined almost exclusively to southeastern Alaska, and to the immediate coast region from Yakutat Bay westward to Alaska Peninsula. As one travels north from Seattle the conditions change slowly in British Columbia, and along the Alaskan coast to Yakutat Bay. The forest consists very largely of hemlocks (coast and alpine) and spruce, with considerable elder, willows, and cottonwoods, some yellow cedar, a sprinkling of red cedar, and probably a few other straggling species. The scanty depth of soil often distorts the tree's growth, so that it makes inferior lumber, though spruces are occasionally found that are from five to six feet in diameter and upward of 150 feet in height. In the Prince William Sound region the other species gradually fail, the hemlock last, leaving the spruce dominant and almost alone from Cook Inlet to the westward.

The interior of Alaska is largely wooded, and

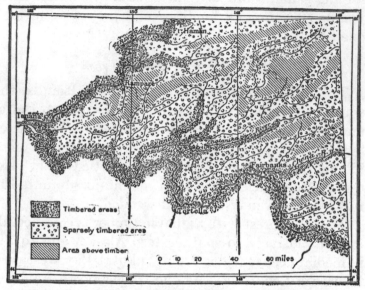

Map No. 5. Distribution of Timber in the Tanana-Yukon Region

though the spruce is the most numerous species, there are large quantities of hemlock, birch, poplar, cottonwood (or aspen), alder, and willow. The Tanana Valley has almost inexhaustible supplies of poplar, spruce, hemlock, and birch, and in the lower valley considerable tamarack. Thousands upon thousands of cords of wood are transported for steamboat fuel from the densely wooded shores of the Tanana to the barren Yukon delta. While there

are enormous areas densely wooded in the Tanana
Valley, yet the timber near the mining camps is rapidly disappearing. The interior limit of timber elevation is unusually high, some trees being found
nearly 5,000 feet above the sea.

The general distribution of the interior forests is
along rivers and adjacent lowlands, as is indicated
by the accompanying map of woodlands in the
Tanana-Yukon region.

While there is considerable timber in the vicinity
of Fort Gibbon, in the central Yukon Valley, yet the
far greater part of the trees are of very moderate
size. Several years since an army contractor had difficulty in obtaining within 75 miles of the post a not
very large number of sizable logs.

In the lake region between Cook Inlet and Bristol
Bay there are well-timbered areas with considerable
large spruce, some said to be over three feet in diameter. The eastern part of Seward Peninsula and the
adjacent shores of Norton Sound are fairly covered
with spruce. The Kobuk Valley is quite heavily
timbered with birch and cottonwood, and Stoney
reports large spruces, one being 60 feet long, with a
butt diameter of 16 inches. The Susitna is well timbered, principally with spruce. The Kanuti Valley
also has considerable forest areas, as well as the Tozi
and the Koyukuk, the latter especially in the lower
reaches where there are many large trees. The Porcupine has a dense growth of birch, spruce, and cottonwood. On the arctic slopes of Endicott Mountains and to the west of Colville River there is much

timber, though of stunted growth and rapidly decreasing toward the ocean.

In short, there are few extended areas in the interior of Alaska where timber fails to meet amply the wants of the miner or settler.

BIBLIOGRAPHY.—Annual Reports and Circulars: Alaska Agricultural Experiment Stations. Annual Reports of Chief of Forest Service, Washington.

CHAPTER XVIII

GLACIER REGIONS

OF all the attractions of Alaska the névé fields, with the various forms and awe-inspiring action of living glaciers, most impress and interest the tourist. This, despite the fact that the most extensive and striking glaciers are not seen by the summer visitors, who very rarely extend their excursions to the surpassingly wonderful regions of Yakutat Bay and Prince William Sound. From year to year, however, the number of visiting students and sightseers must steadily increase along the shores of the Gulf of Alaska, where glaciers far surpassing those of Europe are accessible with the utmost comfort, at moderate expense, and by sea voyages of three or four days.

The high and sharply uprising mountains of British Columbia and southeastern Alaska are the recipients of heavy snowfalls from the moisture-laden ocean winds, and, in consequence, the loftier peaks and valleys are ice-laden with small glaciers. These are of various types, the Alpine, the valley, or the overhanging Piedmont ice sheets covering and projecting from shelves on the mountain-sides.

As one passes Wrangell the glacier formations increase in extent, and pushing down the mountains many approach the level of the sea. The numerous and deeply penetrating fiords usually terminate in gorges, which are filled with rivers of moving ice. They are mostly dead glaciers, retreating and vanishing from year to year, under changing conditions which cut them off from their functions as live glaciers, of discharging ice masses into the open sea.

In Le Conte Bay, near the mouth of the Stikine River, is the most southerly of the live glaciers, debouching from a narrow fiord whose rocky walls rise from 4,000 to 5,000 feet within a few miles.

Some distance farther to the north, in Stephens Passage, are two beautiful ice fiords, Holkham or Sumdum, and Taku.

Of the Sumdum Bay, which he considers one of the most interesting of all the Alaskan fiords, Muir says:

A hundred or more glaciers of the second and third class may be seen along the walls, and about as many snowy cataracts, which, with the plunging bergs, keep all the fiord in a roar. The scenery in both the long arms of the bay and their side branches is of the wildest description, especially in their upper reaches, where the granite walls, streaked with waterfalls, rise in sheer massive precipices, like those of Yosemite Valley, to a height of 3,000 and even over 4,000 feet.

Of her early visit to Taku, Miss Scidmore writes:

That day on the Taku Glacier will live forever as one of the rarest and most perfect enjoyment. The grandest objects in nature were before us, the primeval forces that mould the face of the earth were at work, and it was all so out of the everyday world that we might have been walking a new planet, fresh fallen from the Creator's hand.

Of Taku Inlet, with its 45 ice streams, great and small, John Muir writes of the discharging glacier:

It comes sweeping forward in majestic curves and pours its countless roaring, plunging masses into a western branch of the inlet, next the Taku River. Thus we have here in one view, flowing into the sea, side by side, a river of ice and a river of water, both abounding in cascades and rapids, yet infinitely different in their rate of motion and in the songs they sing—a rare object lesson, worth coming far to learn.

The true glacier region begins to the west of Lynn Canal, along the shores of which, however, are most beautiful dead glaciers, such as Davidson and Mendenhall, and from Cross Bay north. The extreme southern limit has been known to many tourists through the excursions in former years, before the convulsions of nature largely disintegrated many of the glaciers, especially the Muir Glacier.

Kate Field thus described this great ice-stream:

Imagine a glacier three miles wide and 300 feet high, and you have a slight idea of Muir Glacier. Picture a background of mountains 15,000 feet high, all snow-clad, and then imagine a gorgeous sun lighting up the ice crystals with rainbow coloring. The face of the glacier takes on the hue of aquamarine—the hue of every bit of floating ice that surrounds the steamer. This dazzling serpent moves sixty-four feet a day, tumbling headlong into the sea, startling the ear with submarine thunder.

Doubtless the most remarkable for its extent, equal in area to the State of Rhode Island, and of unsurpassed beauty in itself and its surroundings, this great glacier and its companions are now rarely visited, owing to the dangers of navigation within Glacier Bay. Of the Muir Glacier Miss Scidmore writes of her last view:

The whole brow was transfigured with the fires of sunset; the blue and silvery pinnacles, the white and shining front floating dreamlike on a roseate and amber sea, and the range and circle of dull violet mountains lifting their glowing summits into a sky flecked with crimson and gold.

From Glacier Bay north to the Wrangell Range, and westward to Kenai Peninsula, about 500 by 100 miles in extent, is the area of greatest glacial abundance, fully nine-tenths of the ice of this continent being found therein. Here are 35 of the 41 known live glaciers, 11 in the Fairweather Range (2 in Lituya and 9 in Glacier Bay), 3 in the St. Elias region, and 16 in Prince William Sound, and 5 on Kenai Peninsula. There are more than 200 known glaciers of interest.

In the St. Elias region is the Malaspina Glacier, of enormous extent, being about 20 by 60 miles in area, and separated from the sea by a strip of forested moraines five to six miles wide, except where its magnificent ice cliffs enter the sea at Icy Cape.

Of the remarkable surroundings of the noble Gardiner Greene Hubbard Glacier, a most active ice river three miles wide, Muir writes:

The scenery about the head of Disenchantment Bay is gloriously wild and sublime, majestic mountains and glaciers, barren moraines, bloom-covered islands amid icy,

Columbia Glacier, Prince William Sound: Front about 300 feet.

(South end, showing contact of glacier with forest.)

swirling waters, enlivened by screaming gulls, hair seals, and roaring bergs. On the other hand, the beauty of the southern extension of the bay is tranquil and restful and perfectly enchanting. Its shores, especially on the east side, are flowery and finely sculptured, and the mountains, of moderate height, are charmingly combined and reflected in the quiet waters.

Prince William Sound is, however, the most remarkable region for glacial phenomena and living glaciers. With Valdez as a base, it offers opportunities for glacial study and observation unsurpassed elsewhere. Since the discoveries of the Harriman Expedition in College and Harriman fiords, it offers 11 known living glaciers in Prince William Sound, of which the most remarkable for size and beauty are: Columbia, about 4 miles wide, 300 feet high; Harvard, Yale, Serpentine, Harriman, and Surprise.

Of Prince William Sound Muir writes:

All the fiords into which glaciers of the first class flow are encumbered, some of them jammed and crowded, with bergs of every conceivable form, which, by the most active of the glaciers, are given off at intervals of a few minutes with loud, thundering roaring that may be heard five or six miles, proclaiming the restless work and motion of these mighty crystal rivers, so widely contrasting with the deathlike stillness and silence of the second-class decadent glaciers.

Of Harriman Fiord, Muir adds:

It is full of glaciers of every description, waterfalls, gardens, and grand old forests — nature's best and choicest Alpine treasures purely wild. Here we camped in the only pure forest of mountain hemlock I ever saw, the most beautiful of evergreens, growing at sea-level, some of the trees over three feet in diameter and nearly a hundred feet high.

Muir considers Columbia fully as imposing though less active than Muir Glacier. In the writer's opinion, it would be difficult to find a glacier more beautiful to the ordinary visitor than the Columbia, with its enormous mass and its wealth of color and form. Its striking background is offset by the frontal environment of flowery meads and noble trees. Few of the glaciers seen by the writer in the north surpass it in majesty, and none equal it in attractiveness of surroundings.

Mrs. Higginson, in her interesting "Alaska," says:

When seen under favorable conditions, the [Freemantle, renamed the] Columbia Glacier is the most beautiful thing in Alaska. One may have seen glaciers upon glaciers, yet not be prepared for the splendor and magnificence of the one that palisades the northern end of this (Columbia) bay.

The glacier has a frontage of about four miles, and its glittering palisades tower upward to a height of from three to four hundred feet.

In ordinary light, the front of the glacier is beautifully blue. It is a blue that is never seen in anything save a glacier or a floating iceberg—a pale, pale blue, that seems to flash out fire with every movement. At sunset its beauty holds one spellbound. It sweeps down magnificently from the snow-peaks which form its fit setting and pushes out into the sea in a solid wall of spired and pin-

Névé of Fairweather Range, and Alsek Glacier.

nacled opal which, ever and anon breaking off, flings over
it clouds of color which dazzle the eyes. At times there
is a display of prismatic colors. Across the front grow,
fade, and grow again the most beautiful rainbow shadings.

Of the glaciers of the interior two may be briefly
mentioned—the Harvey, two by eight miles in size,
and the Fidéle, both in the Mt. McKinley region.
Of the latter, Cook writes:

The lower edge is seven and a half miles in width, its
length forty miles. The lower ten miles are so thoroughly
weighted down by broken stone that no ice is visible.
It is thus the largest interior glacier of Alaska, and it
probably carries more moraine material than any other
glacier in the world.

Of the life of the glaciers, Professor George Davidson, in his "Glaciers of Alaska," says:

There has been a general recession of the glaciers
through the Aleutian Islands, the Peninsula of Alaska,
and from Cook's Inlet to Portland Canal; except where
they come directly or almost directly upon the broad
ocean.

The evidence of advance seems clear at Taylor Bay,
just inside Cape Spencer, at Icy Strait, since the survey
of Whidbey; but the recent topographical survey by the
United States Coast and Geodetic Survey shows a retreat
behind the terminal moraine which it has left as a record.

The Malaspina Glacier has filled and obliterated the Icy
Bay of Vancouver and Tebenkof; the recent Canadian
survey indicates that the glaciers of Lituya Bay have
shortened the deep arms described by La Pérouse; and
La Pérouse Glacier upon the ocean shore shows positive

signs of advance, according to the reports of the Harriman Expedition of 1899.

Nevertheless, in this region of advance the immense ice blockade at the head of Yakutat Bay, so well described by Malaspina and confirmed by Tebenkof, has been carried away, and the Hubbard and Turner Glaciers now discharge into the sharp bend of the fiord at the head of the bay.

The Geological Survey, in its *Bulletin* 526, gives the investigations of Grant and Higgins of the coastal glaciers of Prince William Sound and the Kenai Peninsula. Fine plates and full descriptions are given in this report. They visited and describe 42 glaciers, of which the live ones, reaching tide-water, are: Aialik, Bainbridge, Barry (including Cascade and Coxe, which unite with it), Bryn Mawr, Blackstone, Cataract, Chenega, Columbia, Harriman, Harvard, Holgate, McCarty, Meares, Northwestern, Pederson (at high tide only), Princeton, Radcliffe, Serpentine, Smith, Surprise, Taylor, Tiger, Vassar, and Yale.

Doubtless there are other live glaciers along the coast of the Gulf of Alaska, but those named are the most accessible for scientific study and tourist visits.

BIBLIOGRAPHY.—Davidson, Glaciers of Alaska on Russian Charts. Muir: Notes on Pacific Coast Glaciers. Gilbert: Glaciers and Glaciation. Tarr and Martin: National Geographic Society's Alaskan Expedition of 1909.

CHAPTER XIX

REINDEER

THE wholesale destruction of land game, the practical extermination of sea game, and the displacement of natives in many places by the influx of miners and prospectors, wrought such disturbances in the economy of native life that the extermination of thousands by starvation was imminent. Among other methods suggested to improve permanently the condition of the natives, especially of the Bering Sea region, was the importation of Siberian reindeer. This action, inspired by Doctor Sheldon Jackson, promises in its results to be the most important benefit ever accorded the natives by the United States.

Doubtless in this, as in other novel and extended enterprises, there were errors of administration and policy, with exaggerated expectations and consequent disappointments, but, as a whole, the policy was wise and the results valuable and far-reaching.

Introduction of Reindeer

In 1889, when many of the Eskimos of the Bering Sea region were suffering from famine—owing to the depletion of sea and land animals on which they fed —and hundreds had perished from starvation, Doctor Sheldon Jackson, a pioneer missionary to the Territory, studied methods for the relief of the natives.

After considering many plans, he decided that the problem could be solved by the importation of Siberian reindeer. He learned from Captain Healy, revenue service, and others that the Asiatic arctic tribes lived comfortably on their herds of tame deer.

His proposition was scouted both by the Alaskans and by others as impracticable and absurd. Commissioner Harris and Doctor Jackson appealed to Congress for an appropriation for the purpose, but in 1890 the legislators viewed the project as ridiculous and refused the money.

Undismayed, Jackson appealed to the generous public, and with a subscription of about $2,100 bought trading supplies—it was known that deer could be obtained only by barter—and aided by Captain Healy visited the Siberian coast and obtained 16 animals in 1891 and 171 in 1892.

When the success of the importation was assured, Congress in 1893 made a small appropriation for the reindeer service. Importations were made from year to year until 1902, when the Russian Government forbade further exportations. By this time 1,280 deer had been brought into Alaska, and so became the progenitors of about 400,000 reindeer, of whom 100,000 have been killed for food and clothing. Rarely in history have the efforts of one man and an enterprise so small wrought equal benefits to an ignorant and starving people.

Methods of Distribution

The policy of the Interior Department, charged with the education of the natives, was wise and successful in distributing the reindeer. To have given them direct to the Eskimo hunters would have meant speedy extermination. The plan devised was carried out by the importation of Lapps, familiar with reindeer, and by the aid of various American missions. The deer were generally distributed in numbers to the missions, and earned by the Eskimo through a system of apprenticeship. Receiving training from the Lapps or other skilled person, an Eskimo apprentice at the close of the first, second and third years of faithful and efficient service received as his own respectively 6, 8, and 10 reindeer. At the end of the fourth year he receives 10 more, assumes entire charge of his herd, and agrees in turn to employ and distribute reindeer among his own apprentices.

There have been three classes of stations: (1) Government, entirely under Federal control; (2) mission, where herds are loaned for industrial training, an equal number to be eventually returned; (3) relief, maintained at suitable points for emergency purposes.

In past years loans or gifts of reindeer have been made to the Congregational missions at Wales and Shishmaref, to the Swedish Evangelical Union missions at Golofnin and Unalaklik, to the Society of Friends missions at Deering and Kotzebue, to the Norwegian Evangelical Lutheran Mission at Teller, to the Moravian Mission at Bethel, to the Catholic

Mission at Holy Cross, and to the Methodist Mission at Sinuk.

The governmental regulations forbade the sale by the natives of females, though it permitted the killing and selling of surplus males. These rules have conserved the native herds. The growth of the industry and the success of the methods was evident in 1914, when 980 Eskimo owned 37,828 herd. The continued increase is shown by the report for 1917, when 1,568 families owned 56,045 deer, against 17,350 by whites, 4,645 by missions, and 3,046 by the United States. In 1921, when the deer were so numerous that they could not be accurately counted, the official report, estimating the reindeer at 216,000, stated that approximately 70 per cent were in the possession of natives. Herds in 1923 were steadily increasing in the following districts: From Point Barrow south along the eastern shores of Bering Sea (except in the Yukon-Kuskokwim delta) to Bristol Bay; in the Kuskokwim Valley; in the upper Kobuk Valley; on the Yukon above Ruby; on the islands of Nunivak, St. Lawrence, Atka, Unmak, Unimak, and the Pribilofs; on Seward Peninsula; in Kotzebue and Norton Sounds, and in the Broad Pass region, west of the Alaska Railroad.

In his report for 1923 the Governor of Alaska stated:

Herds are now found near all of the principal settlements from the Arctic to the Pacific Ocean. The total number of reindeer in Alaska is now estimated at 300,000, of which about 200,000 are owned by the natives themselves. In certain sections they represent little value to the natives. Steps must be taken for the handling of the industry on a business basis.

Commercial exploitation has commenced, to the advantage of both native and the Territory.

Transformation of Eskimo Life

While the original object of the reindeer importation was to feed and clothe the Eskimo, its effect on their life has been astonishing. Hamilton, the chief of the Alaskan Education Bureau, testified:

Within less than a generation the reindeer industry has advanced through one entire stage of civilization, the Eskimo inhabiting the vast grazing lands from Point Barrow to the Aleutian Islands. It has raised them from the primitive to the pastoral stage, from nomadic hunters to civilized men, having in their herds of reindeer assured support for themselves and opportunity to acquire wealth.

It was the earliest and perhaps only governmental action providing, by the introduction of a new industry, practical vocational training adapted to community needs, and resulting in training a primitive race into independence and responsible citizenship.

To-day enterprising Eskimo hold reindeer fairs each year, do business with white settlements, have bank accounts, adopt improved methods of sanitation, purchase American clothing and food, and in some instances have built good frame houses from imported timber.

Commercial Exploitation

The enormous increase in the herds naturally led to the introduction of commercialism. The Eskimo were allowed and encouraged to sell their surplus male deer, the Lapps naturally desired to profit from their labors, and so a trade in the skins and particularly in the palatable meat of the reindeer grew up. The industry in time became important, and the largest corporation, the Lomen Co., became owners of nearly 50,000 deer. The extent of the trade, that of supplying the Seattle and other markets with the desired meat, was limited only by the storage capacity of the steamers navigating Bering Sea. The completion of the Alaska Railroad offers facilities for great extension.

Not alone have the companies benefited by this new business, but the Eskimo have greatly profited therefrom. It was soon learned by the companies that the hides of the deer were steadily decreasing in value from insect attacks, and that the size, quality, etc., of the reindeer were in many cases evidences of deterioration of the stock. Such conditions naturally arose in stock-raising conducted unscientifically by ignorant and often inefficient owners.

Remedial Methods of Stock-Raising

Fortunately, Congress listened favorably to the representations of experts, and, recognizing the importance of reindeer as a future meat supply for the Pacific coast region, made an appropriation for the

By courtesy of U. S. Bureau of Education.

Eskimo and Their Reindeer Teams.

purpose of a thorough investigation of the reindeer problem.

The Biological Survey, under Nelson, caused to be established at Unalakleet, on Norton Sound north of St. Michael, a well-equipped laboratory as headquarters. The investigations were conducted under the direct charge of Doctor S. Hadwen, who had an efficient set of skilled assistants. The programme on the reindeer's life covered diseases (ordinary and bacterial), parasites, and way of combating them, grazing conditions, forage plants, herd management, range methods, interbreeding with caribou, slaughter dressing and shipping, and indeed all matters deemed valuable in modern systems of stock-raising. The field investigations covered 15 months of field work, under trying and exhausting conditions, and accumulated knowledge that must be of incalculable value in the future of Alaska's reindeer industry.

The survey indicates that the successful evolution of the industry demands white supervision, co-operation as to markets, transportation, and cold storage, allotments for grazing, brand registry, distribution for salting, line fencing in some cases, and a system of company herds.

Description

The animal is thus described by Doctor S. Hadwen:

The typical reindeer of Alaska (*Rangifer tarandus*) is colored approximately as follows: The neck and shoulders are a grayish white, becoming darker on the back, and shading into the much darker sides of the abdomen and hind-quarters; the legs are dark to almost black; around the root of the tail there is a whitish area that descends between the legs; the head is dark except for the muzzle, and the mane, which becomes long in the winter, is almost white. The average full-grown reindeer stands about 13 to 13½ hands high, and measures about 7 feet from nose to tip of tail.

White and spotted reindeer are common in Alaskan herds. . . . Reindeer and caribou are the only members of the deer family in which both sexes have horns.

Forage of the Reindeer

The current belief that the reindeer feeds only on moss is incorrect. More than 200 kinds of plants grow on the summer ranges of Alaska, and a large number are eaten. Hadwen states:

The value of the different kinds of range forage plants varies greatly with the stage of growth, and probably to some extent to the tastes of the animals. As a rule reindeer prefer green vegetation and fresh growths and are fond of variety. They feed upon a great number of range plants, but in winter graze especially upon mosses, and in summer upon green vegetation (sedges, browse, grasses, and weeds). In spring they seek the earliest green vegetation, and feed on green growth throughout the summer. In fall and winter they feed on dry vegetation of various kinds and on lichens and mosses, but prefer the lichens known as *reindeer moss*, which, having made new growth in the fall, are fresher and probably more palatable.

The most important summer plants in order are sedges, willows, and mosses, followed by birch and

Alaska tea. In winter the order runs: Reindeer and Iceland moss, sedges and grasses, followed by various inferior mosses.

Necessarily, herds are moved inland in winter. About 30 acres of range are necessary for each deer. With the increasing herds the time has come when there must be rules for the control of special areas, which should be by a permit system, whereby definite grazing areas are allotted.

This problem will be difficult of equitable adjustment. The recommendation is made by Hadwen:

Anticipating the filling up of the ranges to their carrying capacity, small owners, particularly the Eskimos, should begin promptly to organize community or cooperative herds to hold the necessary grazing areas.

The development of the reindeer industry will eventually be an important factor in the food supply of the Pacific States. Promising as it is in present conditions, it is evident that it will require wise legislation and prudent administration to secure the best results. It is estimated that Alaska has sufficient grazing ground for several millions of deer. Under past percentages of growth there may well be a million deer in Alaska before 1950, which will present problems well worth national attention and study.

BIBLIOGRAPHY.—Annual Reports, Biological Survey Department of Agriculture. Hadwen & Palmer: Reindeer in Alaska. Bulletin 1089, Department of Agriculture.

CHAPTER XX

FUR FARMING

MANY years since it was evident to fur traders that the natural increase of the land fur-bearing animals in Alaska was inadequate to the demands made on the stock by the general public. Exact data are wanting as to the number of each species trapped, but that the field was over-exploited is beyond question. So urgent were the demands that the pelts of these animals marketed since Alaska became part of the United States had values exceeding $20,000,000.

Foxes are the most productive in values of the land animals, and regarding them there is evidence. It was testified by an expert before the Congressional Committee, investigating in 1921 conditions in Alaska, that the Russian catch of these animals in 122 years numbered 589,834, while in 51 years the United States had taken 745,795—11,565 annually as against 4,835.

The same authority continuing said:

Alaska is our most valuable fur-bearing possession. The industry ranks third in importance, only exceeded by those of fishing and mining. The success attained with the reindeer industry should be an incentive. Many lines give just as great promise of success, and one of these is fur farming in all its branches, which is capable of unlimited expansion. This work will make an otherwise barren area a region of much value, both to individual citizens and the commonwealth.

The extent to which the fur-farming industry has been developed is not accurately known, but the number of breeding farms certainly exceeds 250, utilizing capital which must exceed $500,000. In the great national forests alone there were in force, in 1924, 173 permits for fox farming. In the Chugach Forest there were 33 farms, while in the Tongass Forest there were 140 farms, covering 78,000 acres of land.

The Biological Survey in 1921 reported that besides 10 islands leased under federal law, there were more than 50 islands occupied for fur-farming purposes on the Aleutian chain. In the Congressional Report of 1921 there were enumerated the names of farmers occupying 119 farms, which are distributed as follows: Southeastern Alaska, 8; southern Alaska, 24; southwestern Alaska, 54; Copper River Valley, 7; Interior Valleys, 26.

The following animals are among those whose domestication and propagation commercially are being undertaken in Alaska: blue, cross, and silver foxes; marten, mink, muskrat, and reindeer (see Chapter XIX). The farming of lynx and beaver has been suggested. The commercial breeding of the muskrat and of the marten is of recent adoption, but in southeastern Alaska applicants for marten farms indicate an increase in this branch of the industry.

Leases and Permits

Under the federal law there are ten islands (Aghiuk, Chirikof, Chowiet, Elizabeth, Little Koniuji, Long, Marmot, Middleton, Pearl, and Simeonof) leased to the highest bidder, at about $200 annually, for five years, by the Biological Survey. Efforts tó obtain legislation on this subject, increasing the number of farms, have failed.

Nelson says:

One drawback to the development of this rapidly growing industry is the fact that many islands along the southern coast lie outside the national forests and the Aleutian Islands Bird Reservation, and remain unoccupied because no legal authority exists by which they may be leased. It is hoped that legislation may be enacted shortly which will render these islands similarly available. This is particularly important in view of the fact that they are of little or no value for any other purpose.

To overcome this drawback as far as the reservations and national forests are suitable for the industry, the Biological Survey and the Forest Service made a co-operative arrangement to cover the use for fur-farming purposes of islands in the Aleutian Chain and along the southern and southeastern coast of Alaska. Under this permit system the occupant pays $25 a year for three years, when a renewal is granted under equitable terms. The islands vary in area from 40 to several thousand acres. Blue foxes literally run free on these islands, while the few black or silver foxes are kept in pens. The success of this system appears from the catch of the Aleutian Chain, where in 1921 1,273 foxes were taken—755 red, 51 cross, 43 silver, 414 blue, and 10 white.

Fox Farming

The primary importance of the fox as a fur-bearing animal is specially shown by the fur industry of 1917. The Alaskan pelts that year of all kinds had a value of $1,338,600. The fur seal stood third, $274,350; lynx second, $296,440; while the fox led with the value of $590,038. It is of interest to note that the most valuable catch of the year was that of the wild red fox, 10,485 pelts, $251,640. In 1922 the red fox still led, 6,111 against 4,414 white and 1,791 blue. Some signs point to over-trapping of the red and white foxes by the use of poison in remote districts.

Fox Farms

The methods and outcome of fox farming are best set forth by the experiences at a large station. The most extensive satisfactory fox farming in Alaska is that which has been carried on for many years on the islands of St. George and St. Paul of the Pribilof group, in Bering Sea. Its successful operation has been due to two causes: First, its freedom from disturbing elements, it being a strictly guarded federal reservation; second, the development of the industry has been brought to its present efficiency by employees of intelligence, who, interested in the biological problems involved therein, have closely studied conditions and introduced conservative methods. Special efforts have been applied to make the colony one of blue foxes only.

The efforts to eliminate the white strain have been very successful. On St. George Island, of the 584 skins taken in the season 1922–1923, only 1 was white; on St. Paul Island there were 205 blue and 21 white. It is interesting to record that the percentages of whites from the two islands fell from 6.4 whites in 1916 to 2.9 in 1922 and 2.6 in 1923. The persistence of a white strain on St. Paul is probably due to the presence of newcomers, white foxes from the mainland who come to the island over the winter ice-pack.

Trapping Methods

The foxes have the run of the islands, and care is taken to avoid alarming the animals, especially during the time when they are caring for their young. When the time for trapping approaches, the animals are induced to come daily into the corral, where their favorite foods are displayed. At suitable times the corral is closed and the foxes are trapped in such manner as not to harm the animal.

From those thus trapped are carefully selected and released the quota for breeding purposes. The breeding fox must be young, sound, pure-colored, and if a male must weigh more than 10 pounds; if a female over 7½ pounds. The foxes are monogamous, and their litters run from 5 to 12.

Food and Feeding

Of their natural diet, Osgood says:

The foxes of the Pribilof Islands seem to prefer birds to any other food. The foxes are adept climbers, and many gulls, puffins, mures, and other cliff-nesting species are secured by the foxes in this way. The bird most commonly eaten is the least auklet, the smallest sea-bird found on the islands. Arriving in millions in May they are pursued relentlessly by the foxes. During the nesting season the eggs of the birds are eagerly and successfully sought. The foxes store large numbers of the eggs, burying them in the mossy tundra. Later the eggs are eaten on the spot, or carried to the young.

The supply of birds and eggs does not cover more than the four months of summer, and the successful propagation of large animals and the securing of good pelts depend largely on the food furnished for the remaining eight months.

Originally the blue foxes of the Pribilof Islands ate in the later season various kinds of vegetation, sea urchins, and such remains of fish and animals as they could find. Systematic feeding was later provided, consisting of oatmeal, seal meat—either raw or cooked,—fish, rice, etc. Mr. Judge states in his valuable report:

The rapidity with which the foxes learned that food would be set out daily at a certain place and time, and the numbers in which they came for it surprised every one on the island.

Commercial Fox Farms

The best private fox farms have been conducted along similar lines to those described above. The financial outcome is the same as in other industries. Nelson states:

Some have made extraordinarily large profits, amounting in a few instances to small fortunes in three or four years. Many others have made a complete failure of the business.

During 1918 from one island were shipped 100 blue pelts, averaging $85 each.

In some places the foxes run wild, and in others are penned by couples. Usually the blue foxes run free, and the black or silver are penned.

An industry of such extent and value should have the protection of law. For the purpose of developing fur farming Nelson recommends "the establishment of a uniform system of permits and rentals," which should in no way be burdensome.

BIBLIOGRAPHY.—Annual Reports of the Chief of Bureau of Biological Survey.

CHAPTER XXI

ALASKAN GAME

WITH material wealth, easy transportation, and improved fire-arms, civilized man has exploited the large game of the world during the past half century so mercilessly and persistently that many species are practically extinct. Among American game may be mentioned the buffalo on land, the sea-otter, and the sea-lion on the ocean.

Devastation among the sea game of Alaskan waters has been enormous in amount and frightful in its results. Elliott states that in the 70 years prior to the cession of Alaska there were annually killed in its waters 10,000 walrus, which were the principal means of subsistence and of life of from 7,000 to 8,000 natives. In 40 years the whalers have practically annihilated the animal in Alaskan seas; the products of $1,027,200 in 1919 fell to $27,200 in 1921, but rose to $409,618 in 1922. The value of sea-game is now of minor importance, except the fur-seal. The sea-otter and walrus are nearly extinct.

Of the effect on the natives of walrus exploitation J. N. Cobb, assistant agent Alaskan Fisheries, reports:

The white hunters rarely make use of anything but the two long, curved tusks, which average about five pounds to the pair. If time permits, the flesh is boiled and the oil saved.

To many of the Esquimo, especially on the Arctic shore, the walrus is almost a necessity of life, and the devastation wrought among the herds by the whalers has been, and is yet, the cause of fearful suffering and of death to many of the natives. The flesh is food for the men and dogs; the oil is used for food, for heating and lighting; the skin makes a cover for the large skin boats; the intestines make waterproof clothing.

The commercial exploitation of other aquatic game, although not so destructive in its outcome, has been fatally successful. From 1881 to 1890 the average annual number of sea-otter caught was 4,784; in 1905, 61; in 1906, 28; and in 1907, 16 only. In similar periods the land-otter decreased from an annual average of 2,730 to 1,889, 1,709, and 1,393 respectively. The beaver from the catch of 6,094 annually fell off to 1,935 in 1905, 1,536 in 1906, and 1,159 in 1907.

The vast area of Alaska, its enormous number of large game, the difficulty of cross-country travel, and the expense of time and effort to hunt such game have been the principal factors in its past preservation.

It would require a volume by itself to consider game conditions in their general aspects, so that brief allusions are here made to the more important species only. These consist of bears, caribou, deer, moose, mountain goats, and mountain sheep.

Bears

Of the thirteen kinds of Alaskan bears recognized by scientists, the general public practically know only four general types: the brown bears, the grizzlies, the black bears, and the polar bears.

The belief that polar bears are numerous in Alaska is not justified by facts. They are very rarely found in the Bering Sea region, and are infrequent even on the Arctic coast, where they confine themselves largely to the polar pack, except when hibernating or when with young.

The grizzlies are of two varieties, whose habits are similar to those of the grizzlies of the United States. The Kenai grizzly has his habitat on the peninsula for which he is named, while the interior species is found most frequently in the Endicott, Nuzotin, and Alaskan ranges, usually near the upper limit of timber.

Black bears roam over all Alaska south and east of the Yukon and Kuskokwim tundras. They are not of excessive size, though the largest of 12 killed on the Alaska Peninsula had an unstretched skin 7 feet 9½ inches long. Quite shy, and their color frequently harmonizing with their environment, they are often located with difficulty. While the coast bears are mostly black in color, those of the interior are not infrequently of the cinnamon variety. Perhaps the most interesting species of this group is the so-called blue or glacier bear of the St. Elias Alps, which is very rarely seen and imperfectly known.

The most numerous and important group is that of the brown bears, which from their dangerous ferocity are widely known. They are the largest carnivorous animals in the world, being approached in size only by the polar bear and by their Kamchatkan relatives. Apparently the largest Kodiak bearskins known are of a Kidder variety, 10 feet, and of a Dall variety, 10 feet 2 inches. Mixter killed one 11 feet 4 inches long, 4 feet 8 inches high.

The brown bear ranges almost exclusively in the coast region, and is found from extreme southern Alaska to the Alaska Peninsula and on islands adjacent thereto. They are not only terrifying from their size and great strength, but have been known at times unprovokedly to attack and kill persons. They are great and skilful salmon fishers, though vegetarians, and carnivorous when the salmon season is past.

The brown bears are divided by scientists into the following species: Kodiak bear, on Kodiak; the Dall and the Kidder bears, on Alaska Peninsula; Yakutat bear, in St. Elias region; Sitka bear, on Baranof Island; and Admiralty bear, on Admiralty Island.

Caribou

The caribou of Alaska are the only ones now found in the United States. Their habitat (see text map in Chapter XXII) is the reindeer-moss regions; largely the tundras and barren mountain ridges. Wherever man comes in numbers the unsuspicious caribou are speedily exterminated or driven away, for they are gregarious, are not keen-sighted, and display scant sagacity in eluding hunters. They keep to the open country and rarely enter timber, so that they are readily found and easily slaughtered. They suffer less from the antler-trophy hunters than from the meat hunters who supply mining camps and prospectors.

Mr. W. H. Osgood, in his excellent "Game Resources of Alaska," from which many of these data are drawn, says of their migrations:

The great herds in the fall of the year perform a more or less regular movement in the nature of a migration, and within certain limits their course of travel and times of arrival at given points are well known. The best known of the large herds is the one which collects along the watershed between the Yukon and Tanana rivers. This herd still numbers from 1,000 to 3,000 or more animals, although levied upon annually by hunters from Fortymile, Eagle, Circle, and the mining towns on the Tanana River. Herds, perhaps equally large, range the little-known arctic slope along the Endicott Mountains.

While hunters usually divide caribou into two general classes, woodland and barren-ground, scientists recognize three species: the Arctic, ranging in northern Alaska; the Grant, on Alaska Peninsula; and the Stone, on Kenai Peninsula.

Alaska Moose

Possibly the giant moose is the most interesting of the large game, for it is not only the largest land animal in America, but is also the largest member of the deer family in the world. The moose is of enormous size, and its weight sometimes exceeds 1,600 pounds. The average spread of their magnificent antlers is

Map No. 6. Distribution of Moose and Deer.

over five feet from tip to tip; there are many recorded spreads exceeding six feet, with a maximum example of six feet nine inches.

As is shown by the map on this page, their range practically covers timbered Alaska, except in the southeast. They are found in quite large numbers in the Yukon Valley, between Circle and Eagle, but are especially numerous on Kenai Peninsula, where favorable environment produces specimens of a size unequalled elsewhere.

Deer

The only Alaskan variety, the Sitkan deer, is exceedingly abundant in southeastern Alaska, where it inhabits the Alexander Archipelago (see preceding text map) and the adjacent mainland from the boundary north to Juneau. Slaughtered by the thousand in past years, the Sitkan deer now bids fair to hold its own under recent game laws.

Mountain Goats

This unique animal is rather of the chamois or antelope type than of the goat family. It has long, pure-white hair, and the horns of both sexes are small (from seven to ten inches in length), recurved and blackish. Its range (see map in Chapter XXII) is almost entirely confined to the coast slopes of the mainland mountains, from Portland Canal north to the western spurs of the Chugach Mountains.

Osgood, in his interesting description, writes:

It lives almost entirely at high altitudes, frequenting steep cliffs, rock-walled cañons, and summits of an even more forbidding nature than those traversed by mountain sheep. To approach a mountain goat successfully is more a feat of mountaineering than of crafty hunting. To get above a white goat is in most cases to get to the ultimate heights.

Mountain Sheep

The pure white Dall variety is the only mountain sheep of Alaska. Especially a mountaineer, the white sheep is only absent from mountains in the vicinity of permanent settlements, whether white or native, and from the Alaska Peninsula and coastal fronts of the Alaskan range.

Of the hunt of the mountain sheep Osgood relates:

They are keen of vision and, unlike most game animals, depend little upon scent for warning of danger; but in spite of this it is no easy task to approach one of these alert, far-sighted animals on an open mountain-side. To those physically equipped for it, hunting mountain sheep is unquestionably one of the greatest sports, and Alaska is one of the best fields for it in the world. To the inspiring and exhilarating joys of mountaineering are added the uncertainties and excitements of the chase.

Hunting and Preservation of Big Game

Of Alaska as a hunting ground Radclyffe writes:

From a sportsman's point of view the country is still a paradise, for big game of various kinds still abounds; and owing to the stringent game laws passed by the United States it appears to be well protected for many years to come.

Of his five months of hunting in western Alaska, Colonel Caine says:

The inducement was the fact that there was one of the finest natural hunting grounds in the world, and one not yet shot out. Was not the Kodiak huge bear the biggest of his species on earth, bar the polar bear? Was not the Alaska moose a veritable giant, with a spread of antlers averaging 12 inches more than his cousins of Canada? And further, was there not the white Alaskan sheep, the most graceful and beautiful of the big-horn family, though not the largest? Besides there were caribou, walrus, seals, sea-lions, wolves, and wolverines.

The preservation of Alaskan game has always been recognized as a subject of great public importance. As elsewhere stated, Congress in 1869 established the Pribilof reservation for the protection of the fur-seal, and at intervals—too long, it must be said—action has been secured to preserve other game. How great was the moral necessity of similar Congressional legislation appears in the brief allusions made in this chapter to the passing of the walrus.

A comprehensive law for the protection of game was passed in 1902, and regulations thereof were made in 1903 as to caribou, walrus, waterfowl, trophies, etc. The effect was practically nil as to walrus, and ineffective in many other ways.

The establishment of the great forest reserves in Alaska was beneficial, directly as well as indirectly, to game preservation, as, under *Forest Regulations*, No. 84, forest officials are charged to co-operate in "the enforcement of local laws for the protection of game."

A great advance was made in the law of May 11, 1908, which divided Alaska into two game districts, one north and one south of latitude 62°, with special seasons for each; establishing a non-resident hunting license, with fees of $50 for citizens of the United States and $100 for aliens, and resident and non-resident shipping licenses, ranging from $5 to $150; authorizing the governor to issue licenses, appoint wardens, establish regulations for the registration of guides, and fix the rates for licensing guides and the rates of compensation for guiding. (Stat. 60th Cong., 102.)

Under the law, game animals include deer, moose, caribou, mountain sheep, mountain goats, brown bear, sea-lions, and walrus; game waterfowl comprise ducks, brant, geese, swans, grouse, ptarmigan, and shore birds.

Land Fur-Bearing Animals

The possibility of the extinction of fur-bearing animals under existing conditions led to the enactment of the federal law of May 31, 1920, under which the jurisdiction of the minor sea-animals was given to the Department of the Interior, while land animals were placed under the Department of Agriculture, except the fox-herd of the Pribilof Islands.

This law recognized the economic importance of the land animals, whose pelts in 1919 exceeded the value of the fur-seals. Under existing laws the value of Alaskan land furs fell to $5,724 in 1899, from which time the annual output increased, with interruptions, to 1923, when furs were shipped from the Territory valued at more than $1,700,000. Nelson estimates that furs used in the Territory and shipped elsewhere make the fur values for that year over $2,000,000.

For many years the field service of the Alaska game law has been administered by the Governor of Alaska, under the Department of the Interior, who appointed game wardens, issued licenses, and commissioned guides, while the Secretary of Agriculture regulated the killing, scientific collections, and breeding sales. This duplicated warden services and created confusion.

In June, 1924, with the approval of the Department of the Interior, the game administration was transferred by Congress to the Department of Agriculture. Now administered by the Biological Survey in combination with the protection of the land fur-bearing animals, which eliminates duplicate warden service and permits additional wardens to be stationed at important points.

Most fortunately the duties relative to the wild life of Alaska have been entrusted to the Biological Survey, under its distinguished chief, E. W. Nelson, who had not only attained international recognition as a conservator of animal life, but had also spent five years in personal exploration and study in Alaska.

Nelson estimates "that the food value of game taken in Alaska each year is not less than $1,000,000, which, added to the $2,000,000 of furs from the land fur-bearing animals, makes a total return of $3,000,-000 from this part of the wild life of the Territory. It is believed that by proper conservation these returns can be largely increased."

The Biological Survey also has charge of the various Federal bird reservations, the largest of which is that covering the entire chain of the Aleutian Islands. These reservations are also being managed in the interests of the natives for food and clothing. The Regulations for the Protection of Land Fur-Bearing Animals in Alaska appear in Table 4.

The chief warden is located at Juneau, and has assistants at Akhiok, Atka, Fairbanks, Igloo, Killisnoo, Unalakleet, Unalaska, and Wrangell. Co-operation of the Foresty, Fishery, Education, Customs, and Coast Guard bureaus aids in enforcing the law.

Hunting Grounds

As to hunting grounds, Capps, of the Geological Survey, considers the Mt. McKinley National Park a game country without rival in America. He says:

Many parts of Alaska are famous for big game, and hunters have come half the way around the world to that Territory to obtain trophies of their skill. It has been my good fortune to visit several of the choicest game ranges in Alaska, notably that east of Nenana River, and the much-praised White River country. Both of these regions are well stocked with game, but for abundant sheep, caribou, and moose over wide areas neither of them compares with the area within the limits of the new game preserve.

During the three weeks spent in the park his diary records as seen by him, 2,677 caribou and 1,310 mountain sheep.

Shiras, who hunts so successfully wild game by

flashlight and camera, says, in connection with his most striking work on Kenai:

Were all of Alaska erased from the map except the Kenai Peninsula and its immediate adjacent waters, there would yet remain in duplicate that which constitutes the more unique and that which typifies the whole of this wonderful country.

This is true of the forest, herbage, wild fruits and flowers, the game and commercial fish, the native and migratory birds, the big game animals and smaller fur-bearers, the minerals and methods of mining, the well-defined mountain ranges and isolated peaks, the foaming cascades, the giant glaciers, the rivers and lakes, the hundreds of unexplored fiords, the green coniferous forests with glistening ponds, the feeding place for moose.

There were "hundreds of animal licks, frequented at different times by deer, caribou, moose, sheep, and goats."

Several weeks spent in studying and photographing moose near Skilak Lake, the network of runways through the birch and poplar thickets, showed very plainly that this was one of the great winter feeding ranges of these animals.

In its isolation the Kenai Peninsula is a great Presque Isle, allowing a marked segregation of northern game. Reports show that the moose have been increasing steadily in recent years, that the white sheep are thriving, and all other game animals except the small fur-bearers and the caribou are holding their own.

While this chapter was going through the press, in January, 1925, Congress has established by an Act (entitled the Alaska Game Law) the Alaska Game

Commission, to protect game animals, land fur-bearing animals, and birds in Alaska. The powers of the Commission cover the methods of taking, of establishing open and closed seasons, and transportation of game. Big game animals are: deer, moose, caribou, elk, mountain sheep, mountain goat, large brown and grizzly bear. Land fur-bearing animals are: beaver, muskrat, marmot, ground squirrel, fisher, fox, lynx, marten or sable, mink, weasel or ermine, land otter, wolverine, polar bear, and black bear including its brown and blue color variations. Game birds are: migratory waterfowl, commonly known as ducks, geese, brant, and swans. Shore birds, commonly known as plover, sandpipers, snipe, little brown crane and curlew, and the several species of grouse and ptarmigan. Use of poison is prohibited. Licenses for fur-dealers are fixed by the Act at $10 for resident, $250 for non-resident Americans, and $500 for aliens. Non-resident hunters pay $10 for small game, $50 for big game or trapping. Fur farmers pay $5 for a license.

The Commission, appointed by the Secretary from residents of Alaska, forms part of the Department of Agriculture.

BIBLIOGRAPHY.—Caine, C.: Summer and Fall in Western Alaska, 1903. Stone, A. J.: The Moose, 1902. Radclyffe, C. R. E.: Big Game Shooting in Alaska, 1903.| Kidder, J. H.: Big Game Shooting in Alaska (Boone and Crockett Club), 1904. Osgood, W. H.: Game Resources of Alaska, 1907 (Year Book, U. S. Department of Agriculture). In *National Geographic Magazine*: Mixter, April, 1909, Hunting the Great Brown Bear; Osgood, July, 1909, Big Game of Alaska; Shiras, May, 1912, White Sheep and Giant Moose of Kenai; Cappa, G., January, 1917, Game Country Without Rival.

CHAPTER XXII

THE ALASKA PENINSULA AND KODIAK

IT may be added that the large ocean steamers do not proceed beyond Seldovia, and that during the open season—from late March to early November—the north and west coasts of Cook Inlet (Turnagain Arm and Alaska Peninsula) are reached by small and somewhat irregular steamers.

The Alaska Peninsula has, indeed, at its northeastern extremity extended areas of lake country, with open valleys and great tundras; but its chief characteristic is the series of lofty volcanic peaks, which continue for a distance of more than 700 miles, from Redoubt southwest to Pogromni. Their sharp abruptness and rocky ruggedness dominate the landscape, the pointed summits being made more striking by the marshy valleys and dreary tundras at their bases, which break the continuity of the range into an irregular succession of isolated cones.

Here the land game, though caribou occupy the land, as shown by the map on the next page, gives way to the products of the sea chase. Unfortunately the palmy days of walrus hunting and otter catching are past, and there are scarcely a dozen permanent Eskimo settlements on the more than 2,000 miles of indented coast along the peninsula. Belkofski, the former headquarters of the sea-otter and other fur trade, has lost its ancient glory and importance.

Nevertheless, the peninsula is an attractive, almost unvisited and unexploited field for the hunter, the naturalist, and especially for the lover of the unusual and beautiful in nature.

Several members of the Harriman Expedition,

Map No. 7.   Distribution of Caribou and Mountain Goats.

landing at Kukak Bay, on the north shore of Shelikof Strait, climbed to the top of the green slope back of their camp, and suddenly found themselves on the brink of an almost perpendicular mountain wall with a deep notch, through which they looked down 2,000 feet into a valley beneath invaded by a great glacier that swept down from the snow-white peaks beyond.

The peninsula extends southwest about 700 miles, from the Iliamna Lake region to the Fox Islands, from which it is separated by a narrow strait. It is a broken, narrow land, lying between the Pacific Ocean and Bering Sea—rarely more than 50 miles from sea to sea, except at the northern base, where it widens to a hundred miles or more.

Along the eastern side, near the ocean, an almost unbroken mountain-range extends, while the greater part of the western regions are lowlands, in which are numerous lakes and extended expanses of morass. While the eastern coast is well known, the western is in part unsurveyed.

Iliamna Lake Country

What is known of this interesting region is derived from the explorations of McKay, Johnson, and Osgood, set forth under the Research chapter. Of his biological reconnaissance from Lake Clark to Cold Bay, Osgood says:

The southeast side of the Alaska Peninsula is extremely mountainous; the mountains are from 3,000 to 6,000 feet in altitude and quite precipitous. They support no trees worthy of the name, but there are some balsam-poplars. On the mountainsides a few tiny spruces, from one to two feet high, rise above the matted mosses, lichens, and small shrubs—alder and dwarf-birch.

Burroughs said of the peninsula:

Now we were to have 2,000 miles without a tree, the valleys and mountains as green as a lawn, chiefly of volcanic origin, many of the cones ideally perfect, the valleys deepened and carved by old glaciers, and heights and lowlands alike covered with a carpet of grass, ferns and flowers.

Hunting over the peninsula nearly a quarter of a century since, to the north of the Shumagin Islands, Stone says:

Most of the mainland was very high, even to the water's edge, and the irregular coast was slashed with narrow fiords that extend inland to the very base of the mountains. I was in the newest and strangest of all the lands of America, yet there are found indications of the habitations of a people who once lived there, obtaining their food from the sea. Few countries ever possessed such valuable and interesting life as this—the very centre of the greatest wealth of furs the world has ever produced.

The whole of the country is more or less mountainous, though the mountains of the peninsula do not form a continuous chain, but are separated in many places by low passes that extend from the shores of the Pacific to those of Bering Sea.

Peninsula Fisheries

The fisheries of Bristol Bay to the north and around the Shumagin and Kodiak groups to the south, have wrought many changes in the life of this region. Business has developed to such an extent that postoffices have been established at Chignik, False Pass, Iliamna, Sand Point, Sanak Island, and Unga Island. Radio stations, of private companies, are operated at Chignik, False Pass, Kvichak, Naknek, Port Moller, Ugashik, and Unga.

Peninsula Petroleum

As set forth in the chapter on Coal and Petroleum, the development of the oil industry is in progress. The fields most promising for petroleum are on the southeastern coast, near Cold Bay.

Natives of the Peninsula

The population is scanty in numbers, and somewhat mixed in stock, half-breeds, and tribal mixtures. The Eskimo occupy the northern base, and extend southward along the east coast to the vicinity of Stepovak Bay. Among their villages in 1920 there were 83 at Egigik, 66 at Iliamna, and 111 at Naknek. There are small settlements of Aleuts on the west coast between Ports Heiden and Moller, and also south of the peninsula in the Shumagin and neighboring groups. Among them in 1920 there were in Morzhorvoi 60 inhabitants, at Sand Point 60, and on Unga Island 313.

The Alaska Division of the Bureau of Education has come to the instruction and improvement of these isolated natives; schools for them have been established at Chignik, Eek, Iliamna, Nugashik, and Port Moller.

Kodiak Archipelago

Among the islands of this group Afognak is interesting, as a fish-culture reservation and for its wooded areas, which caused it to be included in the Chugach National Forest. There are several hundred inhabitants, who have a large Greek chapel, some cattle, flocks of domestic fowl, and thriving vegetable gardens that supplement the usual means of livelihood by fishing.

Large, rugged, and commercially important, Kodiak is one of the most widely known of the Alaskan Islands. It is the site of the first trading post; the scene of cruelty and repression as to its natives, and was first to have a church founded and a school opened. Kodiak lost its prestige when the headquarters of the Russian Company was transferred to Sitka. With its sea-otter catch sadly reduced and its population decimated by disease, Kodiak entered unpropitiously within the circle of American civilization, and long held to Russian ways and interests.

Its present population of nearly a thousand— Americans, Russians, Creoles, and Indians—live principally on fishing, though there are some few otter taken. Its Karluk River is the most famous salmon stream in Alaska, and its canneries afford the primary means of subsistence for the natives.

To many Americans the island is best known through its enormous beast, the great Kodiak bear— the largest species in the world.

Except on the eastern coast the island is treeless, but its smooth, rounded hills are covered with luxuriant verdure. During the brief summer season the island is most beautiful, the emerald surfaces being brilliant with countless wild flowers in great variety. Cattle thrive; grain does not advance beyond the forage state; vegetables do well. Ample supplies for

By courtesy of National Geographic Society.

Galloway Cattle on Kodiak Island.

comfortable living are to be had from the large store of the Northern Commercial Company in the village. There is a fine church, and both the United States and the Greek Church maintain schools.

Burroughs alludes to the island as a pastoral paradise, and says of Kodiak:

So secluded, so remote, so peaceful, such a mingling of the domestic, the pastoral, the sylvan, with the wild and rugged; such emerald heights, such flowery vales, such blue arms and recesses of the sea, and such a vast green solitude stretching away to the west and to the north and to the south! Bewitching Kodiak, the spell of thy summer freshness and placidity is still upon me.

Economic Conditions

More than any other native community the archipelago has grown into modern conditions, and its prosperity has been enlarged by the activities of the federal, territorial, and corporative organizations.

Since 1908 the Department of Agriculture has maintained on Kodiak an experiment station, whose efforts have been largely along stock-raising lines. The grazing season is long and the herds of Galloway and Holstein-Friesian cattle have increased normally and developed finely. For many years the Bureau of Fisheries has given much attention to the conservation of the profitable fish industries. The Afognak Fish Reservation has saved the salmon from commercial depletion, while the natives have been given permits allowing them to utilize the catch. On Afognak Lake the Bureau of Fisheries has long maintained a hatchery, from which in 1922 there were taken 62,000,000 of salmon eggs.

Several corporations are engaged in the salmon and cod fisheries of the waters of Kodiak.

The village of Afognak, population 308 in 1920, has a post-office and a territorial school for mixed white and native children. On Kodiak, the village of Kodiak, 374 inhabitants, has a post-office, territorial school, and a wireless station. Uyak has a wireless station and a post-office.

The population of the entire Kodiak district in 1920 was 1,465, of whom many are either whites or half-breeds. Aleut is the predominant native stock on Afognak and the northeastern part of Kodiak. Elsewhere it is Eskimauen.

BIBLIOGRAPHY.—Department of the Interior: Annual Reports on Minerals of Alaska. Department of Agriculture: Annual Reports, Biological Survey. Department of Commerce: Annual Reports, Bureau of Fisheries, and of Alaska Fisheries and Fur-Seal Industries.

CHAPTER XXIII

THE ALEUTIAN ISLANDS

THERE is little known of the Aleutian Islands except as to the Fox Island group, adjacent to the Alaska Peninsula. From first to last their history has been one of exploitation since, in 1745, Michael Novidskof, in search of the sea-otter, reached Attu in his open frail craft. Fired by a cupidity that no danger could appall, other Russian traders pushed untiringly eastward in moss-calked, skin-sewn shallops, until the long line of Aleutian Islands, extending eastward nearly 800 miles, fell within their knowledge and under their rapacious control.

Some of these islands were then densely populated, aggregating in the early days nearly 30,000 natives, and their inhabitants throve on the sea-otter and other sea game. With rapacity and exploitation rampant they decreased with the vanishing game, and scarcely numbered 1,500 on the islands in 1900. Elliott tells us that in 1885 in the 800 intervening miles between Unalaska and the western boundary there were only three small native settlements—Umnak, 130, Atka, 230, and Attu, a few over 100 souls— in all less than 500 natives, with six or seven white men.

Indeed, the islands are neither attractive in their general appearance nor comfortable in occupation for white men. It is a region of almost continual fog and clouds, with low summer temperatures and high winter winds. About one day of seven or eight is clear at Unalaska, while the island temperatures rarely exceed 65° in the warmest month (usually July), and fall to as low as from 10° to 22° in March.

The chain is divided into five groups, which from east to west are: (1) Fox Islands; (2) Islands of the Four Mountains; (3) Andreanof Islands; (4) Rat Islands; and (5) Near Islands. The last-named group is within a few miles of the Commander Islands —pertaining to Siberia—of which Bering Island is best known.

Except a few of the Fox Islands, the whole chain is treeless. To the west the vegetation usually consists of mosses, grasses, and lichens, though in sheltered valleys and near the hot springs there are found scrubby shrubs, and more or less extensive patches of berry plants.

As set forth elsewhere, the islands are of volcanic origin. Stern and desolate in appearance, their general features are bold, crater-marked peaks, rugged highlands, which are intersected by narrow, dividing valleys which give shelter to foxes and other minor fur-bearing animals—the principal land life.

As a rule the approaches to the islands are marked by equally rugged reefs, which make navigation of the coastal waters difficult and dangerous.

The scanty land game, hunted incessantly by the natives, owing to the practical extermination of the sea-game, needed protection from outside aggression, so the whole Aleutian Chain was made into a Bird Reservation. This reservation called forth the statement of an Alaskan governor, who, in the interest of local hunters, favored its discontinuance, and stated that this protective law was unenforced. Natives, however, are allowed to kill all kinds of game for food and clothing. Under this restriction, however, the reports for 1923 state that wild game is increasing as a whole.

Of the Fox Islands, the easternmost Aleutian group, Unalaska is the largest and by far the most important. Dominated by the volcano Makushin, 5,961 feet, it is not quite so barren as the other Aleutian Islands to the west, and its fiord-indented shores and volcanic-ridged valleys are picturesque to the eye. Its principal town, Iliuliuk, is more generally known as Unalaska, and with the adjacent Dutch harbor has served as a port of call for the early Nome shipping and all other craft doing business in Bering Sea.

In olden times the headquarters of the Russian Church and the centre of the fur-trade, Unalaska, yielded slowly and reluctantly to American influences, which are to-day fully recognized. Gradually it attracts to it drifting natives, mining prospectors, and fishing employees. Its importance has been largely affected by these varied interests. The population was 317 in 1890, 428 in 1900, 281 in 1910, and 299 in 1920. The establishment of a radio station at Dutch Harbor, Unalaska Island, has lately increased its importance.

The proximity of the Seal (Pribilof) Islands, the navigation of the Bering Sea, and the development of the salmon fisheries have given the Fox Islands new life and added importance. Mail and telegraph facilities have brought this region into regular relations with the outside world. There are post-offices at Unalaska and Akutan, and radio stations at Dutch Harbor (Unalaska Island), and Akutan. Reindeer herds have been established and are flourishing at Umnak and Unalaska. While the population in 1920 of the whole Aleutian Chain was only 730, there were 66 on Akutan, 46 on Biorka, 83 on Umnak, and 299 on Unalaska.

From the mineral standpoint this group is unimportant. Although gold has been prospected at Unalaska, neither that nor the sulphur deposits there and on Akun have been developed. The ever changing volcanic peaks of Bogoslof, and the beautiful volcanoes of mountainous Uminak are described in the chapter on volcanoes, as are also those of the uninhabited group of Four Mountains.

Andreanof Islands

The activities of this group of about 20 islands centres in the Island of Akutan. Under the beneficent control of the Bureau of Education, there is here in operation a school for the natives, a herd of reindeer for their vocational training and future food supply, and both a radio station and a post-office. Atka is the most westerly of the Aleutian Islands,

Grewingk Island (born in 1883), Bogoslof Group, Bering Sea.

(Volcanic islands appear and disappear from year to year.)

having a settlement under special care of the Federal Government. It is in longitude 174° West, within about 200 miles of the Eastern Hemisphere.

Rat Islands

This group of about a dozen islands is not permanently inhabited, but is visited in summer for its game. Here thrive foxes of various kinds—blue, red, and cross. Most of the islands are in the eastern hemisphere.

Near Islands

This group in latitude 58° N., longitude 173° E., is best known to the public by the island of Attu, through the striking statement that it is farther west of San Francisco than that city is west of Eastport, Maine.

Originally famous for its blue foxes, its sea otters and other game, and especially for its beautiful woven-grass baskets, the glory of Attu and its contented, primitive people has passed. Exterminated sea game, its depleted land animals, its degradation from unprincipled sea-hunters, explain why Attu is now practically uninhabited.

Condition of Aleutian People

The native inhabitants of these islands are Aleuts, who once numbered many thousands, but loss of sea game and consequent famishing conditions have driven many eastward to the islands bordering the

Alaska Peninsula. Except in the extreme eastern islands, the Aleuts now eke out a very wretched existence by hunting and fishing.

The establishment of the Aleutian Bird Reservation, which has been criticised as deleterious to Alaskan development, and as injurious to resident Aleuts, appears to have been controlled in the interests of the natives.

Thereon Nelson reports:

In the Aleutian chain the use of the islands for fox-farming is being granted to the natives free of charge, owing to their lack of resources and to the difficulty of maintaining themselves, but the regular rental is charged for occupation by others.

The game regulations likewise favor free action by the Aleuts in regard to food and clothing.

The blue fox thrives wild on the extreme westerly Isle of Attu, and from that point several of the Shumagin Islands, Chernabura, Simeonof, etc., have been stocked with moderate success. The extension and development of this industry is desirable as one of the much-needed means to enable the Aleuts successfully to meet changed conditions of Alaskan life.

The latest description of Attu is that given by the American round-the-world fliers, who visited the island in May, 1924, and were detained by bad weather. They considered Attu as "Not only the uttermost point of America, an island on the edge of nothing, but its inhabitants are of the lowest breed of human life belonging to North America."

The population of Attu is exactly 39, all Aleuts, of whom 24 are women and girls.

The harbor is well sheltered, with mountain all around—extinct volcanoes. The village consists of three wooden shacks, of which one is the little Russian church, which the Aleuts attend. The others belong to the two men who control the trading rights of both Attu and Atka.

There are a number of native huts, burrows under the surface of the ground. The roofs, half-domed shape, are of dirt and sod. Each hut has a single window. From 6 to 8 cook, eat and sleep in a space about 8 by 10 feet. This space is divided into two tiny rooms—one filled with clothes, harpoons, jerked meat, and dried fish. In the living-room—shut off by a curtain of skins—old Aleut women, with their wrinkled, weather-beaten faces, make garments out of hides, or weave the world-famous Attu baskets, both rare and expensive.

There are prospects that the Aleutian chain may be gradually utilized for economic purposes, among which is stock raising. An initial step has been taken in the introduction of 2,000 sheep, for which industry certain of the islands are suitable. The few reindeer distributed by the Government on certain islands do not appeal to the Aleuts. For endless generations the Aleuts have lived on the previously abundant game of the northern seas, and the present generation does not take to a herdsman's life, as do the Eskimo.

An unfortunate condition exists, for the United

States has abandoned the Aleuts of the easterly islands—wards of the nation under the Russo-American treaty of cession—to the exploitation of traders, confining federal activity to the annual visit of the coast-guard cutter for a few summer days.

Degraded as are the Aleuts of the present day, as reported, that they have spiritual aspirations is shown by their attendance at their dilapidated, Russian church. Yet the United States leaves these few hundred people, practically an alien no-land folk, scattered over the Aleutian chain some 800 miles in length, as not of us. They are without doctors, without nurses, without medicines, without schools, without any vocational training, without any semblance of law or organized government, without any aids for moral or spiritual uplift. It would be incredible, if it were not true, that rich and Christian America thus neglects its own people—every one of whom was born in a nation flying an emblem of democratic freedom—the Stars and Stripes.

The United States should have the same humane policy as Canada, whose efficient patrol force, established permanently at suitable points in its arctic archipelago, gives care, advice, education, law, and relief to every one of its primitive tribes.

CHAPTER XXIV

SCIENTIFIC FIELDS OF RESEARCH

WITH the material development of Alaska there have risen many questions in which a thorough knowledge of so-called purely scientific character has been of great economical importance. Researches as to climatic and geologic conditions, once discouraged by the Federal authorities in the Territory, are now pursued as indispensable to successful mining operations. As elsewhere mentioned, the work of the United States Geological Survey has progressed with astonishing rapidity, owing to its recognized bearing on the exploitation of material resources, which thus elicits liberal governmental support.

The United States Bureau of Fisheries has also been able to add much relative to subjects allied to the duties which have devolved on it in connection with the great and remunerative industries over which it exercises a general and indefinite supervision. Similarly, the various bureaus of the Department of Agriculture have improved every opportunity to extend scientific knowledge of the vast and most imperfectly known regions of the Territory. Officers of the army, of the navy, of the Coast and Geodetic Survey, of the Census Bureau, and of the Revenue Marine Service, living up to the high standards of modern civilization, have very materially contributed to the world's knowledge by investigating and reporting on all matters, though foreign to their duties, falling under their observation during Alaskan service.

It is obvious, however, that subjects pertaining to the domain of pure science have received scant support from the United States as regards Alaska.

It is not surprising, therefore, to know that the most extended scientific researches in Alaska have been those made independently of the government. Reference is had to those made possible by the liberality and broadmindedness of a well-known citizen, Mr. E. H. Harriman, whose private expedition of 1899 was accompanied by many distinguished scientific men as his guests.

The history of the Harriman Expedition has been published under the supervision of Doctor C. Hart Merriam, in volumes that are highly creditable to all concerned, whether viewed from the standpoint of typography, reproductions, its popular form, or the scientific treatment. In this work Professor Dall, in his valuable article of "Discovery and Exploration," says:

While the sublime scenery of the southern coast will long be the goal of tourists, we may confidently anticipate for years to come a rich harvest for the scientific explorers and naturalists whose good fortune may lead them to the fascinating study of the virgin north.

The Biological Survey, of the Department of Agriculture, has made biological reconnoissances of Cook Inlet, 1900, Yukon River region, 1899, and base of

Alaska Peninsula, 1902, and thus materially contributed to the previous scanty data as to fauna and flora of these almost unknown localities.

The investigations on the Alaska Peninsula were "important as a meeting ground of some of the life areas of the borders of the Hudsonian and Arctic zones." Here, also, is the only locality at which normally meet the Aleuts, the Eskimos, and the Athapascans. The delimitation of the coniferous trees, and of the tundra areas, was supplemented by careful observation of the fauna, which disclosed the presence of 34 land mammals and 136 species of birds.

The Yukon reconnoissance resulted in an annotated list of 171 species of birds, and of 52 mammals, including a few noted in adjacent Canadian territory. Among these were 9 new species and subspecies of mammals, and 3 new forms of birds.

In the Cook Inlet region notes were made as to 24 mammals, 77 birds, and 1 batrachian. The future thorough examination of this region would doubtless add much, as the English hunter, Radclyffe, says:

As a happy hunting ground for ornithologists I can recommend the valley of the Aniakchak River, since nowhere in Alaska did we find such a variety of sandpipers, waders, and ducks as frequent this region.

With innumerable demands on its funds, the Smithsonian Institution has given some attention to Alaska through the investigation of the fauna and flora of the early geological periods, especially of extinct animals.

Among the many attractions that the vast expanse of the Yukon watershed offers to students and lovers of nature, perhaps there is none more fascinating than the search for extinct mammals. The world's knowledge of remains of extinct vertebrates in Alaska began with Otto van Kotzebue's discovery, in 1816, of the remarkable ice-cliffs in Escholtz Bay, where teeth and bones of the mammoth were found. Similar discoveries were made in this region by Beechey in 1827–1828, by Seeman with Kellett in 1848, and by Dall in recent years. The remains thus found comprise the mammoth, the horse, bears, deer, and the musk-ox. From time to time trappers and prospectors have found similar remains at various points in the Seward Peninsula, thence north to the Point Barrow region, and east to the valleys of the upper Koyukuk and the central Yukon.

The scientific search for further remains has been prosecuted under the Smithsonian Institution by Mr. A. G. Maddren in 1904, and by Mr. C. W. Gilmore in 1907. The journey of Maddren proved most interesting. It involved small-boat travel on the Great River and its tributaries during the long summer period of starless nights, almost uninterrupted sunlight and balmy airs, amid such aspects of nature, varieties of experience and vicissitudes of camp life as are scarcely equalled elsewhere.

Maddren made a journey of nearly 300 miles through an unknown country, across the drainage basins of the Ungalik, Inglutalik, and Kobuk Rivers, starting from Kaltag on the Yukon. He was accompanied by an assistant, with two Eskimo packers and guides, though aided for 50 miles by two additional packers. Of his outfit he says:

The camp equipment for this trip was reduced to the minimum. It consisted of a tent made of balloon silk, weighing 12 pounds, measuring 8 feet square on the floor, with a waterproof canvas ground cloth. A light robe made of four large caribou skins sewed together served as a common mattress for all, and a blanket apiece completed the bedding. Three kettles, a frying-pan, with a tin cup and spoon apiece, were all the utensils found necessary. The provisions carried, exclusive of the supplies required for the two additional packers, consisted of 150 pounds of flour, 30 pounds of rice, 30 pounds of beans, 60 pounds of bacon, 25 pounds of sugar, 3 pounds of tea, 2 pounds of baking-powder, and 2 pounds of salt. Seventy pounds to each man, or an average of $2\frac{1}{2}$ pounds per man per day. This supply, supplemented by a few fish and a number of ptarmigan shot from day to day with a .22-calibre rifle, proved ample.

Of the fossil animals discovered in Alaska the most interesting is the Northern Mammoth, or fossil elephant, which evidently roamed, with the bison and the horse, through the entire watershed of the Yukon River, the Seward Peninsula, Kowak Valley, and the Kotzebue Sound region. The largest mammoth tusk is probably that found by Seeman, in 1848, at Escholtz Bay, which weighs 243 pounds: its base had a circumference of 21 inches, and though broken at the point its length was 11 feet 6 inches. It is possible that another tusk, which is 12 feet 10 inches long, may be larger, while the Fort Gibbon imperfect tusk of 10 feet 4 inches, though broken at both ends, may equal the two others in size. Several species of bison have been found, as also remains of the horse, musk-ox, reindeer, bear, and beaver.

Ice-Cliffs

The ice-cliffs of Alaska are worthy of special scientific investigation, both on account of their remarkable formation and also to explain fully the phenomena which have given rise to various differing opinions.

Their discoverer, Kotzebue, describes the ice-cliffs as masses of the purest ice, of the height of a hundred feet, which are under a cover of moss and grass. . . . The covering of these mountains, on which the most luxuriant grass grows, is only half a foot thick, and consists of a mixture of clay, sand, and earth.

Beechey declared that Kotzebue was mistaken, and reported that the cliffs were not mainly ice, but were simply ice-faced.

Seeman, in 1848, justified Kotzebue's views, saying:

The ice-cliffs . . . are from 40 to 90 feet high, and consist of three distinct layers. The lower layer is ice, the central, clay, containing fossils, and the uppermost, peat. The ice, as far as it can be seen, above ground, is from 20 to 50 feet thick, but is every year decreasing.

Hooper, in 1880, thought that both Kotzebue and Beechey were partly in error. W. H. Dall visited them the same year, 1880, and after careful examination reports: "It appeared that the ridge itself, 2 miles wide and 250 feet high, was chiefly composed of solid ice overlaid with clay and vegetable mould." He adds: "It certainly remains one of the most wonderful and puzzling geological phenomena in existence."

In his explorations in 1884, Lieut. J. C. Cantwell discovered similar cliffs along the Kowak River, which he reports to be navigable for 375 miles. He says:

Among the many novel and interesting features, none were more striking than a remarkable series of ice-cliffs observed along the banks of the river about 80 miles from the mouth. . . . One cliff measured by sextant angles showed 185 feet. The tops of the cliffs were superposed by a layer of black, siltlike soil from 6 to 8 feet thick, and from this springs a luxuriant growth of mosses, grass, and the characteristic arctic shrubbery, consisting for the most part of willow, alder, and berry bushes, and a dense forest of spruce trees from 50 to 80 feet high and from 4 to 8 inches in diameter.

Fossil Plants

The fossil flora of Alaska also offers wide, interesting, and almost untouched fields of investigation and exploration. F. H. Knowlton, United States National Museum, has shown that of 115 forms of fossil plants collected in Alaska, no less than 46 are peculiar to that region. Of the 64 having an outside distribution, 39 species are found in Greenland, Spitzbergen, and Sakhalin Island, thus indicating synchronous deposits in the four semi-arctic regions.

The family of oaks, chestnuts, etc., furnish 22 species, the conifers 18 species, and the willows 13 species. Practically every part of Alaska offers opportunities for extension of our knowledge of fossil plants.

Among research work in recent years the Geological Survey leads. While its work is geological, yet its efficient officials contribute in their special papers much matter of special interest to other branches of science. As usual the Smithsonian Institution adds much, its late work including the ethnological studies of Fewkes on the material cultures shown in the houses of Alaskan aborigines; Waterman's survey of the totemic monuments of the Territory; Aldrich's great entomological collection of 10,000 insects covering the fauna of the seacoast, humid mountains, and interior valleys to the north of the Gulf of Alaska; and others. Apart from its annual research work, the biological survey adds Stejneger's studies of the fur-seal of the Pribilof and adjacent islands. Hawkes, of the Canadian Geological Survey, describes the Inviting-In Feast of the Alaskan Eskimo. The most important work by private efforts has been that of the National Geographic Society in its five expeditions in connection with the Katmai eruption, elsewhere described. Besides volcanic studies it made extensive collections in the domain of botany, geography, and geology.

There are few departments of science which would not profit by the work of specialists in the Territory. The language and customs of the vanishing natives, the determination of life zones of existing fauna and flora, the solving of glacial progression or withdrawal —these and many other investigations would be most interesting, even if without practical bearing on material matters. It is to be hoped that more and more the inclinations and efforts of American scientists may be turned to Alaska, where important results may be expected and professional reputation may be gained.

BIBLIOGARPHY.—Knowlton: Fossil Flora of Alaska. Smithsonian Institution, No. 998. Maddren: Smithsonian Exploration in Alaska, 1904, No. 1584. Gilmore: Smithsonian Exploration in Alaska, 1907, No. 1807. Osgood, W. H.: Biological Publications, Department of Agriculture, No. 19. Biological Reconnaissance of Yukon Region, No. 21. Natural History of Cook Inlet, 1901, No. 24. Biological Reconnaissance of Base of Alaska Peninsula, 1904.

CHAPTER XXV

MOUNTAINS

In his nature studies, Ruskin says of great mountains:

They divide the earth, not only into districts, but into climates; and cause perpetual currents of air to traverse their passes in a thousand different states; moistening it with the spray of their waterfalls, closing it within clefts and caves, where the sunbeams never reach, till it is as cold as November mists; then sending it forth again to breathe lightly across the slopes of velvet fields, or to be scorched among sun-burnt shales and grassless crags; then drawing it back in moaning swirls through clefts of ice, and up into dewy wreaths above the snow-fields.

The beauty and force of this description must strongly appeal to those who have visited the stupendous land masses—the Fairweather, the St. Elias, the Wrangell, the McKinley, and the Alaskan mountain ranges—which extend in an immense semicircle of more than a thousand miles from the Sitkan region to the end of the Alaska Peninsula.

In their abrupt rise from the sea, in their length as an uninterrupted mountain chain, in their contiguous areas of luxuriant vegetation and utter desolation, in their striking contrasts of volcanic lava and arctic snows, in the extent of their overlying and debouching glaciers—the Alaskan mountains offer wondrous aspects of nature, unmatched within an equal area by any other mountain masses of the world.

Nor are all Alaskan mountains of one class or of uniform pattern. The routine tourist sees the forested, purple-peaked and snow-touched mountains of the Inside Passage, and the smooth-based, naked sierras of Lynn Canal. Beyond lie other and more striking types: the towering summits of ice-clad Fairweather, the jagged-peaked, ice-beset St. Elias Alps, the huge mass of Wrangell, the graceful, rounded, green slopes of Kodiak, the symmetrical volcanic cone of Pavlof, and the majestic, snow-crowned American monarch—McKinley.

It must not be thought that these grand and awe-inspiring mountain landscapes are inaccessible to the ordinary traveller, or even difficult of access. They are all reached in brief time and under comfortable conditions. Even the magnificent group in McKinley National Park, Mts. McKinley, Foraker, and Russell, are accessible from the Alaska Railroad over a forest road.

There are four important mountain ranges, supplemented by subordinate groups. Except the volcanic Aleutian range they are mountains of recent crustal uplift, modified by erosion.

The Rocky Mountain extension crosses northern Alaska as the Endicott range, nearly parallel with and about 200 miles inland from the Arctic Ocean. It decreases in elevation from about 8,000 feet near the Canadian frontier to 1,000 feet at Kotzebue Sound.

The Coast range, consisting of the Fairweather and St. Elias Mountains, has a mean altitude exceeding 10,000 feet, and includes within its limits the most remarkable and extended glacier fields in America. Though of higher average elevation than the St. Elias group, the Fairweather range is of more limited area. Its principal peaks are La Pérouse, 10,750 feet, Lituya, 11,832, and Fairweather, 15,292 feet, all rising, as it were, from the very sea, their steep declivities covered by great glacial sheets. The beauty and splendor of these mountains are beyond description, and in the mind of the writer unsurpassable. Mrs. Higginson writes of them:

In all the splendor of the drenched sunlight, straight out of the violet sparkling sea, rose the magnificent peaks of the Fairweather Range and towered against the sky. No great snow mountains rising from the land have ever affected me as did that long and noble chain glistening out of the sea.

However, the St. Elias range is still more remarkable through its combination of glacial fields and mountain masses. There are in this range nine peaks whose elevation exceeds 10,000 feet—Augusta, Cook, Hubbard, Huxley, Logan, Newton, St. Elias, Seattle, and Vancouver. Mt. Logan is the highest, 19,539 feet, but as it is not visible from the ocean St. Elias, 18,024 feet, is the dominating feature of the landscape, and is visible under favorable conditions about 150 miles from the sea. Its base washed by the Pacific Ocean, the main peak springs precipitously

McKinley; the Monarch of American Mountains.

(View about 50 miles distant.)

upward. Stupendous in its environment, as well as in its height, St. Elias beggars description. On near approach its beauty is enhanced by a bordering hem of pure white, the Malaspina Glacier, which follows the shore line for nearly seventy miles.

Of St. Elias, Russell wrote:

At length the great pyramid forming the culminating summit of all the region burst into full view. What a glorious sight! The great mountain seemed higher and grander and more regularly proportioned than any peak I had ever beheld before. The white plain formed by the Seward Glacier made an even foreground, which gave distance to the foot-hills forming the western margin of the glacier. Far above the angular crest of the Samovar Hills in the middle distance towered St. Elias, sharp and clear against the evening sky. So majestic was St. Elias that other magnificent peaks scarcely received a second glance.

The Wrangell Mountains are a group of irregular volcanic formation, with a mean elevation of 10,000 feet. They are separate from the Coast range, and cover an area of about 100 by 50 miles in extent. The main peaks are unsymmetrical lava cones, of which eight, Blackburn, Castle Peak, Drum, Jarvis, Regal, Sanford, Wrangell, and Zanetti, exceed 10,000 feet in height. It is known that there are quite a number of unnamed peaks that are of similar high elevation. The highest two of the known peaks are Wrangell, 14,005, and Blackburn, 16,140 feet. As later mentioned, Wrangell is an active volcano and with its neighbors forms a detached group, doubtless the eastern results of the volcanic forces that have played such prominent parts in the formation of southwestern Alaska.

Mrs. Higginson considers the Wrangell Mountain views from Copper Valley "unsurpassed in the interior. Mount Drum, sweeping up splendidly from a level plain, is more imposing than Wrangell and Blackburn (from 2,000 to 4,000 feet higher). Glacial creeks and roaring rivers; wild and fantastic cañons, moving glaciers, gorges of royal purple bloom, green valleys and flowery slopes, the domed and towered Castle Mountains, the lone and majestic peaks, cascades spraying down sheer precipices—all blend into one grand panorama of unrivalled inland grandeur."

The Alaska Range forms the southern boundary of the Yukon Basin, and extends from the International Boundary (where the mountains are named Nutzotin) westward, in a semicircle, to the region west of Cook Inlet. The range has a well-defined crest line, from 8,000 to 10,000 feet in elevation, which is unbroken for about 200 miles. Four peaks— Foraker, Russell, Spurr, and McKinley—are above 10,000 feet, the last-named 20,464 feet, being the highest peak of America.

South of this range are the Chugach Mountains, of which Muir says:

The entrance to the famous Prince William Sound disclosed to the westward one of the richest, most glorious mountain landscapes I ever beheld—peak over peak dipping deep in the sky, a thousand of them, icy and shining, rising higher, higher, beyond and yet beyond another, burning bright in the afternoon light, purple cloud bars above them, purple shadows in the hollows, and great breadths of sun-spangled, ice-dotted waters in front. . . . Grandeur and beauty in a thousand forms awaited us at every turn in this bright and spacious wonderland. But that first broad, far-reaching view in the celestial light was best of all.

The Aleutian Range, which extends southwest from Cook Inlet to the end of the Alaska Peninsula, is composed of typical volcanic cones, which are treated in the following chapter on volcanoes.

It is to be noted that the larger number of high peaks are in the eastern part of Alaska, in the Alaska, Chugach, Fairweather, McKinley, St. Elias, and Wrangell Mountains. West of 153° of longitude there is no peak above 10,000 feet. Possibly the absence of lofty peaks on the Alaska Peninsula and in the Aleutian Chain is due to the frequent volcanic action in those regions.

The following list gives such peaks more than 10,000 feet high as are now known. Doubtless in later years the list will be somewhat enlarged.

Alaskan mountains exceeding 10,000 feet in height:

	Feet
Alverstone, St. Elias group	14,493
Augusta, St. Elias	13,918
Bear, Wrangell Range	14,650
Blackburn, Wrangell	16,140
Boan, Wrangell	16,420
Crillon, Fairweather	12,725
Castel Peak, Wrangell	10,314
Cook, St. Elias	13,755

	Feet
Deborah, Alaska Range	12,540
Drum, Wrangell	12,000
Fairweather	15,300
Florence, Chugach Range	11,610
Foraker, McKinley group	17,000
Goode, Chugach	10,600
Hayes, Alaska	13,950
Hess, Alaska	12,030
Hubbard, St. Elias	14,950
Huxley, St. Elias	12,560
Iliamna, Cook Inlet	10,020
Jarvis, Wrangell	12,230
La Pérouse, Fairweather	10,750
McKinley	20,300
Marcus Baker, Chugach	13,250
Natazhat, Wrangell	13,440
Quincy Adams, Fairweather	13,560
Redoubt, Cook Inlet	10,200
Regal, Wrangell	13,400
Root, Fairweather	12,860
St. Elias	18,024
Sanford, Wrangell	16,210
Seattle, St. Elias	10,175
Spurr, McKinley	11,070
Vancouver, St. Elias	15,676
Wrangell	14,000
Zanetti, Wrangell	12,980
Chugach Peak, unnamed	11,720
" " "	12,023
" " "	12,200
" " "	12,300

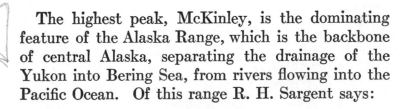

The highest peak, McKinley, is the dominating feature of the Alaska Range, which is the backbone of central Alaska, separating the drainage of the Yukon into Bering Sea, from rivers flowing into the Pacific Ocean. Of this range R. H. Sargent says:

Words fail to express one's impression of the Alaska Range when viewed under favorable circumstances. In 1906 I had such an opportunity as is rarely experienced, from the western slope of the Talkeetna Mountains. Below lay the broad, level valley of the Susitna River, beautifully carpeted in the deep green of the conifers, while here and there a shining patch of light, outlining a lake, broke the monotony.

Across the valley, 50 miles away, the Alaska Range arose, rugged, angular, and formidable, its cold gray serrated peaks often resembling clusters of spires. Back of them Mt. Dall, Mt. Russell, and Mt. Foraker stood like white-clad guardians to their chief, Mt. McKinley, towering grand, superb. The horizon from the south to the northeast gave the grandest panorama imaginable. Far away in the distance could be seen the volcanoes Iliamna and Redoubt, on the western shores of Cook Inlet, while at the other extremity Mt. Hayes towered high above everything.

Considering that the mountains of southern Alaska are mostly glacier-covered, it might be thought that the mountains of the far north would be at least covered with snow perpetually. Riggs in making the boundary survey between the United States and Canada, reports: "The Arctic Range runs very close to the coast at the boundary, the foothills coming to within a mile or two of the Arctic Ocean. The higher summits are about 7,000 feet, and are perfectly bare of snow in summer. A peculiar feature of this range is the large amount of coral and other sea fossils to be found."

Mountain Climbing

There is no peak in Alaska that offers an insuperable obstacle to its being climbed. Fay, an authority on mountain climbing, after alluding to four unsuccessful attempts to ascend Mount St. Elias, says of the successful ascent by the Duke of Abruzzi: "Its remoteness from civilization in a sub-arctic waste, its whole altitude above snow-line, made St. Elias an inviting substitute for an Himalayan goal. Less as an ascent difficult *per se* than as a most skilfully arranged campaign, and as a training school for its leader, does this ascent take a place among the most important of mountain climbing." The Duke tells his story in "Ascent of Mount St. Elias."

Dun relates his experiences in climbing Wrangell in *Harper's Magazine*, March 1909.

Cook's claim to have ascended Mount McKinley has been thoroughly discredited. The credit for reaching the summit of this, the highest of North American mountains, belongs to the late Archdeacon Stuck, who reached the top on March 14, 1913.

Miss Dora Keen, after failing to reach the top of Mount Blackburn in 1911, renewed her attempt in 1912, and was successful on May 19.

CHAPTER XXVI

VOLCANOES

THOUGH viewed by the general public as a semi-arctic territory, yet Alaska affords the most striking phases of volcanic activity to be found in the western hemisphere, whether of ancient or recent times.

Doctor C. Grewingk, the best authority on Alaskan volcanoes, wrote in 1850:

We know of no more extensive theatre of volcanic activity than the Aleutian Islands, the Alaska Peninsula, and the west coast of Cook Inlet. Here, within the limits of a single century, have all the known phenomena occurred: the elevation of mountain chain and islands, the sinking of extensive areas of the earth's surface, earthquakes, eruptions of lava ashes and mud, the hot springs, and explosions of steam and sulphuric gases.

Of the three types—eruptive or true volcano, semi-eruptive, and uplift without eruption—Akutan, Makushin, and Shishaldin are illustrative examples of the first, while Bogoslof and Grewingk pertain to the last-named class.

Of the Alaskan volcanoes as a whole, Grewingk writes:

There are no descriptions of streams of burning lava. Eruptions within historic times have consisted of ashes, stones, and liquid mud, seldom occurring within the true craters.

He adds that the only lava-made islands are St. Matthew, St. Michael, Stuart Islands, the Pribilof group, and perhaps Umnak.

Colonel Caine says of his visit to Cook Inlet:

During the first three months (June to September, 1902) Redoubt poured forth at intervals dense clouds of smoke and vivid sheets of flame, blackening the usually virgin slopes of snow on its sides with dark-gray volcanic dust. [He adds that according to local reports Wrangell broke out violently at that time.]

Of Pavlof, and the adjacent mountain country, at the west end of Alaska Peninsula, John Burroughs ("Summer Holidays in Alaskan Waters") writes:

The twin volcanic peaks of Pavlof rise from the shore to an altitude of seven or eight thousand feet, one of them a symmetrical cone with black converging lines of rock cutting through the snow; the other more rugged and irregular, with many rents upon its sides and near its summit, from which issued vapor, staining the snow like soot from a chimney. Sheets of vapor were also seen issuing from cracks at its foot near sea level (in 1899).

That this volcano has recurring phases of activity is evident from the statement of Captain Radclyffe in "Big Game Shooting in Alaska," who says that in July, 1903:

Mt. Pavlof suddenly burst out with a series of terrific explosions, which were repeated every five minutes, sending up clouds of steam and smoke, and shaking the ground around for miles.

Of the Aghilan Pinnacles, a remarkable succession of black, castellated rocks west of Pavlof Volcano, Burroughs says:

A strange architectural effect amid the wilder and ruder forms that surround them, as if some vast, many-sided cathedral of dark gray stone were going to decay in the mountain solitude. Both in form and color they seem alien to everything about them. Now we saw them athwart the crests of smooth green hills, or fretting the sky above lines of snow. Their walls were so steep that no snow lay upon them, while the pinnacles were like church spires.

The twin volcanoes, Pogromni, 6,500 feet, and Shishaldin, 9,387 feet high, are on Unimak Island, at the end of Alaska Peninsula. Of them John Burroughs writes:

Our first glimpse was of a black cone ending in a point. . . . It seemed buoyed up by the clouds. . . . There was nothing to indicate a mountain. Presently the veil was brushed aside, and we saw both mountains from base to summit and noted the vast concave lines of Shishaldin that swept down to the sea, and that mark the typical volcanic form. The long, graceful curves, so attractive to the eye, repeat on this far-off island the profile of Fujiyama, the sacred peak of Japan. The upper part, for several thousand feet, was dark—doubtless the result of heat, for it is smoking this year.

Mrs. Higginson well describes it:

In the absolute perfection of its conical form, its chaste and elegant beauty of outline, and the slender column of smoke pushing up from its finely pointed crest, Shishaldin stands alone.

One night in 1900 the writer saw the overhanging clouds of Shishaldin all aflame from volcanic action, and again saw the peak's graceful outlines by day, and finds it in form and beauty second, if at all, to the typical volcanic peak of Mayon, in far-off Luzon.

From 1825 to 1829, Pogromni (destroying desolation) and Shishaldin were violently active at intervals, new craters and fissures appearing with masses of red-hot lava, recurring flames, showers of ashes and stones, with other volcanic phenomena. Fortunately there has been no recurrence of violent action.

Bogoslof was formed by crystal uplift in May, 1796, when, after indications of volcanic disturbances, an observer on Unimak saw far out on the sea a black object, and there appeared the volcano Castle Peak.

Large flames of such brilliancy that on the island (twelve miles distant) night was converted into day, and an earthquake (occurred) with thundering noises, while rocks were occasionally thrown on the island from the new crater.

After three days the earthquake ceased, the flames subsided, and the newly created island loomed up in the shape of a cone. About eight years elapsed before the island was sufficiently cooled to permit its examination.

In 1883 a companion volcano, New Bogoslof—now called Grewingk—was born. The history of its rapid and extraordinary changes in size and shape appears in the records of the fourteen visits and examinations between 1883 and 1899. When discovered, September 27, 1883, by Captain Anderson, it was "then in active eruption, throwing out large masses of heated rocks and great volumes of smoke, steam, and ashes, which came from the apex and from numerous fissures, of which some were below the surface of the sea."

Captain Healy, of the *Corwin*, four times visited the island. He states that, in 1884,

Both peaks were inaccessible on account of the steam and fumes of sulphur in which they were enveloped. One night the volcano in the darkness presented a most extraordinary spectacle. The summit was enveloped in a bright sulphurous light, which burst forth from rifts in its side and shone out against the black sky, making a scene both beautiful and impressive.

Doctor C. Hart Merriam, from whose comprehensive account these descriptions are drawn, twice visited Bogoslof. Of the island, in 1891, he says:

The shape of the island did not in any way suggest a volcano, there being no cone and no true crater. . . . The new volcano was enveloped in steam, which issued from thousands of small crannies, and poured in vast clouds from a few great fissures and craterlike openings. . . . The steam was usually impregnated with fumes of sulphur. . . . Most of the rock was hot and pools of hot water were found on the beach.

Merriam's comments as to the absence of a true crater accord with the theory of Grewingk that:

The falling in of mountains on the east coast of Bering Sea, the apparent swelling and bursting of whole sections of islands, are indications pointing to formation of peaks, craters, and crevices by elevation.

In 1906 a third island was added to the Bogoslof group, being first seen on May 26. Doctor C. H. Gilbert says of this visit:

We were astonished to find that Fire (Grewingk) Island was no longer smoking and that a very large third island had arisen half way between the other two. It was made of jagged, rugged lava and was giving off clouds of steam and smoke from any number of little craters scattered all over it. Around these craters, the rocks were all crusted with yellow sulphur.

The new cone, occupying much of the space between the two older ones, was somewhat higher than either, but 300 feet would be an extreme figure. There was no evidence of any crater.

Its bases undermined by the unceasing action of sea currents and storm waves, its cliffs wasting through wind and precipitation, its external material suffering disintegration by alternate action of super-heated steam and arctic cold, and its structural stability impaired by uplifting and shifting internal forces, the entire Bogoslof group bids fair within a century wholly to disintegrate and disappear, as has the adjacent volcanic Ship Rock that antedated Old Bogoslof as an illustration of plutonic action in these seas.

The history of the Bogoslof volcanoes, since their unusual activities in 1909, has been in accord with previous phases. Islands and bays, peaks and rugged lava-masses alternate with astonishing frequency. Munger in his "Jack in the Box" (*Nat. Geogr. Mag.*, March, 1909) well terms it the most wonderful island in the world.

Only two volcanoes are known in eastern Alaska,— the smoking peak of Wrangell and the inactive cone of Edgecumbe, Sitka. The longest extended and most remarkable volcanic belt of the world is that which Griggs terms "The Aleutian Chain,"—which practically connects the seismic systems of Asia and North America. This consists of an almost unbroken series of volcanic peaks, extending more than 1,200 miles—from Spurr Peak, west of Cook Inlet, southwest through the entire Alaska Peninsula, and thence westerly along the Aleutian Islands to Little Sitkin. There is scarcely an island in this chain, great or small, without an active cone or a dead crater.

In the Aleutian Chain there are 36 known volcanoes, and Griggs names 17 other peaks, which, doubtless, have been active in the past. Fortunately, far the greater number of these volcanoes are inactive, but it is to be noted that the remarkable eruption of Katmai was from a peak not formerly numbered among the dangerous volcanoes. The active cones are those on the Alaska Peninsula, or the adjacent westerly islands of Uminak, Unalaska, and Unmak.

Of the Aleutian Islands it is to be stated that in 1920 Bogoslof volcanoes were quiet and both water and lava were cold. The five cones of Atka, two of Amnak, and one of Unalaska have been quiescent ever since American occupation. Far to the west

Gareloi yet flames, but not with violence. On Uminak there are 11 craters, and three volcanoes, of
which the twin Isanotskis and Pogromni have been
silent for a century. Shishaldin, of whose cone
Griggs says it is the most perfect in the world,
confines its activities to infrequent clouds of smoke
by day and of flame at night.

Volcanoes of the Alaska Peninsula

While threatening, the volcanoes at the base of the
peninsula, west of Cook Inlet, have never done dam-
age. A most violent eruption was that of Augustine,
which in 1883 blew off its top, leaving a great jagged-
rimmed crater. For several months, by daily clouds
of dense smoke, and its nightly flames, Augustine
made more or less anxious the settlements fifty miles
distant. The most striking features of this region are
the volcanoes of Iliamna, 10,020 feet, and Redoubt,
10,200 feet, the loftiest of the volcanoes of the chain.
Of them Griggs declares: "The perfection of their
conical forms is evidence enough that neither has
ever suffered a great eruption." Iliamna in 1867 by
an eruption covered Kodiak with an inch of ash. The
eruption of Redoubt in 1902 showered the country
for many miles around with dust.

Volcanoes of the Katmai District

The eruption of Mount Katmai in 1912, one of the
greatest of historic times, drew international attention to the volcanoes of Alaska. Until that time

By courtesy of the National Geographic Society. Mt. Katmai, Before and After the Eruption.

(White upper line shows crest before eruption.)

Katmai was a name on the map, being shown as a triple-peaked mountain, with elevations of 7,500, 7,360, and 7,260 feet. It was not recognized as a volcano, although there is little doubt that it is the mountain, which as the natives said, smoked occasionally, on which account they named their village Katmai.

The scientific researches, full descriptions, and detailed published accounts of this remarkable eruption are due entirely to the foresight, energy, and persistent efforts of the National Geographic Society, which has spared neither labor, money, nor pains in this work. Its six expeditions were led first by G. C. Martin, in 1912, and the four others by Doctor R. F. Griggs.

Martin's excellent description of the scenes following the eruption were published in the *National Geographic Magazine*, February, 1913. Doctor Griggs's reports and scientific publications were followed in 1922 by his "The Valley of Ten Thousand Smokes," a beautiful volume published by the National Geographic Society.

The following summary, from an unpublished account, by Doctor Griggs sets forth the principal points:

On June 6, 1912, Mt. Katmai blew up. The eruption was one of the half-dozen greatest within historic times. the explosions were heard at Juneau, 750 miles away. Ash fell as far as Puget Sound, and at Kodiak, 100 miles from Katmai, it was ten inches deep; total darkness prevailed for three days.

The inhabitants of the Kodiak district suffered abject terror, but there were no fatalities. The inhabitants of Katmai village, fortunately absent fishing, have abandoned their ruined village, and were removed to a location west of Chignik.

Just before Mt. Katmai exploded, the valley, through which ran the old trail across the peninsula, burst open in many places, and a great mass of incandescent material poured through the fissures. This molten magma was surcharged with gases like the distinctive clouds which emanated from Mt. Pelée. Flowing down the valley under gravity, it filled an area more than 50 square miles in extent, with a deposit of fine ground tuff.

After the extension of solid material, the valley continued to emit gases in great volume, forming millions of fumaroles, which constitute one of the most awe-inspiring spectacles. This feature of the eruption was discovered by the expedition under me in 1916, and the basin was named "The Valley of Ten Thousand Smokes." Subsequent expeditions in 1917, 1918, and 1919 were despatched by the society, and the results published in popular accounts in the *Magazine* and scientific results in technical papers and in a volume by the Society.

The wonders of the Katmai district, which in time will attract thousands of annual visitors, have been saved from despoliation by the action of President Wilson, who, in 1918, proclaimed it a National Monument. This wonderful district contains more than a million of acres and its area exceeds that of Rhode Island.

Within the Katmai district are the volcanoes of Katmai, Mageik, 7,250 feet, Martin, 5,000, Knife Peak, 7,800 feet, Novarupta, about 3,500 feet, and

Mt. Katmai Crater.

(The tiny central spot is the crater of about 40 acres 'n area. The wall in the background rises 3,700 feet above the valley.)

Trident, 6,790 feet. To the northeast are the cones of Douglas, Fourpeaked, and Kugak, and to the west, Peulik. Far down the peninsula are the volcanoes of Venaminof and others, ending at the terminus with the striking peak of Pavlof, whose smoking signal ever gives warning of possible future eruptions.

Of the volcanic community of Asia and America, Doctor Griggs says: "Directly in line with the prolongation of the Aleutian Chain are the volcanic Commander Islands, carrying our chain over to the shores of Kamchatka, where it meets a line of very lofty and notable volcanoes running down through the Kurile Islands to northern Japan."

BIBLIOGRAPHY.—Griggs: The Valley of Ten Thousand Smokes.

CHAPTER XXVII

INHABITANTS—THE WHITES

DEFINITE information as to the population of Alaska is not obtainable, and among the reasons therefor are the rapid and frequent changes necessitated by Alaskan industries. Including those engaged in the fishery industries, it is believed that the summer population is fully 15,000 greater than that in winter, when the demand for skilled labor falls off greatly. For instance, in the summer industry of the fisheries there were employed in 1922, 21,974 persons, of whom only 4,192 were natives. The winter placer mines of 1921-1922 were worked by 1,800 less men than those in summer. The Governor in his report of 1923 states that an increase is now indicated, and a larger and more stable population is to be expected.

Census Reports

The population of Alaska by the last five censuses was as follows: 1880, 33,426; 1890, 32,052; 1900, 63,592; 1910, 64,356; 1920, 55,036. In the report of 1920 the term white refers to pure-blooded white persons. The white persons were: 1900, 30,493; 1910, 36,400; 1920, 27,883. Of the whites in 1920, 16,286 were native born, while 11,597 were foreign born. Divided between the sexes there were 20,586 males and 7,297 females. Foreign countries contributing more than a thousand were: Canada, 1,716; Norway, 2,169; Sweden, 1,688. The decrease in 1920 was due to two causes,—numerous volunteers for war service and the closing of many mines due to increased cost under war conditions.

Married whites numbered 18,522, and those single 11,274. As bearing on permanency it is to be noted that in 1920 the school attendance numbered 6,455, 46.7 per cent, as against 4,631, 40.1 per cent in 1910. The illiteracy fell from 0.9 per cent in 1910 to 0.6 per cent among the whites of native parentage in 1920. Inability to speak English fell from 3.8 per cent in 1910, to 1.0 per cent in 1920. These figures show a white population very largely American, British, Germanic, and Scandinavian, with an unusual high degree of literacy and homogeneity of language. Of the 361 white farmers, no less than 335 are of American, British, German, or Scandinavian nationality.

Alaskan Legislation

The general character of a new community is indicated by the laws that they enact and enforce. The constructive and progressive laws of Alaska are remarkable for a new territory, necessarily heterogeneous in its population. Among Alaskan laws may be named the following: Forbidding sale of tobacco to minors, pensions to dependent mothers, rescue of lost persons, establishing citizenship schools for aliens, care of insane, excluding minors from poolrooms, home for destitute pioneers, punishing white slavery and seduction, workmen's liens and compensation, safeguarding miners, regulating drug sales, forbidding narcotics, and an eight-hour law. Early forbidding sale of liquor to natives, by a territorial referendum Alaska established a rigid prohibition law against either sale or gift of intoxicating liquor, prior to the Federal law. When Congress, regardless of its treaty obligations, refused relief to natives dying of epidemic, Alaska appropriated $93,000 for that purpose, though in distressed financial condition.

Local Accomplishments

In addition to the establishment of many thousand homes and economic plants, they have upbuilt eighteen incorporated towns, whose assessed value in 1923 was $19,668,952. The East may well envy Alaskan administration where the town tax varies from eight to twenty mills. Most of these towns have churches, schools, electric lights, water, telephones, radio or telegraph, libraries, social clubs and theatres. Sanitary conditions and climate are such that the normal mortality of Alaska is the lowest in the United States.

Alaskan Patriotism

Before a Congressional Committee a witness testified: "The Alaska people gave more men to the war than any other community in the United States, according to its population. They contributed a great deal more in thrift stamps during the war, and at the present time (1921) are contributing more than any other community in the United States. In the matter of the Victory Loan they were second only to Delaware in their subscription, in proportion to population."

Contrary to the oft-expressed opinion, the Alaskans are neither reckless, dissipated, nor lawless. In the main they are law-abiding, hard-working, and temperate men. The rapid and successful development of the Territory has been the outcome of intelligent, persistent struggles on the part of self-respecting communities that are above the average of those in the United States proper. The writer has been familiar with mining camps and frontier settlements for forty years, and has never elsewhere seen the equal for high qualities of manhood that are usually found in Alaska. This is doubtless due in large part to the fact that Alaska is not a "poor man's country," as only men of some means can even reach the country, while considerable money and credit are necessary for the smallest ventures.

Tourists and prospectors travel everywhere without danger to life or person, though the adventurous can readily find associates of kindred and vicious qualities, if so inclined. It may be added that sojourn among the natives entails danger only on the rarest possible occasions, the killing of a peaceable white man by a native being almost unknown in recent years.

Russian Citizens

The descendants of the Russian settlers have generally a mixture of native blood through intermarriages in the past centuries. Apparently very few of them are classed as white under the rigid distinction drawn by the officials of the census. It seems that the same view is taken by the local authorities, for the schools in several settlements are classed as "white and mixed." Sitka has its own school as an incorporated town and doubtless there are many children of pure Russian stock. Among the white and mixed schools in unincorporated settlements those with the largest enrolments are Unga, 62, Kodiak, 87, Afognak, 51, and Kenai, 97.

Of the Kodiak archipelago Martin says: "The inhabitants of Kodiak and Afognak are mostly descendants of Russians. The largest settlements are Kodiak—formerly St. Paul—and Afognak. The former is well known as one of the quaintest and most attractive towns on the Alaskan coast. The town has long lived upon the memories of its former glories as capital during the early occupation and of the prosperous sea-otter days." Both these towns have Russian churches and follow the orthodox faith.

CHAPTER XXVIII

INHABITANTS — NATIVES

By the census of 1920 there were 26,558 (all kinds of natives) against 25,331 in 1910, an increase of 5 per cent in ten years. By linguistic stock in 1920 there were 2,942 Aleuts, 4,657 Athapascans, 13,698 Esquimauian, 524 Haidan, 3,895 Tlingit, and 842 Tsimshian. It is probable that there were slight decreases in the Athapascan, Haidan, and Tlingit stocks, and increases in the other elements.

The inclination to regard marriage as a permanent condition is indicated by the fact that out of 5,162 married native women there were but 42 divorced, 0.6 per cent as against 2.1 per cent among the whites. Increase in school attendance was shown by 40.4 per cent of those under twenty years in 1920, while in 1910 the attendance was but 37.4 per cent. It should be remembered that school facilities are not within reach of all natives. There has been a decrease of illiteracy, the percentage of 71.4 in 1910 falling to 56.4 in 1920. This followed the increased school opportunities.

Native Characteristics and Distribution

Aleuts

Though numbering less than 3,000, the Aleuts are probably the most interesting of the natives, as having acquired certain benefits of civilization, with minor elements of its vices. Dwelling on the Aleutian Islands, with the seas as their field of occupation, they live largely on fish, varied in summer by a diet of berries and wild-fowl. Their peculiar cellarlike and sedge-covered huts are comfortable and fairly well-kept. On the larger and more accessible islands the construction of framed houses and the presence of gaudy lithographs, coal-oil stoves, granite ware, and cotton prints display the taste of the natives and the influence of the trader. The Aleut is docile, peaceful, a good husband and father, honest and industrious. Baptized in the Greek Catholic Church, and visited at least annually by a priest, he is fond of festivals and ceremonies, which are infrequently marked by excesses. Largely influenced by the church, which uses a mixture of Russian and Aleut in its ceremonies, they have not taken kindly to American speech or education. However, the past neglect of the United States along these lines has been largely responsible for such existent conditions.

In the early days of the American occupation, W. S. Dodge, collector of customs, described them thus: "These people reside in towns and live principally from the products of the fur-seal, sea-otter, and fox. They have a language of their own, but nearly all talk the Russian tongue. They have schools and churches; nearly all read and write. Many are highly educated, even in the classics. The fur company reposed great confidence in them. One of their best physicians was an Aleutian; one of their best navigators was an Aleutian." As shown later, their civilization, prosperity, and decent life have nearly vanished under American control.

The remnant of the Aleutian race occupy the Aleutian Islands—about one-third of them; the Unga and adjacent islands have another third. The remainder are spread over the western and northwestern Alaska Peninsula, with detached communities on the Kenai Peninsula, on Afognak and northeastern Kodiak. One remote settlement, gradually wasting away without mail, school, reindeer, drag out a wretched existence at Attu, almost on the coast of Asia,—almost utterly ignored by the United States.

Haidas

Numbering 524 in 1920, the Haidas are a northern extension of the Indians of the Queen Charlotte Islands. Their clean and orderly villages are known to the tourists of southeastern Alaska, with whom the women play a brisk trade in basketry, hats, ornamental carvings, and curios, many imported from the States. The men are skilful fishermen and good navigators, but the Haidas play no real part in Alaskan native life. A vanishing race, their huge canoes, totemic designs, and cedar houses are of the past. The Haidas occupy the southern half of the Prince of Wales archipelago, immediately north of the Canadian boundary.

Eskimo

The Eskimo are a peaceful and docile people, trustful and generous in their relations with others.

They have been quick to adopt such civilized methods as are specially applicable to their habitat and life methods.

The testimony before a congressional committee said: "The Eskimo people are intelligent and industrious. They maintain several co-operative trading-posts, and own over 100,000 reindeer. Some are educated to a degree that qualifies them to occupy the positions of teachers under the Bureau of Education. They have decided mechanical ability, as is shown by their success in the manual training work. They are chiefly valuable as a people who occupy, and are satisfied with, a portion of our national domain which will not be demanded by any other people, and who make that domain valuable. They are a strength and an economic asset to the Nation."

Nelson, commenting on the extended and radical recommendation made to Eskimo owning reindeer, for their proper treatment, said that it was gratifying to note "the open-minded way in which a number of herdowners are already putting in effect the improved methods suggested."

The Eskimo inhabit the entire coast region of Alaska on the Arctic Ocean, Bering Sea, the northeastern parts of the Alaska Peninsula, and the greater part of Kodiak Island. Probably one-half of the Eskimo live in the tundra and sea region of Bering Sea, from Norton Sound southward to the environs of Bristol Bay. Nearly 4,000 live in the delta of the Kuskokwim.

Athapaskans

Although the census officials include all natives under the term Indian, the Athapaskans are the only true Indians in Alaska. Although they are usually hunters and fishermen, yet they at times have done good work as woodmen, and have been very efficient pilots in navigating the Yukon and Tanana rivers. These Indians are a branch of one of the most important and widely distributed tribes of North America. The Alaskan communities are a westerly offshoot of the Athapaskans of the Mackenzie valley. Although numbering but 4,657 in 1920, they cover practically all the hunting grounds of the Yukon watershed—the delta excepted—the upper regions of the Kuskokwim, and the entire watersheds draining into Cook Inlet and the Gulf of Alaska. They are nowhere gathered in large numbers, but perhaps one-fourth of the Indians are in the Nenana district, Tanana watershed. Epidemics and famines have seriously reduced their numbers. Contact with civilization means steady dimunition in numbers.

Metlakatlans

The Tsimpsean Indians, under the leadership of their devoted missionary, William Duncan, immigrated in a body from near Port Simpson, British Columbia, to obtain greater religious liberty, to Alaska in 1887. On March 3, 1891, Congress set apart the Annette Islands, now popularly known as

Metlakatla, as a reservation "for the use of the Metlakatlan Indians and those personally known as Metlakatlans, who have recently emigrated from British Columbia to Alaska, and such other Alaskan natives as may join them."

The town of Metlakatla is perpetual evidence of the soundness of Governor Swineford's judgment regarding the capabilities of Alaskan natives. They labor at fishing, in the cannery, in the saw-mill, live industriously and exemplarily in the clean, well-ordered, and picturesque village that is the work of their brains and hands. They have built a church, a schoolhouse, town-hall, guest-house, sawmill, cannery, several stores, and many comfortable dwellings —in short, they are a community that does not compare unfavorably with any white settlement in Alaska in thrift, comfort, and order.

Repeated efforts to reduce the size of the reservation and open it to whites have so far failed, and should fail. Their isolation has been a most favorable factor in the prosperity of the Metlakatlans, and complete success can only be expected in Alaskan missionary work through rigid separation of whites and natives. Missionaries recognize almost universally that the whites seek natives largely for exploitation. In late years the Tsimpseans have greatly prospered, though a few have abandoned communal life. The community is self-governing, and its business success is shown by a net revenue in 1918 of $70,253 from its fishing and other industries.

Tlinkits

The habitat of the Tlinkit Indians extends from the southeastern boundary of Alaska to the mouth of Copper River. In consequence he is the Alaskan Indian, as far as the experience of the summer tourist extends. There are twelve subdivisions of the tribe, but in general the Tlinkits are divided into two clans: the Wolf, which has minor branches, such as Bear, Porpoise, Eagle, etc., and the Raven, to which belong the Frog, Owl, Sea Lion, and Salmon. Marriages are invariably made between members of different clans, as those of the same clan are assumed to be within prohibited degrees of consanguinity.

Hereditary chieftains and slaves formerly filled the upper and lower tribal positions, but slavery is now extinct and the claims to higher station and power on account of birth are steadily weakening.

Originally marine nomads, with settled habitats in winter alone, these Indians have, under changed conditions, become permanent in their residences. The original disinclination of the men to work has disappeared under the stimulus of artificial wants, so sedulously fostered by the whites and favored by native women. The mechanical skill of the men is well known, having in the past been applied to the carving and erection of artistic totem poles, the construction of large log houses, and especially in the building of war canoes, usually from a single huge tree, and their elaborate carving and ornamentation. These huge canoes, capable of carrying sixty to seventy warriors, are now rarely seen, giving way to small boats fitted for sea and coast fisheries. The totem poles, formerly ornamented by elaborate and curious carvings, related in a manner to their clan connections, family history, and pedigrees. While small totems are now made for trading and sale, yet the old order of family coat-of-arms, as one may say, has passed among the younger generation. The skill in copper forgings, once so highly prized, has yielded to cheap iron and steel from the trader.

The women were once famous for their closely woven, plant-dyed blankets of mountain-sheep wool, the cherished form of personal wealth, but now they apply the least work consistent with the untrained demands of summer tourists to imported wools colored by aniline dyes. Similarly, there has been marked decline in the basketry methods and styles, which formerly were so artistic and pleasing.

In short, the Tlinkits have changed from a war-like, proud people to the positions of hewers of wood and drawers of water. They live through labor in the saw-mills, canneries, and fisheries, that are the main industries of the Sitkan Archipelago, supplemented on the part of the women by shrewd and profitable curio trade with the summer tourist. Gradually the natives are engaging in the minor operations as miners, wherever the union does not emphatically forbid. Industrial training, along with their peculiar gifts, is hesitatingly but fairly well received, especially by the men, and the Tlinkit has become a valuable factor in the development of southeastern Alaska, justifying the faith of the first American Governor, A. P. Swineford, who, in his annual report for 1885, writes:

All the natives are self-sustaining. They are far superior intellectually, if not in physical development, to the Indian of the plains; are industrious, more or less skilful workers in woods and metals. They yield readily to civilizing influences, and can, with much less care than has been bestowed on native tribes elsewhere, be educated up to the standard of a good and intelligent citizenship.

General Condition of the Natives

This subject seriously engaged the attention of the writer from 1900 to 1908. Three journeys from the Canadian boundary to Nome, through the valleys of the Yukon and Tanana, and two others to Prince William Sound and the Skagway region, while constructing the telegraph system of Alaska, were supplemented by an inspection of all military posts, while commanding general. The fatalities of the 1900 epidemic, the failure of game, both land and sea, and the diversion of the activities of the natives came under my eye. Missionaries, army officers, river and woodyard men, hunters, teachers, fur-traders, miners, and natives were consulted, and gave their varying views freely.

In 1905 the writer, at the request of the late Ethan A. Hitchcock, then Secretary of the Interior, also made a personal study of the problem, during an inspecting tour through Alaska. It appears certain that general and indiscriminate charity is not only undesirable, but also deleterious in its effects. My official recommendations looked especially to encouraging the Indians to help themselves. To this end it was suggested that there should be employed Indian inspectors, whose moral influence should be strengthened by clothing them with a certain coercive authority. Such inspectors should be medical men with the true missionary spirit. Their specific duties were to furnish treatment to natives remote from medical aid. There was to be instruction in, and enforcement of, sanitary methods, supplemented by industrial training suited to the environment; finally there was to be the minimum of food and clothing issues, restricted to most urgent needs.

These suggestions appear to have had weight, for the Bureau of Education furnished the following year medical supplies and text-books to eleven Indian villages destitute of medical means. The Secretary of the Interior also set aside $5,000 to be spent by officers of the army in affording relief in emergent cases of great destitution and need.

Medical investigations, directed by the writer at two widely separated points—Haines Mission and Eagle—disclosed shocking conditions of disease and sanitation. At one place more than half the natives were afflicted with contagious diseases—tuberculosis (48 per cent) and trachoma (7 per cent). Twenty-four per cent of the children die as infants and 16 in childhood. The investigations covered over 600 Indians. The natives were reported at one place as largely free from prejudice, "tractable, easy to teach, and eager to learn."

Many high officials of the nation have publicly deplored the condition of the natives, and President Taft, when Secretary of War, officially recommended legislative action in his annual report of 1906, saying: "From time to time during the past four years the War Department has been called upon to extend relief to destitute natives. This destitution (he adds) is owing to increasing scarcity of game, and the decline in the run of the salmon, due in large measure to the ingress and encroachments of the whites, and from the ignorance and improvidence of the Indians themselves." He recommended: "The adoption of radical measures of relief not only from a standpoint of humanity, but from that of the moral obligation and honor of the nation."

Every thoughtful man must realize the moral duty of this nation toward those whom we have materially, morally, and physically injured—especially to those of the extreme northwest. To these natives, Professor W. H. Dall, an authority from his extended associations with them, covering with intervals 40 years, pays the following deserved tribute:

The men of the Yukon had, like other men, their careers, affections, tragedies, and triumphs. The valley whose rim enclosed their world was as wide for them as our world is for us. It is certain that for their world they had worked out problems which we are still facing with trepidation in ours. No man went hungry in a Yukon village. No youth might wed until he had killed a deer,

as token that he could support his family. The trail
might be lined with temporary caches, yet no man put
out his hand to steal. Men were valued by their achieve-
ments and their liberality.

Such were the men of the Yukon, to whom civilization
and the greed of gold brought drink, disease, and death.
The fittest has survived, but the fittest for what?

What, if anything, does the General Government
owe the natives of Alaska, and in what form shall
the payment be made? It is a problem great in its
moral as well as in its practical aspects. Having
largely destroyed their food supplies, altered their environment, and changed their standards and methods
of life, what does a nation that has drawn products
valued at $1,000,000,000 owe to the natives of Alaska?
Will this nation pay its debts on this account?

What our Christian nation did not do is past history. In 1919 more than 1,500 natives died of epidemic influenza, imported from the States. Congress,
disregarding its treaty with Russia, refused to appropriate for the relief of its suffering wards: Alaska was
not a political factor. Despite business depression
the whites of Alaska spent $120,000 for aid. The
natives did their duty, and when in certain settlements every adult died, the Eskimo communities
adopted 250 orphans. And the 200 natives of Unga
the previous year raised $1,400 for the Red Cross.

Citizens Remedy the Nation's Neglect

What every Alaskan historian knows of the continued and gross neglect of the United States to care

for the uncivilized natives of the Territory,—obligated by treaty with Russia, was recited in testimony before a Congressional Committee in 1921.

For more than 30 years, from Portland Canal to Point Barrow, the natives were made drunkards by the freely sold rum of American exploiters. The murder and rapine of helpless men and women went unpunished. Rights to life, education, and property were absolutely ignored. Thousands died of starvation owing to the unchecked debauchery; on St. Lawrence Island whole villages perished to a man. Other thousands were left unrelieved on the verge of starvation. That so many of the natives have survived is due to their vigor and ability.

The recommendations of men like Roosevelt, Root, Hitchcock, and Taft were disregarded or largely minimized.

Fortunately there is yet a public conscience among us. When the nation failed in its treaty obligations and in its duties of humanity, individual citizens took up the almost helpless task. Through their unselfish exertions the main bodies of Alaskan natives are now self-supporting. Little by little Congress has listened to their urgings, and has thus been stimulated to provide in part and inadequately for the education of the youth, and the medical care of the sick.

The labors of the teachers and missionaries, elsewhere briefly recited, form a bright page in the otherwise dismal story of the dealings of a Christian nation with its native wards in Alaska.

CHAPTER XXIX

EDUCATION AND MISSIONS

AMERICAN polity looks to the universal education of the people at public expense and under government control, leaving religious instruction to private initiative. The United States for a quarter of a century was, however, equally indifferent to both the moral and the mental training of Alaskan natives, which thus devolved entirely on the liberality and activities of Christian men and women, until in very recent years means and methods of secular education were evolved.

Under the Russian régime, education in Alaska was confined to a few religious and secular schools. The first, connected with Russian Greek Church missions, confined its efforts to training native priests; and the latter class, under the Russian-American Company, practically educated selected natives and half-breeds for employment as mechanics, navigators, and ship carpenters, but these training-schools fell into decay about the time of the cession.

It should be added that the natives of Kodiak and several of the larger Aleutian Islands have been regularly educated since that great and noble Russian, Father Veniaminof, systematized the work and increased its efficiency by devising and publishing an Aleut-Russian grammar, which is yet in use.

American governmental control left to absolute

neglect for 18 years the important question of education, in connection with other similar administrative problems that pertain to every Christian and self-respecting nation. Stimulated by appeals from officers of the army, American missionary societies were not entirely neglectful of Alaska's necessities, and in 1877 the Presbyterians, through their agent, Doctor Sheldon Jackson, established schools in southeastern Alaska, their example being soon followed by other missionary societies.

The Alaska Commercial Company maintained under its control an English school on the Seal Islands, but the educational privileges of the Pribilof natives have been very greatly improved since the islands became a closed governmental reservation.

The United States was finally forced by public opinion to a tardy and meagre assumption of its duties toward the natives—obligations assumed under the treaty of cession and also necessitated by regard for national morality.

In accordance with the law of May 17, 1884, the Secretary of the Interior, in 1885, charged the Commissioner of Education with the "needful and proper provision for the education of the children of school age in the territory of Alaska, without reference to race." The pitiful sum of $25,000 was appropriated, and for the following ten years the school system, pecuniarily unable to install its own plant, was maintained largely by contracts with the missions, which generously supplemented the deficient support of the nation.

American Schools

The question of education was brought indirectly to public attention by the influx of whites into the Territory in 1898, which necessitated the establishment of civil government in Alaska. In the law of June 6, 1900, for this general purpose, provision was made authorizing incorporated schools, which should be maintained by 50 per cent of the so-called Alaska Fund arising from license fees collected within their corporate limits.

In 1901, Congress withdrew all national support for education, and the expense of all schools devolved on Alaska, to be met from license moneys. Better counsels prevailed later, and by the law of January 27, 1905, regarding roads, schools, and the insane in Alaska, the education of white children devolved on local officials, while that of the natives remains under the Secretary of the Interior and at the expense of the United States, which appropriated $315,000 for this purpose in 1924.

Public schools are now of three kinds—town, territorial, and native. Those of incorporated towns, Juneau, Eagle, Nome, Valdez, Ketchikan, Skagway, Anchorage, Cordova, Douglas, Fairbanks, Haines, Nenana, Petersburg, Seward, Sitka, Tanana, and Wrangell, are managed by directors, elected by the people. They are supported by 25 per cent from federal licenses of the town, and 75 per cent from appropriations made by the territorial legislature.

Incorporated Schools

Seven of the incorporated towns maintain four-year high schools, which are fully accredited to the University of Washington. Most other towns have high-school courses from one to three years. The cost of these schools in 1923 was $100 per capita, of which 25 per cent comes from town-federal licenses and 75 per cent from territorial appropriations. More than 80 per cent of the 113 teachers are graduates of either normal schools or colleges; their average salary is $1,675. The total enrolment of pupils in 1923 was 2,652 with an average attendance of 2,111.

In four settlements there are night schools to prepare foreigners for citizenship. From an enrolment of 89—12 being women—composed of 25 nationalities, 28 were prepared in one year for citizenship.

Unincorporated Villages

There are 56 white and mixed schools outside of incorporated towns. Such schools are maintained at an annual cost of $104 per capita, by territorial appropriations. The salaries of the teachers average $1,385. The enrolment of pupils in 1923 was 1,175 (68 high school), with an average attendance of 883.

The quality and success of Alaskan schools are evident by the census of 1920, when of 24,822 whites over 10 years of age, only 464 were illiterate, 1.9 per cent. Few if any of the States have a record superior to this.

These Territorial schools lead up to an institution of higher education, the Agricultural College and School of Mines, established at Fairbanks and open to both sexes. The College offers five courses, which are being supplemented: Agriculture, home economics, general science, civil engineering, and mining engineering.

Schools for Natives

The natives of Alaska are educated by the U. S. Bureau of Education. Their schools are maintained by federal appropriations, which in 1924 amounted to $355,000, about $88 per capita. The direction of this important work is under a superintendent, stationed at Seattle. He has under him 5 superintendents and 144 teachers. The most northerly school is at Point Barrow, on the shores of the Arctic Ocean, and the most westerly at Atka, one of the Aleutian Islands. Besides English and ordinary elementary subjects, special emphasis is laid on carpentry, home economics, gardening, and sanitation.

For supervision Alaska is divided into five school districts, under a superintendent. They are the northwestern, including ten schools, one hospital, and the reindeer herds on the shores of the Arctic Ocean and regions tributary thereto; the Seward Peninsula, 11 schools and reindeer herds of the Peninsula; western district, 17 schools, 1 hospital, and reindeer herds region bordering on Bering Sea; central district, 22 schools, 2 hospitals, and reindeer herds in central Alaska and on the Aleutian Islands; southeastern district, 15 schools and 1 hospital in southeastern Alaska. It is estimated that educational facilities are offered to 60 per cent of the natives, as many as can be reached under present appropriations.

Hamilton, acting chief of the Alaska Division, points out that one district is twice the size of Illinois; that many schools are beyond regular transportation and mail service; that special attention must be given to children on whom the future of the native races depends.

In 1923 75 schools were in operation, with an enrolment of about 4,000.

The success of the system is shown by the report of the census of 1920, when the percentage of illiterates above ten years of age had dropped from 71.4 in 1910, to 56.4 per cent in 1920, among the natives. Of those under 25 years of age the percentage dropped from 50 to 34. As illustrative of the benefits accruing from education among the natives may be mentioned the establishment of segregated villages, of co-operative establishments, of entrance into professional and avocational work. At one time a survey of 88 native villages showed that among their residents were 47 teachers and preachers, 53 engineers, and 119 carpenters. Entrance into literature was shown by the issue at Nome of *The Eskimo*, which regularly contains native contributions in English.

The general conditions of the native population are set forth in a separate chapter.

Missions

The enduring bases of missionary work in Alaska were laid by that remarkable man, Innocent Veniaminof, who died as Primate of Russia. Laboring assiduously for 19 years, 1823–1842, as missionary and priest in Alaska, he exerted an extraordinary influence over all natives that came under his personal supervision.

The treaty of cession provided "that the churches which have been built in the ceded territory by the Russian Government shall remain the property of such members of the Greek Oriental Church resident in the territory as may choose to worship therein." Although its Russian communicants very largely departed, the Greek Church, to its great credit, kept alive for 12 years in Alaska, under alien and discouraging conditions, the feeble flame of Christian faith; even now the Russian Church pays five-sixths of the salaries of its Alaskan priests. To this day the Russian Church maintains its active and financial interest in Alaska, and its bishops and priests still officiate in churches at Sitka, Kodiak, Unalaska, and St. Michael, besides keeping up its mission work at Ikogmut and elsewhere.

In addition to the Greek cathedral at Sitka, there were, in 1900, 7 parishes and 34 minor churches with 27 chapels. Their field of operation lies largely on the fringing islands of southern Alaska and in the Aleutian Archipelago—from Sitka to Atka, the Seal Islands, and the western Aleutians, though it

has establishments in the valleys of the Yukon and
Kuskokwim. Yearly visits are made by priests to
minor settlements where there are but few natives.
Those who think that the Greek Church is dead
in Alaska will be surprised to learn that in 1890,
although there were missions representing 11 faiths,
the Greek Church had 10,335 communicants as
against 1,334 of Protestant faiths and 498 Catho-
lics. Of the 10,509 who were within the pale of the
church in 1905, only 59 were Russians and they
mostly clergy. Criticisms regarding Greek formalism
and the efficiency of its clergy are often heard, but so
are similar disparaging remarks in Alaska as to the
consistency of doctrine and practice as set forth in
the lives of missionaries and teachers of other faiths.
The Christian and tolerant view of the local head of
the Greek Church is shown by the recommendation
of the Alaskan bishop in 1905, that Russian and
Aleutian should be replaced by the English language
in all exercises. Changed conditions in Russia will
impair the prosperity of the Greek Church in Alaska.

Protestant Missions

Suffice it to say, that as a body the representatives
of the various churches in Alaska are devoted, self-
sacrificing men and women, who labor faithfully and
strenuously for the welfare of the natives, often under
the most discouraging and trying circumstances. The
advent of American churches into this field came
after 12 years of hesitation, and then through the

efforts of the United States army. Sheldon Jackson says: "Christian women, wives of army officers stationed at Sitka and Wrangell, were continually writing to their friends concerning the need of missionaries." With the aid of General (then Captain) S. P. Jocelyn, United States army, the first Indian church outside of the Greek pale was opened at Wrangell in 1876. The next year a soldier, whose name is unknown, wrote General Howard, asking that some church send a minister to guide and instruct these Christian Indians. This letter was sent to Doctor Sheldon Jackson, who made such prompt and effective representations that he was sent, in 1877, to institute the first Presbyterian mission in Alaska. The number eventually increased to six—Wrangell, Sitka, Hooniah, Howkan, Haines (all in Sitkan Alaska), and at Point Barrow. The most important work for uplifting the Indians, practically as well as spiritually, has been the development and extension of the Sitka Industrial School, in which ex-Governor Brady was for many years the dominant and inspiring spirit. There are accommodations for about 160 pupils, both boys and girls, who are trained industrially and religiously. Formerly the pupils were from Sitka or adjacent islands, but they now represent three tribes and are recruited from distant points in southeastern Alaska.

The efforts of the Baptists in Cook Inlet, on Copper River, and Prince William Sound, have been supplemented by establishing an orphanage at Wood Island, Kodiak. Of the six missions of the Methodists, the

St. James Mission, and Native Children, at Tanana, Central Yukon.

most important is a girls' home at Unalaska, which, with the Baptist orphanage, has done much to make useful and honest the lives of the helpless waifs, for whom otherwise there were scant hopes of the future.

The Swedish Lutheran Church has three missions —at Yakutat, Golofnin, and Unalaklik—while the Norwegian Lutherans took station at Teller. The last three missions have become especially important from their association with reindeer work, later mentioned.

The most northern mission, at Point Barrow, was opened by the Presbyterians. As Point Barrow is a whaling centre, has a trading post, and is occupied as a governmental relief and life-saving station, it is a highly important outpost, and the mission influence is correspondingly necessary. Altogether, the Presbyterians have established 16 churches, of which 12 are for natives.

The Moravians have a mission at Kwinak village, at the mouth of the Kanektok. They also opened two missions, Bethel and Carmel, under contract with the United States Bureau of Education, to establish schools in connection therewith. Bethel was founded in 1885, near the Eskimo village, Mumtrelak. Its usefulness has been largely increased in late years by its herd of reindeer, which in 1907 numbered about 2,100. Carmel was opened in 1866, near the Eskimo village Kanulik on the Nushagak River. In addition to its religious work it has instituted industrial schools for boys and for girls, which have materially benefited the Eskimo who, to the number of several thousands, live in that region.

The Society of Friends, beginning operations at
Douglas City, extended their work to the Kotzebue
Sound region, where they have at present three missions—Deering (now an important mining centre),
Kotzebue, and Kikiktak. They have given much
practical instruction and are actively interested in
training apprentices for the reindeer, which, to the
number of 845 and 1,193 (in 1907) head, were collected at the two latter stations. The Kotzebue
school had the largest enrolment in 1907, 120 pupils,
of any federal school.

The Kinegnak mission at Cape Prince of Wales,
and that on Shismaref Inlet, are supported by the
Congregationalists. The Eskimo villages of King-
egan and Kinegnak, of several hundred natives, from
their association with whalers, liquor smugglers, and
prospectors, have great need of guidance. The institution of this mission has been supplemented by a
government school with 105 enrolled pupils, and a
reindeer station, in which there were 1,261 reindeer
in 1907.

Though late in entering the field, the Episcopal
Church has pursued its Alaskan work with great
vigor. It opened a mission and school at Anvik in
1887, and has steadily extended its operations in the
shape of schools, hospitals, and churches, occupying
23 stations in 1908. Alaska was organized as a
missionary diocese in 1888, but its first bishop, P. T.
Rowe, was not ordained until 1895. With his diocesan residence at Sitka, Bishop Rowe has stimulated
missionary zeal by extraordinary personal efforts in

the field. He has made winter journeys of thousands of miles, following the sledge through Alaskan cold and darkness to encourage the missions on Bering Strait, and in the valleys of the Tanana, the Yukon, and the Koyukuk. The most promising of missions lately established is that on the Koyukuk, which, from its isolated position, is free from the disadvantages inseparable from those at or near white settlements. The conditions of the service, despite Bishop Rowe's personal efforts, are indicative of the great difficulties under which missionary work is done by all churches. Of the 23 stations in 1908 there were no less than 8 vacant, while 3 had only a native helper.

Fidelity, faith, courage, above all practicality and administrative ability, are essential qualities for missionary work in Alaska, where climate, environment, and isolation are all adverse to successful work.

The most striking and favorable results through mission work among the Tsimpseans are in evidence at Metlakatla, the Indian community transferred from British Columbia, some 50 miles to the eastward, in 1887. Mr. Henry S. Wellcome, an able and warm-hearted champion in their days of oppression, in his most interesting "Story of Metlakatla," says:

This people, only thirty years since, consisted of the most ferocious Indian tribes, given up to constant warfare, notorious for treachery, cannibalism, and other hideous practices. Mr. William Duncan, with rare fortitude and genius, began single-handed a mission. He educated them and taught them Christianity in the simplest manner; at the same time introducing peaceful industries; and by these means he wrought in a single generation a marvellous transformation. Where blood has flowed continually he founded the model, self-supporting village of Metlakatla, of one thousand souls, that will compare favorably with almost any village of its size in England or America for intelligence, morality, and thrift.

Catholic Missions

In addition to its labors elsewhere in Alaska among the white population, the Catholic Church has contributed greatly to the material as well as to the spiritual advancement of the natives of the valley of the Yukon, especially at Nulato and Kosereyski (usually known as Holy Cross), near the Yukon delta. Conditions for spiritual improvement are not very favorable at Nulato, where the shifting native population of about 300 are materially affected by the trading operations conducted in that vicinity. While the former troubles arising from liquor dealers have largely passed since the enactment of the prohibition law by the Alaska Legislature, yet there still remain the disturbing elements of traders, prospectors, and river men—an environment somewhat irreligious.

Great benefits and extraordinary success have resulted from the work of the fathers and sisters at the Holy Cross Mission. The mission was wisely established on the north bank of the Yukon River, opposite the native village of Kosereyski on the southern shore. Believed by many to be unsuited

Holy Cross Mission, Lower Yukon Valley.

(Remarkable for its successful agricultural work.)

to the prospective industries of agriculture and stock-raising, failure was forecast by observers.

However, this mission, established in 1886, is a striking illustration of what can be done in an unfavorable environment by unremitting labor, zeal, and intelligence. Nearly fifty acres of land have been brought under intensive cultivation, and the resulting wealth of forage, flowers, and vegetables has been such as to excite the admiration of all visitors.

The Jesuit fathers supervised the construction of substantial log buildings for houses, schools, and church; brought the land into successful cultivation; constructed and operated a steamboat; and introduced profitable methods of fishing.

The sisters meanwhile taught several score of native girls the rudiments of primary education; instructed them in methods of household economy and of healthful sanitation; instilled a knowledge of womanly duties suitable to their environment; and inculcated lessons and life-methods of moral value.

In recent years the Catholic Church has increased its activities in Alaska, and its missionary force now consists of 13 priests, 10 brothers, and 20 sisters. It now maintains three mission schools, at Akularak, Holy Cross, and Pilgrim, where about 400 native children are educated and cared for, as also are adults in its hospitals, when necessity arises. A Catholic hospital is also maintained at Ketchikan. The action of Congress in enacting a law that hereafter no federal appropriation whatever shall be used for education in a sectarian school obliges all the Alaskan missionary establishments to depend entirely for their support on the religious bodies specially interested therein.

CHAPTER XXX

TRADE AND TRANSPORTATION

PROBABLY there is no practical phase of Alaska that is so little known as that of transportation in and out of the Territory, whether it be of mail or telegram, of passenger or freight. The completion of the Alaska Railroad entirely changed the old transportation systems, especially for the Yukon Valley and Seward Peninsula.

Routes of Travel

There is but one starting point for Alaska—Seattle; and there are three direct and sharply differing routes to various regions—to southeastern Alaska, to southwestern Alaska, and to Seward Peninsula.

To southeastern Alaska are the steamship lines that run, through the Inside Passage, to Skagway, touching at Ketchikan, Wrangell, and Juneau regularly, and occasionally at other ports. The through voyage lasts from four to five days in all seasons, and the first-class fare is $30.*

Southwestern Alaska (from Cordova westward to Seward) is reached by direct steamers in five to eight days, and the first-class fare is $45. The ports

*Fares given are, of course, liable to change.

thus reached are Cordova, Valdez, and Seward, with calls at adjacent ports occasionally. This region is also reached from Seattle via Juneau and the Inside Passage by 3 or 4 boats each month, in 10 to 12 days; some steamers run through, and in other cases a change at Juneau is necessary. The boats from Juneau touch at Sitka, Yakutat Bay, Cordova, Orca, Valdez, Seward, and occasionally at other points, as far west as Seldovia. At Seward there is a connecting steamer about the middle of each month, that runs to the Cook Inlet ports, and to Kodiak, ending its voyage at Unalaska (Dutch Harbor). In summer it runs beyond Unalaska to Bristol Bay.

Seward Peninsula and adjacent regions are reached direct only during the open season of four months, from early June to early October. In the open season this ocean voyage of 2,740 miles is made in 8 to 10 days, the first-class fare being from $75 to $100, according to accommodations; second-class, $65; steerage, $35. Steamers leave Seattle from about June 5 to October 5; and they return from Nome from about June 20 to October 15. In 1908 there were 74 steamers which arrived and cleared at Nome during the season. There are few now.

Winter travel in and out of Seward Peninsula lasts from early November to the beginning of April. It commences only with frozen streams and ends with the break-up of the rivers in the Tanana and other southerly valleys. Travel is by private dog-teams via Unalaklik, up the frozen Yukon River to Tanana, and over the ice of the Tanana River to Nenana, the northern terminus of the Alaska Railroad. Thence the route is via Seward, which is an open winter port in frequent and regular communication with Seattle; first-class fare, $45. Travel between Seward and Fairbanks, 468 miles, is by rail.

Railroad Routes

The Alaska Railroad is now the main line for traffic of the greater part of the Territory. Seward Peninsula necessarily depends for its freight, and for most of its personal travel, on the summer steamers. Owing to the discontinuance of the American commercial boats on the Yukon, the upper valley must turn to Canadian steamboats for summer freight and travel until the United States provides therefor. The same conditions possibly confront the settlements in the Koyukuk. At present, as elsewhere stated, the Alaska Railroad has a summer boat running between Fairbanks, on the Tanana, and Holy Cross, on the lower Yukon. Winter travel and mails between Fairbanks, Seward Peninsula, Kuskokwim valley, the Koyukuk Valley, and the upper Yukon depend as before on sledge teams, the airplane or other extemporized service.

The Copper River Railroad provides facilities between Cordova and the lower watershed of Copper River and the settlements of Prince William Sound.

The Alaska Railroad provides for the adjacent regions in the valleys of the Matanuska, Susitna, and Tanana, and the Cook Inlet country. The Alaskan territorial road programme, looking to the expenditure of one million dollars annually for needful roads, will in time provide roads that will be feeders for the railroad and connections of remote mining regions therewith—such as the upper Kuskokwim, Bristol Bay, upper Tanana, Koyukuk Valley, and Alaska Peninsula.

Trade

The development of the resources of Alaska has not been unmarked by corresponding benefits to the United States in general, and to the Pacific Coast in particular. Economic writers have frequently and potently set forth the great importance of the trade of the Orient as an indispensable factor in the future prosperity of this nation, and none will gainsay the soundness of their reasonings. Meanwhile there has sprung into existence an Alaskan trade which is simply enormous in its extent—time and circumstance considered.

Doubtless there are many who will learn with surprise that, as shown by the Statistical Abstract of the United States, 1908, the exportations from the United States to Alaska in 1907 aggregated $18,402,-765, which increased to a maximum in 1918, and in 1923, after the post-bellum depression, amounted to $30,000,000.

It may be added that the Alaskan trade demands no special methods of manufacture or of packing, and that it deals only in the best of merchandise, as the question of freight charges enters so largely

St. Elias Alps, and Disenchantment Bay.

in the cost to the consumer. All shipments are carried in vessels of American register, an additional advantage to our national interests.

"The Monthly Summary of Commerce," for June, 1923, gives the shipments of merchandise from the United States for the fiscal years 1921 to 1923, which were in value as follows: 1921, $27,323,972; 1922, $23,625,161; 1923, $29,981,604. The articles shipped in 1923 were: Animals and animal products, except wool and hair, $4,042,105; vegetable food products, oil seeds, expressed oil and beverages, $3,773,785; other vegetable products, except fibres and wood, $1,259,448; textiles, $3,225,228; wood and paper, $2,346,331; non-metallic minerals, $2,179,887; metals and manufactures of, except machinery and vehicles, $7,765,306; machinery and vehicles, $2,981,082; chemicals and allied products, $1,393,230; miscellaneous, $1,015,202.

Shipments of merchandise (gold and silver not included) from Alaska to the United States: 1921, $54,126,718; 1922, $36,775,870; 1923, $52,984,275. Shipments of domestic gold and silver: 1922, $6,681,020; 1923, $7,496,319.

Trading Companies

Although the Alaskan trade is no longer a monopoly, yet it is practically controlled in the interior by several large corporations. The oldest and best known of these is the Northern Commercial Company, which, founded in 1868, was the pioneer of

Yukon trade and navigation. For 20 years, as the Alaska Commercial Company, it was the lessee of the Pribilof seal islands, but it now practically confines its operations to the trade of the Yukon watershed. Its local headquarters at St. Michael command the admiration of every Alaskan. At that point are operated a shipyard, hotel, general store, warehousing, machine and repair shops, a laundry, and, of all things, a cold-storage plant—for the imported fresh meat. There are complete facilities for the handling and transfer of the thousands of tons of freight that are necessarily transshipped here to the river steamboats navigating the interior waters. In addition to the great plants and warehouses at St. Michael, Tanana, Dawson, and Fairbanks, they operate large trading stores at Bettles on the Koyukuk, at Delta on the Tanana, and at Eagle, Circle, Rampart, Kokrines, Nulato, and Andreafski on the Yukon. Inevitably great changes are being wrought in the operations of this company, due to the construction and operation of the Alaska Railroad.

Second in the field was the North American Trading and Transportation Company, whose activities are mainly displayed in the Klondike trade at Dawson, the Tanana trade at Fairbanks, and on the upper Yukon from Eagle to Tanana (Fort Gibbon). The amount and variety of the stocks carried by these companies are matters of surprise to Alaskan tourists, whose needs and comforts are thoroughly and reasonably subserved by them throughout interior Alaska.

Military Telegraph Service

This service reaches nearly all places of size in the Territory, and speedily serves almost every important permanent industry as well as the promising mining camps. The only extended areas that are without a military telegraph are Alaska Peninsula, the Kuskokwim watershed, the Yukon delta, the Point Barrow region, and the Koyukuk Valley. These areas are comparatively unimportant, as 75 per cent of the white population of Alaska are within an hour of a cable, a telephone, or telegraph office, so that at will they can speedily communicate with their friends of the outside world. Less than 10 per cent of the settled whites are 50 miles distant from such service.

The cables from Seattle reach, through Sitka and Valdez, every important Alaskan port from Ketchikan to Seward, on Kenai Peninsula. The connecting land lines from Valdez extend northeast to Eagle, there connecting with the Dawson system, and northwest to Fairbanks, Tanana, and St. Michael, while wireless sections reach Nome, Circle, and Eagle. Supplementary private systems of telephone reach all the large mining camps near Nome and in the Fairbanks region, while there are connecting railroad systems at Seward, of the Alaska Central, and at Cordova, of the Copper River Railway.

General G. M. Randall suggested the land lines for military purposes, and to Secretary Root is due the credit of the first cable system—to Skagway. The line of the army built the land lines under the supervision of technical experts of the Signal Corps.

While the entire responsibility for route, construction, equipment, installation, and operation rested by law on the writer, then Chief Signal Officer of the army, the enterprise would have dragged for years but for the far-seeing and helpful policy of Mr. Root, one of the great American War Secretaries.

Special difficulties—practical and theoretical—demanded unusual energy and high professional skill from the field workers. In solving these problems, on which the completion and operation of the system depended, high credit is due to Colonel (now General) James Allen, and to Major (now General) Edgar Russel, for the construction, equipment, and installation in a practically uncharted ocean of the longest American cables ever laid—aggregating over 3,000 miles, more than enough to cross the North Atlantic. Similar credit is due Captains G. C. Burnell, G. S. Gibbs, and William Mitchell, for line location and construction under Arctic conditions through hitherto unknown areas of Alaska. Finally Captain L. Wildman equipped, installed, and operated a wireless system—largely of his own invention—between St. Michael and Nome, the first commercial, long-distance, and regularly operating wireless system in the world—now in its 22d year of continuous and uninterrupted service.

The Congressional appropriations for these lines aggregated $1,352,132, and about $1,000,000 additional was involved in the army transportation used, and in the pay, clothing, and subsistence of the soldiers engaged in the construction, operation, and maintenance of the lines. As a rule such initial construction work, in regions apart from centres of civilization, involves ever-enlarging expenditures to meet unforeseen conditions, but in this work the ability and loyalty of the officers and men of the Signal Corps were equal to the task. Despite difficulties inherent on work in a practically unknown environment, the system was built, without either deficiency or additional appropriation, from the sums originally estimated.

Failure was freely forecast, the scheme being impracticable, and if built its expenses would swamp the treasury: fortunately neither prediction was verified. Its value to the Government has been enormous, which before saw local officials in Alaska absolutely without restraint. A telegraph to Nome in 1900 would have saved the American nation a sorrowful chapter in its practically stainless record as to the federal judiciary.

Commercial business was equally difficult to control, extravagant in its expenses, often inadequate, dilatory, and inefficient. The lines were thrown open to commercial business, to the advantage of the nation, of the Territory, and of the individual. The business done, astonishing even to optimists in its amount, best indicates the value of the system.

The writer was derided for estimating a possible revenue of $100,000 annually, and the receipts for 1903, $1,934.32, were viewed as large. The last fiscal year, 1924, they amounted to $268,000 besides government business on which the tariff was $137,400.

It is not infrequently said that corruption is rife in the public service, especially in Alaska. Let it be noted that these telegraph tolls, of over three millions of dollars, have in their entirety passed through the hands of American soldiers—enlisted men—and the total loss by embezzlement is but $361.69. This insignificant loss was through a sergeant—who deposited $75 the day he deserted—who was receiving $1.50 per day for doing the telegraphing and accounting for about $18,000 a year of tolls received; this in a town where skilled workmen were paid $15 per day, and laborers $8 to $9 per day.

Modified in the past few years, the army system now consists of 3,736 miles of submarine cable (1099 being old cable), 840 miles circuit land lines, and 18 radio stations.

Radio Stations

Besides the 18 stations of the Signal Corps, the United States maintains through the navy the following radio stations: Cordova, Dutch Harbor (Unalaska), Kodiak, St. George, St. Paul, Seward, and Sitka. The Bureau of Education has stations on the Aleutian Islands at Akutan and Atka, which have no mail facilities.

Large vested interests in Alaska have established a large number of private radio stations, of which there were about 60 in 1922. They are principally operated by the corporations engaged in fishing or mining.

Mail Facilities

Though neglected for many years as to its postal needs, and largely dependent on the Canadian facilities via Dawson, Alaska is now most liberally provided with mail service. The mails for the interior and northwestern Alaska are necessarily irregular of delivery during the months of April, May, and October, when travel is most difficult pending the formation of the autumn ice and of the spring break-up.

Southeastern Alaska and the coast from Yakutat to Seldovia are well cared for during the entire year. Alaska Peninsula and Unalaska receive a monthly mail by coast steamers running west from Valdez, or Seward, starting about the middle of each month; this service is extended during the salmon season to the Bering sea-coast at Nushagak. In winter the Kuskokwim regions are supplied by the monthly mail carried overland from Cold Bay, Shelikof Straits, from November to April. A similar winter service runs from Kenai north to Hober.

The summer mails for Seward Peninsula go direct to Nome by steamer during the four months of open season—June to early October.

All classes of mail are dispatched from Seattle throughout the year to points in southern Alaska; but considerable mail is thence routed to Vancouver and goes north by Alaskan steamers of the Canadian Pacific Railroad.

While unlimited weights go to Nenana at all times, from that point north the winter mails are carried over a series of routes on which the weights are limited, preference being given first to letters and postal cards; second to single newspapers and magazines. Mails are dispatched in winter twice a week from Nenana and Tanana for Yukon River points, and once a week for the Seward Peninsula points.

In 1924 there were 167 post-offices in Alaska, of which 86 were money-order, and 13 postal savings depository offices. The most northerly office is at Point Barrow, the most westerly at Wales, Seward Peninsula, and the most southwesterly at Unalaska. No service is provided for the Aleutian Islands west of Unalaska, yet this is part of the United States.

CHAPTER XXXI

THE CANADIAN KLONDIKE

THIS famous gold-producing district owes its development to the discovery of rich placers on Bonanza Creek in August, 1896, by G. W. Cormack, and by Henderson on Gold Bottom Creek.

The extreme richness of the ground attracted immediately thousands upon thousands of gold seekers, whose tragic toils, sufferings, and endurance made historic the mountain passes of Chilkoot, Chilkat, and White, as well as the lakes and rapids of the upper Lewes and Yukon, through which they descended by rudely built boats to Dawson, at the confluence of the Klondike and the Yukon.

The construction of the White Pass Railway, 1898 to 1900, from Skagway to the foot of the dangerous White Horse Rapids, and the establishment of a connecting line of steamers thence down the Yukon, make the journey of to-day one of delightful pleasure surrounded by modern comforts, through regions of picturesque beauty, and past many incipient settlements where hunting, fishing, and agriculture are the principal means of subsistence. Trains run between Skagway and White Horse, over the White Pass Railway, every week-day throughout the year, and well-furnished boats leave White Horse for Dawson about three times a week, from May to September. The traveller usually passes a night at White Horse, a thriving frontier town.

The journey is made from Seattle to Dawson in about 8 days in summer and 12 days in winter. The downward voyage from White Horse is made in less than 2 days, and the upward trip from Dawson in less than 4 days. Winter travel between White Horse and Dawson is by four-horse sleighs over a well-built trail of 300 miles, and is made in 6 days, travel being by day only.

Dawson is the capital of Yukon Territory, and is the social, financial, and trade centre of the Klondike and other adjacent mines. It passed long since from the status of a mining camp to that of a modern city. It has churches, schools, libraries, hospitals, banks, clubs, assay offices, telephones, electric lights, power plants, newspapers, and water-works. The commissioner, governor by courtesy, here supervises the executive functions of government, the judiciary administers justice, and the well-known Northwest Mounted Police efficiently preserve the public peace, enforce the laws, and arrest the criminals, of whom, contrary to oft-expressed opinions, there are few and those of the minor order.

The Klondike mining district includes the basins of the Klondike, Indian, and McQuestion Rivers, an area of about 800 square miles. The mines in the Bonanza precinct, distant from 12 to 15 miles from Dawson, are reached by stage or by the Klondike Mines Railway.

The very rich placers are practically exhausted, and the low-grade gravels have very largely passed under the control of large corporations, which are adopting the most efficient and economical systems of exploitation. Extensive ditches have been constructed, the best modern machinery imported, and systematic, carefully planned methods of placer mining are now in operation. The practical wisdom of such policy is evidenced by the increase in the output for 1908, which materially exceeded that of 1907. Dawson has decreased in population in late years, and but for systematic mining with machinery its decadence would have been much greater and it would have speedily culminated in a deserted district. It now looks forward to an era of moderate prosperity.

The days of extraordinary bonanzas, whereby the laborer of yesterday became a wealthy man of to-day, have passed, and the Klondike is no longer a poor man's country.

Of Klondike mining, Brooks said several years since:

It was the exploitation of these almost fabulously rich and relatively shallow gravels that brought the Klondike gold output up with a bound, and it is their quick exhaustion that has caused an almost equally rapid decline of the annual yield. There are still extensive bodies of lower-grade gravels to mine in the Klondike, but these can be developed only by means of extensive water conduits or by dredging. Mining in the Klondike has passed its zenith, whereas in Seward Peninsula the maximum yearly output is still to be reached.

The Canadian Government has endeavored to restore the early prosperity of the Klondike by aiding in building ditches, railways, and otherwise.

The Canadian Yukon Mineral Production

The most productive district has been the Klondike, where the aggregate value of gold mined to include the mining year ending March 31, 1923, has been since 1898, $179,532,134.

The output by years was as follows: 1898, $3,072,-773; 1899, $7,582,283; 1900, $9,809,465; 1901, $9,162,-083; 1902, $9,566,340; 1903, $12,113,015; 1904, $10,-790,663; 1905, $8,222,054; 1906, $6,540,007; 1907, $3,304,791; 1908, $2,820,162; 1909, $3,260,283; 1910, $3,594,251; 1911, $4,126,728; 1912, $4,024,237; 1913, $5,018,412; 1914, $5,301,308; 1915, $4,649,634; 1916, $4,458,278; 1917, $3,960,207; 1918, $3,266,019; 1919, $1,947,082; 1920, $1,660,450; 1921, $1,246,486; 1922, $1,125,705; 1923, $1,240,806.

It will be noted that the introduction of modern methods of hydraulic and dredging machinery reached its maximum in 1914, since which year there has been an almost uninterrupted decrease.

Copper Mining

The development of rich copper deposits in the Whitehorse district was very promising, and the annual products for the years 1912 and 1913 approximated $300,000 in value, but with decrease in prices the output fell to $92,000 in 1915. Under stimulus

of war demands the product attained values of
$764,000 in 1916 and $668,650 in 1917. Low prices
and increased cost of mining have temporarily
stopped production.

Silver and Lead

The total silver product of $1,700,000, up to 1920
averaged about $80,000 annually, though varying
largely from year to year. The placer mines produced
about 90 per cent until 1920. In the year 1921, the
output of $246,288 was the maximum to date. This
increase was due to the development of the rich
high-grade silver-lead ores in the Mayo area, north
of the Stewart River. This area is the most promising mineral district of Canadian Yukon. The region
is reported to be rich in gold-placers, gold-quartz,
and galena ore carrying high values in silver.

The population of the Yukon Province fell from
8,512 in 1911 to 4,157 in 1921, but is said to have
since increased. Fisheries are becoming of importance and the trade in furs exceeds $300,000 annually.

BIBLIOGRAPHY.—Canada: Mineral Production, Annual Reports, Department
of Mines, Ottawa.

CHAPTER XXXII

TOURIST TRIPS

THERE are four Alaskan trips that can be especially recommended to tourists from the standpoint of time, expense, and attractiveness. The Inside Passage from Seattle to Skagway is the best known, the shortest, and most largely followed. The Prince William Sound and the Yukon-Nome trips, though longer, are more thoroughly comprehensive and desirable. The Alaska Railroad makes accessible the marvels of McKinley Park, though some frontier travel is involved.

To intending tourists Gannett humorously says:

If you are old, go by all means; but if you are young, wait. The scenery of Alaska is much grander than anything else of the kind in the world, and it is not well to dull one's capacity by seeing the finest first.

Inside Passage

The Inside Passage is the local name applied to the coast and sheltered waterways connecting Seattle and Skagway. Emerging from Puget Sound the steamer skirts the east shore of Vancouver Island, crosses Queen Charlotte Sound, again seeks the quiet inside waters as far as Dixon Entrance, whence it passes into the inland channels of Alexander Archipelago. Save in two stretches of 40 and 20 miles, respectively, there is no opportunity for an ocean swell. This extraordinary comfort of navigation is enhanced for voyagers by a continuity of fascinating landscapes, of the most varied and novel character. John Burroughs tersely describes it as a thousand miles "through probably the finest scenery of the kind in the world that can be seen from the deck of a ship—the scenery of fiords and mountain-locked bays and arms of the sea."

Nine fortunate voyages in regular steamers, which are scarcely less comfortable than the excursion boats, have made the writer familiar with external aspects and local topography, without, however, giving him power adequately to describe or correctly to classify its moods and brilliancy, its majesty and beauty. Suffice it to say, that during each of these four-day voyages his attention was steadily engrossed in the varied and magnificent landscapes which are best likened to a moving panorama of nature's masterpieces.

Though occasionally touching at Vancouver, the regular steamer ordinarily makes but one stop, Port Townsend, in the 720 miles from Seattle to Ketchikan. Thence to Skagway, Wrangell is the ordinary, Juneau and Treadwell the regular, port of call. The excursion steamers, which carry no local passengers, make the round trip in 11 days, stopping also at Metlakatla, Taku Glacier, Sitka, and occasionally at other points of interest, as may be scheduled.

To me the landscape has never been twice alike, with its shifting lights, changing seasons, and varying weather, affording the same pleasure for study and observation as a beautiful woman in her capricious moods. Along the Alaskan coast the elements of sea and mountain, of glacier and forest, of crag and vegetation, take on such subtle qualities of beauty and tenderness, of grandeur and picturesqueness as to bewilder the traveller when he pauses to analyze and compare.

Yesterday, the Gulf of Georgia entranced with its displays of form and color. To-day, the rocky shores, the jagged reefs, and swirling currents of Seymour Narrows appall. To-night, the Greville Reach seems most fascinating of all. To-morrow, the beauties of Naha Bay will seem to excel. Then with crescendo emotions one absorbs the perfection of Wrangell Narrows, the unsurpassable views of Frederick Sound, only to find later some aspect of nobler character at Taku Glacier or in Lynn Canal. Description is beyond the powers of the writer, who asks attention to a few words from gifted lovers of nature.

Mrs. Higginson, in her interesting "Alaska," writes:

Of the fiords tributary to Millbank Sound, innumerable cataracts fall sheer and foaming down their great precipices; the narrow cañons are filled with their liquid, musical thunder, and the prevailing color, the palest green, reflected from the water underneath the beaded foam.

These fiords are walled to a great height, and are of magnificent beauty. Some are so narrow and so deep

that the sunlight penetrates only for a few hours each day
—eternal mist and twilight fill the spaces. Covered with
constant moisture, the vegetation is of almost tropical
luxuriance.

John Burroughs, in the "Harriman Alaska Expedition," says:

A scene such as artists try in vain to paint and travellers
to describe; towering snow-clad peaks far ahead of us,
rising behind dark blue and purple ranges, fold on fold
and all aflame with the setting sun. The solid earth
became spiritual and transcendent.

Miss Scidmore, one of nature's keen observers,
says:

Of all the lovely spots in Alaska commend me to the
little land-locked Naha Bay, where the clear, green waters
are stirred with the leaping of thousands of salmon, and
the shores are clothed with an enchanted forest of giant
pines, and the undergrowth is a tangle of ferns and salmon-
berry bushes. Of all green and verdant woods I know of
none that so satisfy one with their rank luxuriance, their
beauty, and picturesqueness.

Again Mrs. Higginson describes a notable reach:

In Finlayson Channel the forestation is a solid mountain of green on each side, growing down to the water.
The reflections are so brilliant and true on clear days,
that the dividing line is not perceptible to the vision. The
mountains rise sheer from the water to a great height,
with snow upon their crests and occasional cataracts
foaming musically down their fissures. We are so close

to the wooded shores that one is tormented with the desire to reach out one's hand and strip the cool, green cedar needles from the drooping branches.

For an account of Taku Glacier, see Chapter XVIII.

In the narrow pass beyond Clarence Strait [says Miss Scidmore] the waters reflected in shimmering, pale blue and pearly lights the wonderful panorama of mountains. The first ranges above the water shaded from the deep green and russet of the nearer pine forests to azure and purple, where their further summits were outlined against the sky or the snow-covered peaks that were mirrored so faithfully in the long stretches of the channel.

Miss Scidmore was as much charmed with Wrangell Narrows as was the writer, for she says:

It was an enchanting trip up that narrow channel of deep water, rippling between bold island shores and parallel mountain walls. Beside the clear, emerald tide, reflecting every tree and rock, there was the beauty of foaming cataracts leaping down the sides of snow-capped mountains, and the grandeur of great glaciers pushing down through sharp ravines and dropping miniature icebergs in the sea. Touched by the last light of the sun, Patterson Glacier was a frozen lake of wonderland, shimmering with silvery lights, and showing a pale ethereal green and deep pure blue in all the rifts and crevices of its icy front.

Through Wrangell Narrows one emerges from scenes of quiet beauty into a domain of impressive grandeur. The attention of most tourists is here drawn entirely to glacial wonders (see Chapter XVIII), to the exclusion of the more general features of this region, which present in unique harmony high peaks, deep fiords, great mountain masses, extended sweeps of ocean, and vast ice-caps. Burroughs simply says: "We sailed under cloudless skies along Frederick Sound, feasting our eyes upon the vast panorama of encircling mountains." These interwoven elements of mountain and sea, of fiord and glacier continue until one passes the serrated cliffs of Lynn Canal and reaches Skagway, the end of the Inside Passage.

The present commercial importance of Skagway, the terminus of the Inside Passage, depends almost entirely on the operations of the White Pass and Yukon Railway, which has there established its headquarters, repair shops, etc. The town has a population of about 1,000, is provided with cable, telephonic, and telegraphic service, is electrically lighted, has good schools, churches, well-stocked stores, attractive homes, and good gardens. Picturesquely situated in an amphitheatre surrounded by high and usually snow-capped mountains, Skagway is the best-known town in Alaska. It will live in history as the base of operations for thousands of adventurous prospectors during the Klondike excitement of 1897–1898. Skagway is a pleasant base for excursions for the lover of the picturesque, the admirer of scenery, the student of natural history or ethnographical subjects. Reasonably near are the Chilkat and Chilkoot villages, with their native hats, baskets, and blankets. Over the White Pass, by rail, through scenery of beauty and grandeur, and along the way once marked by scenes of human misery and courage, one reaches in a few hours the lake sources of the Yukon. Near by also are the glaciers of Davidson, Mendenhall, and others, which will richly repay a visit. Along the foaming rapids of Skagway River, with its flowery banks, or up the winding paths to the mountain forests, the flowery glades, and sylvan lakes, there is surprise upon surprise at the delights and beauties that hourly break in on one, while wandering in the delicious summer weather of the Alaskan wonderland.

Prince William Sound

The Inside Passage is wonderfully attractive, but it yields in grandeur of beauty to the Prince William Sound route, which should always be taken, via Juneau, unless want of time absolutely forbids. One thus sees the best of the Inside Passage, from Seymour Narrows to Juneau, branching westward from the last-named town to Sitka, and thence along the incomparable Fairweather Range to the crowning mountain glory, St. Elias, and westward, from Yakutat Bay to Valdez, the wonderful Columbia Glacier and its sisters of Harriman Fiord. Thence to Resurrection Bay, the Kenai Peninsula, and Cook Inlet, is the end of this voyage, which can be extended to the westward by another steamer.

With comfort and clearness one views from Cross Sound to Cook Inlet a series of lofty mountains, extensive snow-fields, great glaciers (the Malaspina

Growing Forest on Malaspina Glacier, near Mt. St. Elias.

skirts the sea for nearly 70 miles), and forest-lined cliffs, such scenery as cannot be elsewhere matched in the world in the same area and distance. (For mountains and glaciers, see Chapters XVIII, XIX.)

The writer's experiences were akin to those of John Muir, who says:

The sail down the coast from St. Elias along the magnificent Fairweather Range, when every mountain stood transfigured in divine light, was the crowning grace and glory, and must be immortal in the remembrance of every soul of us.

Of Yakutat Bay, Mrs. Higginson says:

To the very head of Russell Fiord supreme splendor of scenery is encountered, surpassing the most vaunted of the Old World. Within a few miles, one passes from luxuriant forestation to lovely lakes, lacy cascades, bits of green valley; and then of a sudden, all unprepared, into the most sublime snow-mountain fastnesses imaginable, surrounded by glaciers and many of the most majestic mountain peaks of the world.

Of Prince William Sound, to the west, John Burroughs writes:

Our route was a devious one: past islands and headlands, then over the immense expanse of the open water, with a circle of towering, snow-capped mountains far off along the horizon; then winding through arms and straits, close to tree-tufted islands and steep, spruce-clad mountains; now looking between near-by dark-forested hills upon a group of distant peaks white as midwinter; then upon broad, low-wooded shores, with glimpses of open meadowlike glades among the trees.

The striking features of the Sound region are set forth in the chapter on glaciers (XVIII), the wondrous splendor being that of Harriman Fiord. This fiord indents the northeast shore of Kenai Peninsula, a land of 9,000 square miles in area that is a sealed book to the ordinary tourist. To the Cook Inlet visitor, however, its thousand miles of bold coast present magnificent scenery—high mountains, rugged summits, deep-cut valleys, and numerous glaciers. Invaded for fur, for fish, for coal, and now for gold, its chief charm lies in its mountain fastnesses, with their abundant game and opportunity of adventure.

Writing of the scenery of the interior of Kenai, Colonel Caine, the English sportsman, says:

The view was sublime. To our right the enormous glacier, from which this branch of Indian River issues, filled up the whole of the head of the deep valley, the precipitous sides of which fell almost perpendicularly to its foot in cliffs a thousand feet high, till it met the skyline ten miles away. Beyond the gorge mountain after mountain stretched away as far as eye could reach, with a glimpse between two peaks of another glacier.

Kenai Peninsula, reached from Seward and other points on the Alaska Railroad, is well worth a special summer season by itself.

Familiar with the beauties and attractions of Kenai, Mr. A. J. Stone * delightfully describes it:

It is a land of magnificent, rugged mountains, and of beautiful rolling meadow lands; a land of eternal fields

* "An Explorer Naturalist in the Arctic," *Scribner's Magazine*, Vol. XXXIII, p. 38.

White Horse Rapids on the Lewes (Upper Yukon) River.

(The rapids so much dreaded by the Klondike pioneers.)

of glistening snow and ice, and of everlasting fires of burning lignite; of frozen moss and lichen-covered plains, and of vegetation that is tropical in its luxuriance; a land of extensive coal-fields, smoking volcanoes, and of earthquakes so frequent as to fail to excite comment among its native residents; of charming, quiet bays and harbors, and of tides and tide-rips among the greatest in the world; of almost endless days in summer, and of long, dismal winter nights; of an abundant animal life both in the water and on the land. Nowhere else in the world does nature exert itself in so many ways as in the Kenai Peninsula.

Of scenery Burroughs writes of Kachemack Bay:

Grandeur looked down on it from the mountains around, especially from the great volcanic peaks, Iliamna and Redoubt, sixty miles across the inlet to the west. The former rises over 12,000 feet from the sea, and, bathed in sunshine, was an impressive spectacle. It was wrapped in a mantle of snow, but it evidently was warm at heart, for we could see steam issuing from two points near its summit.

The Klondike Yukon

The completion of the Alaska Railroad has very largely eliminated the steamer service on the Yukon and the wonderful boat journey of some 2,300 miles on this magnificent river, from White Horse Rapids to St. Michael, is usually impracticable.

It can however be made with delays and frequent changes. The Canadian boats run regularly in summer from White Horse to Dawson; thus one sees the great gorges and wonderful rapids of the upper Yukon.

From Dawson there are occasional freight steamers to
Fairbanks, passing Fort Yukon with its midnight sun.

From Fairbanks the steamer service of the Alaska
Railroad runs to Holy Cross, the Catholic Mission.
A launch service takes one to St. Michael and thence
across Norton Sound to Nome, where one enters the
new Eskimo world of Seward Peninsula and Kotzebue Sound.

McKinley Park

This public reservation, dominated by the highest
peak of the continent, is now within tourist reach.
Travel is by steamer from Seattle to Seward, where
the railroad takes one luxuriously to a station adjacent to the park. A day's journey by horse, or wagon
over a forest trail takes one into this wonderland.

The railroad managers also arrange for journeys to
the wondrous Valley of Ten Thousand Smokes, and
to various points west of Cook Inlet, where one is in
the land of volcanoes elsewhere described.

There is also offered what is called "The Golden
Belt-Line Tour," costing about $200. Leaving the
ocean steamer from Seattle at Seward, one travels by
train 370 miles to Fairbanks, 320 miles by automobile over the Richardson Highway to Chitina, and
130 miles by train to Cordova, where the ocean
steamer is rejoined.

CHAPTER XXXIII

PRODUCTS, ACTUAL AND POTENTIAL

1867–1924

SUCH various opinions have been expressed as to the present value of Alaska, and of its future development, that a brief presentation of facts and estimates is desirable for the consideration of those interested in the Territory. These data are presented along four lines:

1. *Local Products Shipped Out of Alaska*

It is impossible to tabulate accurately all of these material contributions. These are drawn from official reports, which are not only reliable, but are recognized as understatements rather than overestimates. The fishery products are valued at $575,000,000 distributed as follows: Salmon, $525,000,000; halibut, $16,000,000; cod, $13,000,000; herring, $10,000,000; whales, $7,000,000; minor fisheries, $4,000,000.

The value of the mineral products is $536,000,000 distributed thus: Gold, $348,000,000; copper, $168,-000,000; silver, $10,000,000; coal, $4,000,000; miscellaneous (tin, lead, antimony, platinum, marble, etc.), $6,000,000.

The receipts from the pelts of the fur-seal amount to $57,000,000.

The pelts of the land fur-bearing animals have contributed over $30,000,000 to the country.

2. Domesticated Animals of Economic Value

The fur-seals of the Pribilof Islands, 700,000 head, have a minimum value of $21,500,000. Foxes on reservations and on fox farms, about $1,000,000 at current prices. The value of the reindeer herds, numbering about 350,000, is estimated by the Governor of Alaska at $8,750,000.

3. Industrial Plants

Railroads built and operated by private enterprise are worth about $35,000,000. The Alaskan investments of the hundred fishing corporations had a value in 1922 of $54,590,000, thus distributed: Salmon, $47,509,000; herring, $3,368,000; halibut, $1,840, 000; whale, $802,000; cod, $778,000; shrimp, $163,000; crab, $130,000. Data as to the numerous and widely separated mining plants are especially deficient, but they must exceed in value $10,000,000.

In 1924 the assessed property of the 18 incorporated towns amounted to $21,500,000; that of other towns and villages must approximate the same figures.

The 17 banks had a capital of $780,000, surplus $607,000, and deposits of $8,374,000 in 1924.

4. Minerals and Other Economic Material in situ

A. H. Brooks, the Alaskan mineral expert, estimated that the gold in placer reserves has a value of

$360,000,000; possibly, he adds, it may be double that. The potential output of gold lodes must run into a hundred million. Unmined copper doubtless reaches hundreds of millions in value. Coal is so abundant in enormous quantities that it must reach seven figures in coming years. The official estimate of the United States Forestry Bureau places the value of the standing timber of to-day—increasing from year to year—at $54,000,000. Agricultural products must have a large potential value, as 1,000 farmers raised in one year 1,340 tons of cereals and root crops.

TABLES

TABLE NO. 1

DATES OF HISTORICAL INTEREST

1648. Deshneff, rounding Asia, navigates Bering Strait.
1731. Gwosdeff discovers the Alaskan coast.
1741. Bering discovers St. Elias region.
1761–1762. Pushkaref winters on Alaska Peninsula.
1778. Cook traces north coasts to Icy Cape.
1783. First permanent settlement—on Kodiak Island.
1792. Baranoff, Director of the Colonies.
1799. Russian-American Trading Company, chartered; granted monopoly for twenty years, renewed 1821 and 1844. Trading posts and missions established at Sitka and elsewhere.
1802. Tlinkits practically annihilated the Russian garrison at Sitka.
1804. Sitka again occupied and fortified.
1816. Kotzebue, discovering Kotzebue Sound, reaches Cape Krusenstern.
1824. Convention between Russia and the United States regarding boundary, fishing, trading, and navigation. Similar treaty between Russia and Great Britain in 1825.
1825. Father Veniaminof begins his missionary work, establishing a school at Unalaska; made a bishop in 1834.
1826. Beechey discovers Point Barrow, northernmost cape of Alaska.
1831. Baron Wrangell, Director of the Colonies.
1832. Lukeen built redoubt on Kuskokwim, named for Kolmakof, who explored the river in 1820.
1833. St. Michael trading post established.
1837. Simpson completes northern coast-line by connecting Return Reef (Franklin, 1826) with Point Barrow.
1838. Nulato occupied as trading post.
1847. Hudson Bay Company descends the Porcupine and builds Fort Yukon.
1848. American whaling established north of Bering Strait.
1850. Beginning of cattle breeding at Kodiak and Cook Inlet.
1855. Rodgers explores Arctic Ocean to 72° 05′ N.
1862. Russian-American Company refused renewal of charter in 1862.
1863. Lukeen ascends (first) the Yukon to Fort Yukon.
1865. Kennicott commences exploration of Yukon for Western Union Telegraph Company.

1867. Russia cedes Alaska to the United States for $7,200,000. United States Army takes possession, establishing posts at Sitka, Tongass, and Wrangell.

1868. United States custom, revenue, and navigation laws extended to Alaska.

1869. Alaska Commercial Company initiates steam navigation on the Yukon.

1871–1880. Dall surveys Alaskan waters and Bering Strait.

1873. Gold discovered in southeastern Alaska (Treadwell and Juneau).

1877. United States troops withdrawn from Alaska, leaving control to United States Navy and Revenue Marine Service.

1881.
1883. { International polar station at Point Barrow, and system of meteorological stations established by Signal Corps, United States Army.

1885. Laws of Oregon extended to Alaska by Congress. Administrative and judicial officers authorized; mining, educational, and other legislation enacted.

1885. Allen explored Copper, Tanana, and Koyukuk regions.

1893. International conference at Paris established six-mile limit for pelagic fur-seal fishery.

1896. Gold discovered in Yukon region, and in Tanana Valley.

1897. United States Army returns to Alaska.

1899. Gold discovered in Nome region.

1899. Modus Vivendi between United States and Great Britain fixed provisional boundary between Canada and Alaska.

1900. Alaska granted civil government, with judicial and other officials and institutions.

1900.
1904. { United States Military Telegraph System built and installed: consisting of cables from Seattle via Sitka to Skagway, from Sitka to Valdez, and Valdez to Seward and Cordova; of over 2,300 miles of land lines from Valdez via Fairbanks and Fort Gibbon to St. Michael, and from Valdez to Fort Egbert (Eagle); and of wireless system from St. Michael to Safety Harbor, near Nome.

1903. Alaskan Boundary Tribunal defined the Alaskan boundary from Portland Canal to the 141st meridian.

1906. Alaska granted representation in Congress, through a delegate.

1906. Convention between Great Britain and the United States provided for surveying and marking the 141st meridian.

1907. Coal lands withdrawn by Executive proclamation.

1910. Oil lands withdrawn by Executive order.

1911. Pelagic sealing prohibited for 15 years by convention between Great Britain, Japan, Russia, and United States.

1912. Sealing on Pribilofs prohibited for five years.
1912. Alaska granted a Legislative Assembly.
1912. Eruption of Mount Katmai.
1914. Coal leasing authorized by Congress.
1914. Congress authorized construction of Alaska Railroad.
1920. Oil land leasing granted by Congress.
1924. Congress enacted law for protection of fisheries.
1924. Halibut treaty between United States and Great Britain.
1925. Congress enacted the Alaska Game Law.

TABLE No. 2

MEAN TEMPERATURES, IN DEGREES FAHR.

Stations	Jan.	Feb.	Mar.	Apr.	May	June	July	Aug.	Sept.	Oct.	Nov.	Dec.
Interior												
Copper Center	—12	4	13	29	45	54	56	53	43	27	5	—4
Fort Gibbon (Tanana)	—16	—5	6	24	44	57	59	53	40	22	—2	—12
Fort Yukon *	—26	—11	—3	20	41	56	61	57	43	18	—7	—24
Dawson (Canada)	—23	—12	4	29	46	57	60	54	42	25	—0	—3
Fairbanks	—15	0	10	29	47	58	61	55	43	25	1	—7
Anchorage	7	17	20	33	43	52	56	54	47	35	17	8
Coast												
Point Barrow	—20	—13	—13	—2	22	36	41	38	32	16	—0	—15
St. Michael	6	1	9	20	33	46	54	52	44	30	16	5
Unalaska (Dutch Harbor)	32	32	34	35	41	46	51	51	47	41	35	32
Valdez	18	22	25	34	43	51	54	51	46	37	25	20
Sitka	32	34	37	42	47	52	55	56	52	46	38	35

* Broken record, combined with Dall River.

TABLE No. 2—Continued

PRECIPITATION, RAIN AND MELTED SNOW, IN INCHES

Stations	Jan.	Feb.	Mar.	Apr.	May	June	July	Aug.	Sept.	Oct.	Nov.	Dec.
Interior												
Copper Center	0.6	0.5	0.3	0.2	0.4	0.9	1.6	1.1	1.3	0.9	0.8	0.6
Fairbanks	0.8	0.4	1.0	0.3	0.5	1.4	1.8	1.9	1.3	0.8	0.7	0.7
Tanana	0.7	0.8	0.7	0.2	0.9	0.9	2.2	2.2	1.4	1.0	0.7	0.8
Eagle	0.3	0.3	0.4	0.7	0.4	1.1	1.9	0.6	1.0	0.5	0.1	0.5
Fort Yukon	0.6	0.6	0.5	0.5	0.7	0.9	0.7	0.7	0.3	0.9	0.4	0.5
Dawson, Canada	0.9	0.8	0.4	0.5	0.8	1.1	1.6	1.6	1.5	1.2	1.1	1.0
Coast												
Point Barrow	0.1	0.3	0.2	0.3	0.3	0.4	0.9	0.9	0.5	0.7	0.4	0.2
St. Michael	0.8	0.1	0.5	0.4	0.9	1.3	1.6	2.4	2.7	1.2	0.7	0.6
Unalaska	5.5	7.1	5.1	3.4	5.1	2.8	2.4	3.3	6.0	9.0	7.0	7.1
Anchorage	1.2	0.9	0.3	0.3	0.6	0.6	1.9	3.1	2.3	2.4	0.8	0.6
Sitka	7.6	6.5	5.6	5.5	4.1	3.4	4.2	7.1	10.2	12.2	9.5	9.0

TABLE NO. 3

LAWS FOR PROTECTION OF FISHERIES OF ALASKA

DEPARTMENT OF COMMERCE
OFFICE OF THE SECRETARY
WASHINGTON

June 21, 1924.

TO WHOM IT MAY CONCERN:

Attention is directed to the following acts for the protection and regulation of the fisheries of Alaska, approved June 14, 1906, June 26, 1906, and June 6, 1924.

AN ACT FOR THE PROTECTION OF THE FISHERIES OF ALASKA, AND FOR OTHER PURPOSES

Be it enacted by the Senate and House of Representatives of the United States of America in Congress assembled, That for the purpose of protecting and conserving the fisheries of the United States in all waters of Alaska the Secretary of Commerce from time to time may set apart and reserve fishing areas in any of the waters of Alaska over which the United States has jurisdiction, and within such areas may establish closed seasons during which fishing may be limited or prohibited as he may prescribe. Under this authority to limit fishing in any area so set apart and reserved the Secretary may (a) fix the size and character of nets, boats, traps, or other gear and appliances to be used therein; (b) limit the catch of fish to be taken from any area; (c) make such regulations as to time, means, methods, and extent of fishing as he may deem advisable. From and after the creation of any such fishing area and during the time fishing is prohibited therein it shall be unlawful to fish therein or to operate therein any boat, seine, trap, or other gear or apparatus for the purpose of taking fish; and from and after the creation of any such fishing area in which limited fishing is permitted such fishing shall be carried on only during the time, in the manner, to the extent, and in conformity with such rules and regulations as the Secretary prescribes under the authority herein given: *Provided,* That every such regulation made by the Secretary of Commerce shall be of general application within the particular area to which it applies, and that no exclusive or several right of fishery shall be granted therein, nor shall any citizen of the United States be denied the right to take, prepare, cure, or preserve fish or shellfish in any area of the waters of Alaska where fishing is permitted by the Secretary of Commerce. The right herein given to establish fishing areas and to permit limited fishing therein shall not apply to any creek, stream, river, or other bodies of water in which fishing is prohibited by specific provisions of this Act, but the Secretary of Commerce through the creation of such areas and the establishment of closed seasons may further extend the restrictions and limitations imposed upon fishing by specific provisions of this or any other Act of Congress.

It shall be unlawful to import or bring into the Territory of Alaska, for purposes other than personal use and not for sale or barter, salmon from waters outside the jurisdiction of the United States taken during any closed period provided for by this Act or regulations made thereunder.

Sec. 2. In all creeks, streams, or rivers, or in any other bodies of water in Alaska, over which the United States has jurisdiction, in which salmon run, and in which now or hereafter there exist racks, gateways, or other means by which the number in a run may be counted or estimated with substantial accuracy, there shall be allowed an escapement of not less than 50 per centum of the total number thereof. In such waters the taking of more than 50 per centum of the run of such fish is hereby prohibited. It is hereby declared to be the intent and policy of Congress that in all waters of Alaska in which salmon run there shall be an escapement of not less than 50 per centum thereof, and if in any year it shall appear to the Secretary of Commerce that the run of fish in any waters has diminished, or is diminishing, there shall be required a correspondingly increased escapement of fish therefrom.

Sec. 3. Section 3 of the Act of Congress entitled "An Act for the protection and regulation of the fisheries of Alaska," approved June 26, 1906, is amended to read as follows:

"Sec. 3. That it shall be unlawful to erect or maintain any dam, barricade, fence, trap, fish wheel, or other fixed or stationary obstruction, except for purposes of fish culture, in any of the waters of Alaska at any point where the distance from shore to shore is less than one thousand feet, or within five hundred yards of the mouth of any creek, stream, or river into which salmon run, excepting the Karluk and Ugashik Rivers, with the purpose or result of capturing salmon or preventing or impeding their ascent to the spawning grounds, and the Secretary of Commerce is hereby authorized and directed to have any and all such unlawful obstructions removed or destroyed. For the purposes of this section, the mouth of such creek, stream, or river shall be taken to be the point determined as such mouth by the Secretary of Commerce and marked in accordance with this determination. It shall be unlawful to lay or set any seine or net of any kind within one hundred yards of any other seine, net, or other fishing appliance which is being or which has been laid or set in any of the waters of Alaska, or to drive or to construct any trap or any other fixed fishing appliance within six hundred yards laterally or within one hundred yards endwise of any other trap or fixed fishing appliance."

SEC. 4. Section 4 of said Act of Congress approved June 26, 1906, is amended to read as follows:

"SEC. 4. That it shall be unlawful to fish for, take, or kill any salmon of any species or by any means except by hand rod, spear, or gaff in any of the creeks, streams, or rivers of Alaska; or within five hundred yards of the mouth of any such creek, stream, or river over which the United States has jurisdiction, excepting the Karluk and Ugashik Rivers: *Provided,* That nothing contained herein shall prevent the taking of fish for local food requirements or for use as dog feed."

SEC. 5. Section 5 of said Act of Congress approved June 26, 1906, is amended to read as follows:

"SEC. 5. That it shall be unlawful to fish for, take, or kill any salmon of any species in any manner or by any means except by hand rod, spear, or gaff for personal use and not for sale or barter in any of the waters of Alaska over which the United States has jurisdiction from six o'clock postmeridian of Saturday of each week until six o'clock antemeridian of the Monday following, or during such further closed time as may be declared by authority now or hereafter conferred, but such authority shall not be exercised to prohibit the taking of fish for local food requirements or for use as dog feed. Whenever the Secretary of Commerce shall find that conditions in any fishing area make such action advisable, he may advance twelve hours both the opening and ending time of the minimum thirty-six-hour closed period herein stipulated. Throughout the weekly closed season herein prescribed the gate, mouth, or tunnel of all stationary and floating traps shall be closed, and twenty-five feet of the webbing or net of the 'heart' of such traps on each side next to the 'pot' shall be lifted or lowered in such manner as to permit the free passage of salmon and other fishes."

SEC. 6. Any person, company, corporation, or association violating any provision of this Act or of said Act of Congress approved June 26, 1906, or of any regulation made under the authority of either, shall, upon conviction thereof, be punished by a fine not exceeding $5,000 or imprisonment for a term of not more than ninety days in the county jail, or by both such fine and imprisonment; and in case of the violation of section 3 of said Act approved June 26, 1906, as amended, there may be imposed a further fine not exceeding $250 for each day the obstruction therein declared unlawful is maintained. Every boat, seine, net, trap, and every other gear and appliance used or employed in violation of this Act or in violation of said Act approved June 26, 1906, and all fish taken therein or therewith, shall be forfeited to the United States, and shall be seized and sold under the direction of the court in which the forfeiture is declared, at public auction, and the proceeds thereof, after deducting the expenses of sale, shall be disposed of as other fines and forfeitures under the laws relating to Alaska. Proceedings for such forfeiture shall be in rem under the rules of admiralty.

That for the purposes of this Act all employees of the Bureau of Fisheries, designated by the Commissioner of Fisheries, shall be considered as peace officers and shall have the same powers of arrest of persons and seizure of property for any violation of this Act as have United States marshals or their deputies.

Sec. 7. Sections 6 and 13 of said Act of Congress approved June 26, 1906, are hereby repealed. Such repeal, however, shall not affect any act done or any right accrued or any suit or proceeding had or commenced in any civil cause prior to said repeal, but all liabilities under said laws shall continue and may be enforced in the same manner as if committed, and all penalties, forfeitures, or liabilities incurred prior to taking effect hereof, under any law embraced in, changed, modified, or repealed by this Act, may be prosecuted and punished in the same manner and with the same effect as if this Act had not been passed.

Sec. 8. Nothing in this Act contained, nor any powers herein conferred upon the Secretary of Commerce, shall abrogate or curtail the powers granted the Territorial Legislature of Alaska to impose taxes or licenses, nor limit or curtail any powers granted the Territorial Legislature of Alaska by the Act of Congress approved August 24, 1912, "To create a legislative assembly in the Territory of Alaska, to confer legislative power thereon, and for other purposes."

Approved, June 6, 1924.

The following sections of an act for the protection and regulation of the fisheries of Alaska, approved June 26, 1906, are still in effect.

AN ACT FOR THE PROTECTION AND REGULATION OF THE FISHERIES OF ALASKA *

Be it enacted by the Senate and House of Representatives of the United States of America in Congress assembled, That every person, company, or corporation carrying on the business of canning, curing, or preserving fish or manufacturing fish products within the territory known as Alaska, ceded to the United States by Russia by the treaty of March thirtieth, eighteen hundred and sixty-seven, or in any of the waters of Alaska over which the United States has jurisdiction, shall, in lieu of all other license fees and taxes therefor and thereon, pay license taxes on their said business and output as follows: Canned salmon, four cents per case; pickled salmon, ten cents per barrel; salt salmon in bulk, five cents per one hundred pounds; fish oil, ten cents per barrel; fertilizer, twenty cents per ton. The payment and collection of such license taxes shall be under and in accordance with the provisions of the Act of March third, eighteen hundred and ninety-nine, entitled "An Act to define and punish crimes in the district of Alaska, and to provide a code of criminal procedure for the district," and amendments thereto.

SEC. 2. That the catch and pack of salmon made in Alaska by the owners of private salmon hatcheries operated in Alaska shall be exempt from all license fees and taxation of every nature at the rate of ten cases of canned salmon to every one thousand red or king salmon fry liberated, upon the following conditions:

That the Secretary of Commerce may from time to time, and on the application of the hatchery owner shall, within a reasonable time thereafter, cause such private hatcheries to be inspected for the purpose of determining the character of their operations, efficiency, and productiveness, and if he approve the same shall cause notice of such approval to be filed in the office of the clerk or deputy clerk of the United States district court of the division of the district of Alaska wherein any such hatchery is located, and shall also notify the owners of such hatchery of the action taken by him. The owner, agent, officer, or superintendent of any hatchery the effectiveness and productiveness of which has been approved as above provided shall, between the thirtieth day of June and the thirty-first day of December of each year, make proof of the number of salmon fry liberated during the twelve months immedi-

* "Department of Commerce and Labor" and "Secretary of Commerce and Labor," wherever they occur in this act, have been changed, respectively, to "Department of Commerce" and "Secretary of Commerce," in accordance with the act of Mar. 4, 1913, creating the Department of Labor.

ately preceding the thirtieth day of June, by a written statement under oath. Such proof shall be filed in the office of the clerk or deputy clerk of the United States district court of the division of the district of Alaska wherein such hatchery is located, and when so filed shall entitle the respective hatchery owners to the exemption as herein provided; and a false oath as to the number of salmon fry liberated shall be deemed perjury and subject the offender to all the pains and penalties thereof. Duplicates of such statements shall also be filed with the Secretary of Commerce. It shall be the duty of such clerk or deputy clerk in whose office the approval and proof heretofore provided for are filed to forthwith issue to the hatchery owner, causing such proofs to be filed, certificates which shall not be transferable and of such denominations as said owner may request (no certificate to cover fewer than one thousand fry), covering in the aggregate the number of fry so proved to have been liberated; and such certificates may be used at any time by the person, company, corporation, or association to whom issued for the payment pro tanto of any license fees or taxes upon or against or on account of any catch or pack of salmon made by them in Alaska; and it shall be the duty of all public officials charged with the duty of collecting or receiving such license fees or taxes to accept such certificates in lieu of money in payment of all license fees or taxes upon or against the pack of canned salmon at the ratio of one thousand fry for each ten cases of salmon. No hatchery owner shall obtain the rebates from the output of any hatchery to which he might otherwise be entitled under this Act unless the efficiency of said hatchery has first been approved by the Secretary of Commerce in the manner herein provided for.

. . . .

SEC. 7. That it shall be unlawful to can or salt for sale for food any salmon more than forty-eight hours after it has been killed.

SEC. 8. That it shall be unlawful for any person, company, or corporation wantonly to waste or destroy salmon or other food fishes taken or caught in any of the waters of Alaska.

SEC. 9. That it shall be unlawful for any person, company, or corporation canning, salting, or curing fish of any species in Alaska to use any label, brand, or trade-mark which shall tend to misrepresent the contents of any package of fish offered for sale: *Provided*, That the use of the terms "red," "medium red," "pink," "chum," and so forth, as applied to the various species of Pacific salmon under present trade usages shall not be deemed in conflict with the provisions of this Act when used to designate salmon of those known species.

SEC. 10. That every person, company, and corporation engaged in catching, curing, or in any manner utilizing fishery products, or in operating fish hatcheries in Alaska, shall make detailed annual reports thereof to the Secretary of Commerce, on blanks furnished by him, covering all such facts as may be required with respect thereto for the information of the Department. Such reports shall be sworn to by the superintendent, manager, or other person having knowledge of the facts, a separate blank form being used for each establishment in cases where more than one cannery, saltery, or other establishment is conducted by a person, company, or corporation, and the same shall be forwarded to the Department at the close of the fishing season and not later than December fifteenth of each year.

Sec. 11. That the catching or killing, except with rod, spear, or gaff, of any fish of any kind or species whatsoever in any of the waters of Alaska over which the United States has jurisdiction, shall be subject to the provisions of this Act, and the Secretary of Commerce is hereby authorized to make and establish such rules and regulations not inconsistent with law as may be necessary to carry into effect the provisions of this Act.

Sec. 12. That to enforce the provisions of this Act and such regulations as he may establish in pursuance thereof, the Secretary of Commerce is authorized and directed to depute, in addition to the agent and assistant agent of salmon fisheries now provided by law, from the officers and employees of the Department of Commerce, a force adequate to the performance of all work required for the proper investigation, inspection, and regulation of the Alaskan fisheries and hatcheries, and he shall annually submit to Congress estimates to cover the cost of the establishment and maintenance of fish hatcheries in Alaska, the salaries and actual traveling expenses of such officials, and for such other expenditures as may be necessary to carry out the provisions of this Act.

.   .   .   .

Sec. 14. That the violation of any provision of this Act may be prosecuted in any district court of Alaska or any district court of the United States in the States of California, Oregon, or Washington. And it shall be the duty of the Secretary of Commerce to enforce the provisions of this Act and the rules and regulations made thereunder. And it shall be the duty of the district attorney to whom any violation is reported by any agent or representative of the Department of Commerce to institute proceedings necessary to carry out the provisions of this Act.

Sec. 15. That all Acts or parts of Acts inconsistent with the provisions of this Act are, so far as inconsistent, hereby repealed.

Sec. 16. That this Act shall take effect and be in force from and after its passage.
Approved, June 26, 1906.

AN ACT TO PROHIBIT ALIENS FROM FISHING IN THE WATERS OF ALASKA *

Be it enacted by the Senate and House of Representatives of the United States of America in Congress assembled, That it shall be unlawful for any person not a citizen of the United States, or who has declared his intention to become a citizen of the United States, and is not a bona fide resident therein, or for any company, corporation, or association not organized or authorized to transact business under the laws of the United States or under the laws of any State, Territory, or district thereof, or for any person not a native of Alaska, to catch or kill, or attempt to catch or kill, except with rod, spear, or gaff, any fish of any kind or species whatsoever in any of the waters of Alaska under the jurisdiction of the United States: *Provided, however,* That nothing contained in this Act shall prevent those lawfully taking fish in the said waters from selling the same, fresh or cured, in Alaska or in Alaskan waters, to any alien person, company, or vessel then being lawfully in said waters: *And provided further,* That nothing contained in this Act shall prevent any person, firm, corporation, or association lawfully entitled to fish in the waters of Alaska from employing as laborers any aliens who can now be lawfully employed under the existing laws of the United States, either at stated wages or by piecework, or both, in connection with Alaskan fisheries, or with the canning, salting, or otherwise preserving of fish.

Sec. 2. That every person, company, corporation, or association found guilty of a violation of any provision of this Act or of any regulation made thereunder shall, for each offense, be fined not less than one hundred dollars nor more than five hundred dollars, which fine shall be a lien against any vessel or other property of the offending party or which was used in the commission of such unlawful act. Every vessel used or employed in violation of any provision of this Act or of any regulation made thereunder shall be liable to a fine of not less than one hundred dollars nor more than five hundred dollars, and may

* "Department of Commerce and Labor" and "Secretary of Commerce and Labor," wherever they occur in this act, have been changed, respectively, to "Department of Commerce" and "Secretary of Commerce," in accordance with the act of Mar. 4, 1913, creating the Department of Labor.

be seized and proceeded against by way of libel in any court having jurisdiction of the offense.

SEC. 3. That the violation of any provision of this Act or of any regulation made thereunder may be prosecuted in any United States district court of Alaska, California, Oregon, or Washington.

SEC. 4. That the collector of customs of the district of Alaska is hereby authorized to search and seize every foreign vessel and arrest every person violating any provision of this Act or any regulation made thereunder, and the Secretary of Commerce shall have power to authorize officers of the Navy and of the Revenue Cutter Service and agents of the Department of Commerce to likewise make such searches, seizures, and arrests. If any foreign vessel shall be found within the waters to which this Act applies, having on board fresh or cured fish and apparatus or implements suitable for killing or taking fish, it shall be presumed that the vessel and apparatus were used in violation of this Act until it is otherwise sufficiently proved. And every vessel, its tackle, apparatus, or implements so seized shall be given into the custody of the United States marshal of either of the districts mentioned in section three of this Act, and shall be held by him subject to the proceedings provided for in section two of this Act. The facts in connection with such seizures shall be at once reported to the United States district attorney for the district to which the vessel so seized shall be taken, whose duty it shall be to institute the proper proceedings.

SEC. 5. That the Secretary of Commerce shall have power to make rules and regulations not inconsistent with law to carry into effect the provisions of this Act. And it shall be the duty of the Secretary of Commerce to enforce the provisions of this Act and the rules and regulations made thereunder, and for that purpose he may employ, through the Secretary of the Treasury and the Secretary of the Navy, the vessels of the United States Revenue-Cutter Service and of the Navy: *Provided, however,* That nothing contained in this Act shall be construed as affecting any existing treaty or convention between the United States and any foreign power.

Approved, June 14, 1906.

YES BAY RESERVATION

An Executive order of February 1, 1906, is as follows:

It is hereby ordered that the hereinafter described land and water areas in the District of Alaska be, and they are hereby, reserved and set apart as a site for a salmon hatchery, subject to the possessory rights of the natives and of persons claiming title through the Russian Government, also subject to the rights of natives to take fish from the waters and fuel from the forests included in the limits of the reservation hereby established to wit:

Yes Lake (otherwise known as Lake McDonald) and its catchment basin, its outlet, and a strip of land one-eighth of a mile wide along each shore thereof; Yes Bay, Back Bay, and a strip of land one-eighth of a mile wide along the shores thereof and a strip of land one-eighth of a mile wide on each side of the old Indian trail.

ANNETTE ISLAND FISHERY RESERVE

Section 15 of the act of March 3, 1891, is as follows:

That until otherwise provided by law the body of lands known as Annette Islands, situated in Alexander Archipelago in Southeastern Alaska, on the north side of Dixon's Entrance, be, and the same is hereby, set apart as a reservation for the use of the Metlakatla Indians, and those people known as Metlakatlans who have recently emigrated from British Columbia to Alaska, and such other Alaskan natives as may join them, to be held and used by them in common, under such rules and regulations, and subject to such restrictions, as may be prescribed from time to time by the Secretary of the Interior.

On April 28, 1916, the President issued a proclamation creating the Annette Island Fishery Reserve. The proclamation provides that—

The waters within three thousand feet from the shore lines at mean low tide of Annette Island, Ham Island, Walker Island, Lewis Island, Spire Island, Hemlock Island, and adjacent rocks and islets, . . . also the bays of said islands, rocks, and islets, are hereby reserved for the benefit of the Metlakatlans and such other Alaskan natives as have joined them or may join them in residence on these islands, to be used by them under the general fisheries laws and regulations of the United States as administered by the Secretary of Commerce.

AFOGNAK RESERVATION

A proclamation by the President of the United States, promulgated December 24, 1892, created the Afognak Forest and Fish Culture Reserve, which is now a part of the Chugach National Forest. The proclamation states that—

There is hereby reserved from occupation and sale, and set apart as a public reservation, including use for fish-culture stations, said Afognak Island, Alaska, and its adjacent bays and rocks and territorial waters, including among others the Sea Lion Rocks, and Sea Otter Island: *Provided*, That this proclamation shall not be so construed as to deprive any bona fide inhabitant of said island of any valid right he may possess under the treaty for the cession of the Russian possessions in North America to the United States, concluded at Washington on the thirtieth day of March, eighteen hundred and sixty-seven.

Warning is hereby expressly given to all persons not to enter upon, or to occupy, the tract or tracts of land or waters reserved by this proclamation, or to fish in, or use any of the waters herein described or mentioned.

ALEUTIAN ISLANDS RESERVATION

By Executive order of March 3, 1913, the Aleutian Islands Reservation consisting of "all islands of the Aleutian chain, Alaska, including Unimak and Sannak Islands on the east, and extending to and including Attu Island on the west," was created and set apart for various purposes, including the encouragement and development of the fisheries.

This reservation was placed under the joint jurisdiction of the Department of Commerce and the Department of Agriculture, and among the matters committed exclusively to the Department of Commerce was jurisdiction over the fisheries. Joint regulations for the administration of the reservation were promulgated April 30, 1921, by the two departments concerned.

These regulations in respect to the fisheries are hereby revoked. The Executive order of March 3, 1913, creating the Aleutian Islands Reservation is still in full force and effect, as specifically stated in the Executive orders of June 7, 1924, which revoked the Executive orders of February 17, 1922, and November 3, 1922, creating the Alaska Peninsula Fisheries Reservation, and the Southwestern Alaska Fisheries Reservation, respectively.

HERBERT HOOVER,
Secretary of Commerce.

TABLE NO. 4

REGULATIONS FOR THE PROTECTION OF LAND FUR-BEARING ANIMALS IN ALASKA

UNITED STATES DEPARTMENT OF AGRICULTURE

BUREAU OF BIOLOGICAL SURVEY

E. W. NELSON, CHIEF OF BUREAU

The act of May 31, 1920, entitled "An act making appropriations for the Department of Agriculture for the fiscal year ending June 30, 1921" (Public, No. 234, 66th Cong.), conferred upon the Secretary of Agriculture the powers and duties theretofore conferred upon the Secretary of Commerce, by law, proclamations, or Executive orders, with respect to any mink, marten, beaver, land otter, muskrat, fox, wolf, wolverine, weasel, or other land fur-bearing animal in Alaska.

Section 1956 of the Revised Statutes, as amended by section 173 of the act of March 3, 1899 (30 Stat., 1253), and by section 4 of the act of April 21, 1910 (36 Stat., 326–327), provides that—

No person shall kill any otter, mink, marten, sable, or fur seal, or other fur-bearing animal, within the limits of Alaska Territory or in the waters thereof; and every person guilty thereof shall, for each offense, be fined not less than two hundred nor more than one thousand dollars or imprisoned not more than six months, or both; and all vessels, their tackle, apparel, furniture, and cargo found engaged in violation of this section shall be forfeited; but the Secretary of Commerce and Labor shall have power to authorize the killing of any such mink, marten, sable, fur seal, or other fur-bearing animal under such regulations as he may prescribe; and it shall be the duty of the Secretary of Commerce and Labor to prevent the killing of any fur seal except as authorized by law and to provide for the execution of the provisions of this section until it is otherwise provided by law.

Pursuant to the authority conferred upon the Secretary of Agriculture under the aforesaid acts of Congress, the following regulations effective July 1, 1920, are prescribed to govern the killing of land fur-bearing animals in Alaska:

REGULATION 1.—DISTRICTS

The climatic and physiographic features of different parts of Alaska vary so greatly that in order to serve the convenience of trappers and the cause of conservation with justice it has been deemed advisable to divide the Territory into three districts, in each of which the conditions relating to fur are comparatively uniform. These districts are shown in the accompanying map and may be described as follows:

District 1 includes the Aleutian Islands, Alaska Peninsula, and neighboring islands, and Southeastern Alaska, mainland and islands, from Yakutat Bay to Dixon Entrance.

District 2 includes the mainland and islands from Yakutat Bay, Gulf of Alaska, Iliamna Lake, and Bristol Bay, northward to the headwaters of the streams flowing into the Arctic Ocean north of the sixty-eighth parallel of north latitude.

District 3 includes the region drained by the streams entering the Arctic Ocean north of the sixty-eighth parallel of north latitude.

REGULATION 2.—UNPRIME PELTS

No land fur-bearing animal shall be killed when its pelt is unprime.

REGULATION 3.—CLOSE PERIODS

Beaver.—The killing of beaver is prohibited in all the districts throughout the Territory until November 15, 1923.

Marten.—The killing of marten is prohibited in all districts throughout the Territory until November 15, 1925.

REGULATION 4.—OPEN SEASONS

The black, glacier, and cinnamon bear, wolf, wolverine, squirrel, marmot, varying hare (rabbit), and Arctic hare may be killed at any time.

The following land fur-bearing animals may be killed in the specified districts during the following open seasons:

District 1:

Muskrat, December 16 to March 31, both dates inclusive.

Otter, mink, and weasel (ermine), December 16 to March 15, both dates inclusive.

Lynx and fox, December 1 to January 31, both dates inclusive.
[NOTE.—Amended Oct. 5, 1920, by Secretary of Agriculture, to read: "Lynx, December 1, to January 31, both dates inclusive. Fox, December 1 to February 28, both dates inclusive.]

District 2:
  Muskrat, December 1, to May 31, both dates inclusive.
  Otter, mink, and weasel (ermine), November 16 to March 31, both dates inclusive.
  Lynx and fox, November 16 to February 28, both dates inclusive.

District 3:
  Muskrat, December 1 to May 31, both dates inclusive.
  Otter, mink, and weasel (ermine), November 1 to March 31, both dates inclusive.
  Lynx and fox, November 16 to April 15, both dates inclusive.

REGULATION 5.—TRAPS

The killing of any land fur-bearing animal at any time by means of the trap or device known as the "klips," or by means of any steel bear trap or any other trap with jaws having a spread exceeding 8 inches is prohibited.

REGULATION 6.—DOGS

The use of dogs for pursuing and killing land fur-bearing animals for which close seasons exist is prohibited.

REGULATION 7.—POISON

The killing of any land fur-bearing animal by means of strychnine or any other poison is prohibited at all times.

NOTE.—The Criminal Code of Alaska (Title 1, chap. 13, sec. 186) provides that all persons concerned in the commission of a crime, whether they directly commit the act constituting the crime or aid and abet in its commission, though not present, are principals, and to be tried and punished as such. By this section any person knowingly selling poison for the purpose of killing land fur-bearing animals is a participator in the crime and is likewise punishable.

REGULATION 8.—SEIZURE OF SKINS

All skins of land fur-bearing animals killed in violation of these regulations found in the possession of any person in Alaska shall be seized by wardens and other officers designated by the Secretary of Agriculture, and such wardens and other officers shall hold said skins for such disposition as shall be ordered by the court having jurisdiction of a suit for condemnation and forfeiture thereof.

Shipments of fur from Alaska, whether shipped as personal baggage or otherwise, will be subject to examination by proper authorities and may be detained if the shipment was made in violation of these regulations.

REGULATION 9.—PENALTIES FOR UNLAWFUL SHIPMENT AND TRANSPORTATION

The following statute (Act Mar. 4, 1909, 35 Stat., 1137–1138) will be strictly enforced:

SEC. 242. It shall be unlawful for any person to deliver to any common carrier for transportation, or for any common carrier to transport from any State, Territory, or District of the United States, to any other State, Territory, or District thereof, any foreign animals or birds, the importation of which is prohibited, or the dead bodies or parts thereof of any wild animals or birds, where such animals or birds have been killed or shipped in violation of the laws of the State, Territory, or District in which the same were killed, or from which they were shipped: *Provided*, That nothing herein shall prevent the transportation of any dead birds or animals killed during the season when the same may be lawfully captured, and the export of which is not prohibited by law in the State, Territory, or District in which the same are captured or killed: *Provided further*, That nothing herein shall prevent the importation, transportation, or sale of birds or bird plumage manufactured from the feathers of barnyard fowls.

. . . .

SEC. 244. For each evasion or violation of any provision of the three sections last preceding the shipper shall be fined not more than two hundred dollars; the consignee knowingly receiving such articles so shipped and transported in violation of said sections shall be fined not more than two hundred dollars; and the carrier knowingly carrying or transporting the same in violation of said sections shall be fined not more than two hundred dollars.

REGULATION 10.—SHIPMENTS OF FURS TO BE REPORTED

Shipments of furs consigned to points outside of Alaska, which may be made at any time, should be reported to the Bureau of Biological Survey, Department of Agriculture, on appropriate blanks which will be supplied for that purpose.

REGULATION 11.—PENALTIES AND FORFEITURES

The penalties and forfeitures imposed will be strictly enforced against all persons who commit acts in violation of law or the regulations promulgated in accordance therewith.

In testimony whereof, I have hereunto set my hand and caused the official seal of the United States Department of Agriculture to be affixed, in the District of Columbia, this 12th day of June, 1920.

[SEAL.]

E. T. MEREDITH,
Secretary of Agriculture.

INDEX

INDEX

327